EARLY ANNALS OF ORNITHOLOGY

EARLY ANNALS
OF ORNITHOLOGY

BY

J. H. GURNEY, F.Z.S.

Author of "The Gannet: a Bird with a History," "A Catalogue of
the Birds of Prey, *Accipitres* and *Striges*," etc.

WITH ILLUSTRATIONS FROM PHOTOGRAPHS AND OLD PRINTS

H. F. & G. WITHERBY
326 HIGH HOLBORN, LONDON

1921

PREFACE.

The idea with which this little volume originated was to collect all the ancient passages about birds, of any special interest, but more particularly those which concerned British Birds, and to string them together in order of date. The preparation of such a book has naturally led to considerable research into the realms of literature, and here I should have been in difficulty but for the help of such good friends as Mr. J. E. Harting, Professor Edward Bensly and Dr. Eagle Clarke. Especially do I hold myself indebted to Mr. Harting for most valuable criticisms, and scarcely less so to Colonel Willoughby Verner, Mr. W. H. Mullens, Mr. A. H. Evans and Dr. Jenkinson.

J.H.G.

KESWICK HALL, NORFOLK.

CONTENTS.

LIST OF ILLUSTRATIONS.

EARLY ANNALS OF ORNITHOLOGY.

CHAPTER I.

PREHISTORIC BIRDS.

Later Stone Age: Prehistoric Drawings.   First Observers of Migration.
Superficial Deposits.

Bird Remains of the Later Stone Age.—In commencing with
the remains of birds attributable to the Stone Age, it must be
stated that there is no intention of attempting to investigate
the voluminous history of that subject in the present volume,
it is one for which the writer is far from being competent, and
moreover it is a branch of science which has been repeatedly
handled by those who have specialised in research of this
kind, and given the world their discoveries, which are accessible to all.   Certain it is that there are few species of birds
now living in Europe, be they of the Order *Steganopodes* or any
other family, of whose Miocene progenitors anything conclusive
can be said, still less can the birds of our era be connected
with that earlier period which is known to geologists as the
Eocene, but as we approach a more modern epoch, remains of
birds become much less rare.   Many there are which are assignable to the Stone Age, and especially to the Later Stone Age, a
period comparatively recent, when the prehistoric Briton had
begun to round off his roughly chipped stone axes and polish
them with sand.   It is to this period, terminating in Britain
about two thousand years B.C., that the remains of Solan Geese,
and other birds discovered in a sea-cave in Durham, belong ;
also some fragments of Solan Geese which were found in 1913
(together with bones of the Great Auk, Razorbill, Guillemot,
Cormorant, Shag, Swan, Wild Goose, Merganser, Gull, Tern,
and Water-Rail) by Mr. Ludovic Mann in the Asilian or
Mesolithic shell-mounds of Oronsay, an island on the west
coast of Scotland.

These mounds, in Mr. Mann's opinion, represent the oldest
known inhabited sites in North Britain, and their age is

B

probably to be computed by tens of thousands of years. But
the bones found in them are not necessarily all of equal
antiquity. " There is no doubt," writes Mr. Mann, " that
at the time these mounds were inhabited the topography of
Britain was somewhat different from what it is at present.
The land was sunk some twenty-five to thirty feet lower into
the sea, but the climate, so far as we can ascertain from
molluscan and from floral remains, was not materially different
from the present climatic position."*

In Denmark a number of Solan Goose bones have been
disinterred, and some in Norway, mixed with the bones of other
birds, all of which have been described by Dr. Herluf Winge.

These remains indicate that there may have been
Gannetries† on the Norwegian and Danish coasts, where also
for the same reason it is thought possible that the Great Auk
bred in the Stone Age.

Prehistoric Drawings of Birds.—Most remarkable are the
ancient representations of birds, which have been discovered
by Colonel Willoughby Verner and the Abbé H. Breuil in the
rock shelves and recesses of caves in southern Spain, where,
protected alike from wind and weather, they have lain unknown
yet preserved for thousands of years. These are of the Neolithic Age, but the Abbé Breuil has been good enough to furnish
information of some caves which contain a few figures of birds
appertaining to the Palæolithic epoch. These he has already
partly published, in conjunction with Señor H. Alcalde del Rio
and Père Lorenzo Sierra, under the title of " Les Cavernes de
la Région Cantabrique, Espagne." At Gargas, in the Upper
Pyrenees, he is acquainted with a beautiful Palæolithic
representation of a bird, perhaps a Crane or Heron ; and at
La Vilera de-El Arab, he knows of a Stork ; while other figures
of birds of similar antiquity have been found at Minateda in
Albacete.‡ These singular drawings are in all probability

* L. M., *in litt.*

† In no English Dictionary is the word Gannetry to be found, yet there
is no reason why it should not be considered English, as much as the commonly
employed terms Rookery, Heronry, and Gullery. They are all names having
the contracted suffix *eyrie* or *aery*, signifying a breeding-place of birds. To
speak of a " Rookery " of Gannets, or a " Rookery " of Penguins seems very
inappropriate.

‡ *See* also Reinach's " Répertoire de l'art quaternaire," p. 23 *et seq.*

the oldest pictures of birds in the world, far exceeding anything which has been found in Egypt, or among the sculptures
of Assyria. The most productive cave which has been
explored, and the only one in southern Spain where birds
have occurred, was that at the Tajo Segura, situated near the
Laguna de la Janda, in the province of Cadiz, which came
under Colonel Willoughby Verner's investigation in 1913–14.
The Abbé Breuil assumes as beyond question that the birds
depicted at the Tajo Segura are of Neolithic origin, in which
case they may be assigned an antiquity of six to eight thousand
years. I am greatly indebted to Colonel Verner for some
of the photographs, which were taken under difficult circumstances. In his interesting account of this cavern and
its drawings* Colonel Verner furnishes the following list of
recognisable outlines of twelve species of birds, viz., Great
Bustard, Crane, Wild Duck, Wild Goose, Raven, Spoonbill,
Flamingo, Purple Gallinule, Glossy Ibis, White Stork, Eagle
and Marsh Harrier, besides others which are doubtful. It is
true the drawings are very crude, but in some instances the
character of the bird or beast is caught in an unmistakable
manner. With Colonel Verner's permission three of the most
characteristic are here reproduced ; these give the Flamingo,
Duck and Purple Gallinule. It is to be observed that they
all represent birds that are to this day characteristic Spanish
species, which is an indication that the *ornis* of Spain has
undergone very little alteration in this great lapse of time.
Neolithic man was more advanced in many ways than we are
apt to suppose, and very cunning in the chase of beasts and
birds, whose habits, from continual watching, were well known
to him. "That Neolithic man," observes Colonel Verner in
one of his articles, "inhabiting this district was a keen
hunter, is proved by his numerous drawings of the beasts
of the chase, notably Red Deer and Ibex ; also by the representations of men armed with bows in pursuit of the same.
All the animals thus shown as having formed his quarry in
ancient times exist to this day in southern Spain. It is the
same with the birds." This undoubtedly adds very much to
their interest in the eyes of a modern naturalist. In the
vicinity of the caves, or at no great distance, there are still

* "Country Life," July 28th, 1914.

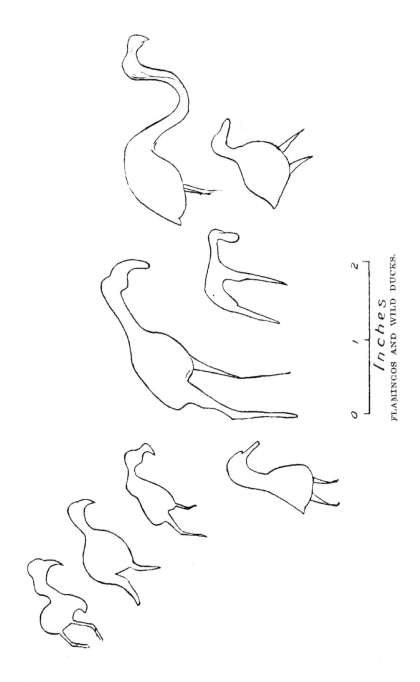

Inches

FLAMINGOS AND WILD DUCKS.

living, to quote Colonel Verner, hundreds of Great Bustards, tens of thousands of Wild Geese and Water-fowl of all sorts, besides Cranes, Storks, and a few Flamingos, also Vultures, Eagles, and Harriers. The ancient inhabitants of the district would therefore have presumably had no difficulty in obtaining them for food. A considerable number of similar cave drawings representing Deer, Ibex, Goats, Horses and Cattle, one of a Bison, and some of Fish, had previously been discovered by Colonel Verner and his indefatigable colleagues in the enormous

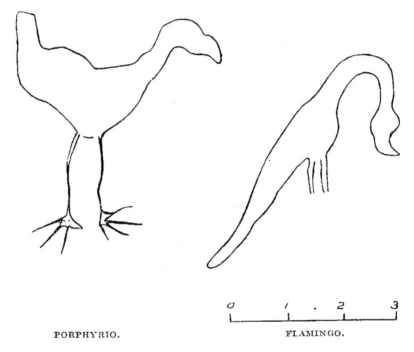

0   1   .   2   3

PORPHYRIO.   FLAMINGO.

cavern of La Pileta in the Serrania of Ronda. Many, if not most of these, are Palæolithic, which gives them a vastly greater antiquity than the birds. Some of the figures are depicted in yellow, some in red and others in black, but the first are the oldest. A few of the best are executed with great fidelity, particularly one fine Wild Goat about eighteen inches long, in black. Others are very imperfect and crude, often the merest outline, but in nearly every case the animal intended can be guessed at. In the opinion of Colonel Verner and others who have studied the subject, the Spanish pictures plainly indicate that Palæolithic man, accustomed to the incessant and intent watching of the birds and beasts upon which he was dependent for food, has shown himself more expert than those who came after him. It is a fact that in knowledge of drawing and colour, when delineating objects of the chase, he has proved to be more advanced than were the men of the Later Stone Age, who many thousand years afterwards left us their examples of Neolithic art.

Animals in the Bronze Age.—The next stage brought under our notice is the Bronze Age. Hitherto the rude and uncultured inhabitants of Great Britain had lived on the wild fruits of the land, and on such fish and small game as they could catch with the help of sticks and stones. While still possessing little or no knowledge of metals, they had to contend with the Wolf, the Wild Ox and the Stag, and also with the Bear and the Eagle. But a great change was produced when they took to fashioning tools, and most likely discovered the art of setting snares for birds. As the Bronze period superseded the age of stone implements, so was it itself superseded in due course, though not until long after, by the use of iron, which prevailed among the Romans, and gave still greater facilities for hunting and bird-catching. It is hardly to be expected that skeletons of birds eaten in the Bronze Age would be preserved, when even the remains of much larger animals have proved unable to resist the process of disintegration.

Ancient Records of Geese, Fowls and Pigeons.—Although as regards antiquity the prehistoric figures of birds, which have been discovered in the cave dwellings of the Neolithic hunters, far exceed any other representations, the ancient pictures of Egypt, and the bas-reliefs of Babylon must not be overlooked. Crude as they are, they afford considerable testimony which can be of use to the naturalist, if only because of their being the earliest evidences of bird-life in that portion of the globe. One of the most significant of these old paintings so far known, is an exceptionally lifelike fresco representing six Red-breasted and White-fronted Geese, to which attention was drawn by the present writer in 1876.* This unique and beautiful relic was obtained by the celebrated excavator, Mariette, from a tomb at Meidoum in Egypt. The slab was assigned by Mariette

* " Naturalist in Egypt." p. 120.

to the fourth dynasty, but in any case it must date from at least three thousand years before the Christian era. It suffices to show that in these two species of Geese a space of more than five thousand years has not been long enough to create any alteration in plumage. There are many other birds besides Geese among the paintings of Egypt, but very few of equal merit and antiquity with this slab.

RED-BREASTED GEESE FROM MEIDOUM.

The Fowl.—But old as is the painting from Meidoum, there exist figures believed by Messrs. Stubbs and Rowe to be ascribable to the Domestic Fowl, which date further back still. In a shrewd investigation of their age and identity, these authors seek to demonstrate that the Fowl was kept and reared by the inhabitants of ancient Egypt prior to 4400 B.C.* In support of their contention, they cite especially two figures, one a painting, the other a statuette, but as their cut of the latter is not quite satisfactory, it is here more correctly reproduced from the Proceedings of The Society of Biblical Archæology.†

* "Zoologist," 1912, p. 1.
† Vol. XXII., p. 270.

If a breed of Fowls was to be had in Egypt, one would expect it to be also existent in Syria, yet whether Fowls are mentioned, or not, in the Old Testament, is a point not settled, commentators being by no means agreed. The Hebrew word *barberim* in 1 Kings iv. 23 is considered by most scholars to mean "fatted fowl," and is so translated in both the Authorised and Revised versions, but some have raised arguments against that reading. It is worthy of notice that the Domestic Fowl is among the few animals which have shown themselves capable of living and multiplying in any and every country, from the equator to the poles : so long have they been under the yoke of man, that they have lost the need of any

STATUETTE OF A DOMESTIC FOWL.

particular climate, or soil. This makes it the more likely that they were early introduced into both Syria and Egypt.

The Pigeon.—Tristram takes the view that the Pigeon, and not the Fowl, is the earliest domesticated bird of which we have any knowledge. In Egyptian records, Pigeons in a domestic condition date back to the fifth dynasty, that is about 3000 B.C., indeed the art of training them as carriers of news was known not a great while later.* No bird is more frequently mentioned in the Old Testament. It was a Dove or Pigeon that Noah chose to send out from the Ark, when the Raven failed, and some early attempt at taming is indicated by the fact of their being offered with domestic animals like the Heifer and the Goat, in sacrifice. It was at least 2000 B.C. when Abraham was bidden to present " a Turtle-dove and a young Pigeon," for those being very likely the kind of birds

* Wilkinson's " Ancient Egyptians," S.S. II., p. 215.

most ready to hand could most easily be offered with the she Goat and the Ram.* Then we recall the reference in Isaiah, " Who are these," exclaims the prophet, " that fly as a cloud, and as the Doves to their windows ? "—*arubbah*—that is " dove-cots " (Is. lx. 8). If the translation is correct, they were a domestic species, and dove-cots, or pigeon-houses are proved to have been coeval with the Kings of Judah.

First Observers of the Migration of Birds.—There are many theories as to the origin and subsequent development of bird-migration, but whatever may have been the source from which it sprang, it is clear that it was going on some thousands of years before the Christian era. It was not likely that this great biannual movement would be overlooked by the ancients, and in fact we have several intimations of their having accurately observed it. There were naturalists in those days as there are now, although the records left behind them be but few.

The first of these is the well-known passage in the Book of Job, " Doth the hawk fly by thy wisdom, and stretch her wings towards the south ? "†

Next we have that graphic Bible story of the miracle of the Quails in Sinai, told in two passages in the Pentateuch, when the Israelites were saved from starvation by great flights of these birds. On the first occasion, for they refer to different dates—in fact, a year apart—the sacred narrative tells how " it came to pass that at even the quails came up, and covered the camp " (Exodus xvi. 13). The expression " at even " is to be noticed, as characteristic of the habits of Quails, which migrate by night, as do most birds.

Again we read in the Book of Numbers, that " There went forth a wind from the Lord, and brought quails from the sea " (Num. xi. 13). The appearance of an unusual number of a migratory species is often to be connected with a high wind, which in this instance Lane supposes to have been the south-western *Khamasin*,‡ an idea supported by a reference to it in the Psalms.§

* Genesis xv. 9.
† Job xxxix. 26.
‡ " Modern Egyptians," II., p. 222.
§ Psalm lxxviii. 26.

Canon Tristram finds that according to calculation the season was spring, and the month April,* in which he is in agreement with Clarke and other commentators. This is the period when all avine migration runs strong, and with Quails in particular, as I can testify.†

The Quails which came to save the Israelites from starvation, therefore, were making their annual journey northwards, only in very unusual numbers, and the sea from which they came, or over which they had passed, was we conclude some portion of the Red Sea.

To the prophet Jeremiah, when remonstrating with backsliding Judah, the periodical return of birds must have been known, or how could he have said, as he did, " The stork in the heaven knoweth her appointed times, and the turtle [dove] and the crane and the swallow observe the time of their coming."‡

Jeremiah, who is believed to have been born, and to have lived, near the Dead Sea, had probably often watched troops of Cranes and Storks passing overhead, as modern travellers have done, in many parts of Palestine.

The above quotations from the Old Testament clearly prove that some, at least, of the Scriptural writers were well acquainted with the phenomenon of migration, nor were the classical poets behind them. Passing over an incidental comparison by Homer of the Trojans to Cranes fleeing from the coming winter,§ there was Hesiod, who lived in the eighth century B.C. and like his great predecessor, knew the Crane. He had probably often watched them, when on passage high in the air, in Bœotia. To Hesiod their cries sounded like a summons to the labourer to plough his land, just as in other countries they have been looked on as the heralds of spring.

Then there was the poet Herodorus (circa 525 B.C.), who though not mentioning Cranes, guessed that the Hawks he

* " Natural History of the Bible," p. 231.
† April 3rd, 1875. Being at Silsilis on the Nile, the lentil fields were found to be full of Quail, so that we could realise on a smaller scale the scene in the Israelitish camp on those two memorable occasions. It was not easy to recover such small birds in the luxuriance of the lentils, when killed, but thirteen couple proved an acceptable addition to our fare.
‡ Jeremiah viii. 7.
§ " Iliad," Bk. III.

saw must have come from some distant land, because they appeared suddenly. Some translators think he meant Vultures, but nearly all birds of prey are migratory, so that is immaterial.

The Swallow was pretty sure to appeal to the poets, and in the fifth century B.C. Anacreon was ready enough to welcome the return of this harbinger of spring. In lines which have been rendered into English by Thomas Moore, he assigns Memphis on the shores of the Nile as its winter retreat. As might be expected, Herodotus, commonly called the " Father of History " (b. 484 B.C.), has something to say about migration which is also fairly definite. He tells us, as if it were an admitted fact, that Cranes, when they fly from the rigours of a Scythian winter, flock into Egypt to pass the cold season. By Scythia he meant the country to the north of the Black Sea ; farther north than that was to him a *terra incognita*.*

Aristotle a Great Naturalist.—But the first to discuss migration in anything like the spirit which moves a modern naturalist was the philosopher Aristotle (384-322 B.C.). He knew that there were many birds which migrated north in summer and south in winter, quitting countries which would have afforded them an insufficiency of food after the autumnal equinox. He also thought he knew that the Crane migrated from the steppes of Scythia to the marsh-lands south of Egypt, where the Nile has its source, *i.e.*, Central Africa. To the Pelican he gave a much shorter range, supposing that it merely shifted from the Strymon in Bulgaria to the Ister River, *i.e.*, the Danube. Aristotle, although he may not have read Anacreon, was quite aware that the Swallow went somewhere, and admits that no one had seen a Turtle Dove in winter. He held that Pigeons and Turtle Doves flocked together and migrated, as did the Swan and the Wild Goose. As to Quails, if the wind was south, it went hard with them in his judgment, but if it were in the north they were bound to have a successful passage. His observations, which contain much truth, must have been partly made at Athens, and partly derived from travellers, but some refer to Pontus in Asia Minor. Aristotle considered

* *See* Rennell's " Geographical System of Herodotus " p 50 *et seq.*

that the Cuckoo went away about the time the Dog-Star (*Sirius*) rose, that is in July, which is correct enough.*

Bones of Birds from Superficial Deposits.—Of no great antiquity are the bones of birds which have been dug up in peat bogs and other superficial deposits in different parts of the British Isles, a list of which is given in the " Ibis " for 1891 (pp. 383-394). Some of them are perhaps open to question as regards their determination.

More than sixty years ago a Pelican's humerus was exhumed in the Isle of Ely, although its identity was not immediately recognised.† This and another of larger size which I obtained through Mr. Baker, at Feltwell in Norfolk in 1869,‡ were thought by Professor Newton to be assignable to *Pelecanus crispus*, an opinion confirmed by the subsequent discovery of a third specimen.§ The first Pelican's humerus was submitted by Professor Newton to Professor Milne-Edwards, who agreed with him that it was that of a young bird, in which ossification was incomplete, a strong indication that it was bred in Cambridgeshire. A fourth Pelican's bone was subsequently reported to Professor Newton from Glastonbury, where later excavations have yielded quite a large number of Pelican remains. These have been fully described in the " Ibis " (1899, p. 351) by Mr. C. W. Andrews, and in " The Glastonbury Lake Village " (Vol. II., p. 631). Mr. Andrews finds that " Many of the bones are greatly broken and the ends much abraded, and in several instances they must have belonged to young birds. This latter circumstance appears to indicate that these birds bred in the neighbourhood, and that they were probably used for food by the inhabitants of the Village." Pelican bones have also been recorded by Dr. Herluf Winge from Danish kitchen-middens of the Stone Age. The peat bogs of the Isle of Ely have further yielded bones of the Beaver, Wild Swan, Wild Duck, Great Crested Grebe, Bittern, and Coot.‖ That the Swan, like the

* Dr. Eagle Clarke attaches much importance to the writings of Aristotle about Migration (" Studies in Bird Migration," Vol. I., pp. 3-5).

† "Proc. Zool. Soc.," 1868, p. 2 ; "Ibis," 1868, p. 363.

‡ " Proc. Zool. Soc.," 1871, p. 703 ; Norwich Nat. Tr., VI., p. 363.

§ " Norwich Nat. Tr.," VII., p. 159.

‖ " Ibis," 1863, p. 364.

Pelican, was a breeder, is most probable. Seven associated bones attributed to *Cygnus musicus* were found at Southery in Norfolk, and a tarsus referable to *C. bewickii* in Monmouthshire.* Bones of the Crane, being large, are not infrequently preserved ; chief among the places where they have been dug up are the fens of Cambridgeshire, and at King's Lynn in Norfolk. These latter, from their condition, seemed to be remains of no antiquity, *see* " Norwich Naturalists' Transactions " (Vol. VII., p. 178). Other bones of the Crane have been found in County Clare, where at the same time certain remnants of the Greater Spotted Woodpecker and Hawfinch were identified.†

---

* " Cat. of Fossil Birds in Brit. Mus.," pp. 107, 108.
† " Tr. R. Irish Acad.," XXXIII., B. pt. 1.

CHAPTER II.

FOURTH TO NINTH CENTURIES.

Fourth and Fifth Centuries : Birds known to the Romans.—*Sixth and Seventh Centuries :* Allusions to Birds in Saxon poetry. —*Eighth and Ninth Centuries :* Birds known to the Later Saxons. Birds eaten by the Picts.

British Birds known to the Romans.—Before dealing with any one particular species, it will probably be both helpful and convenient to take a general survey of British birds, beginning, that nothing may be overlooked, with the earliest times. By a survey is here meant an examination of all such records and facts as are likely to throw any light on ornithology in its broadest sense. It is hoped that something of utility may in this way be adduced, but the task is not altogether an easy one, and can only be achieved with the help of a good library, and with the assistance of friends. First, it will enable us to mark the gradual rise of ornithology. For a while the study of natural history is almost non-existent : then we begin to trace the pursuit of it by a few. Having overcome the indifference of the Saxons and passed the period of the Norman's ignorance so far as relates to birds, in all matters apart from hawking, ornithology at length begins to see light. Progress is very slow throughout the fourteenth and fifteenth centuries, but in the sixteenth, discovery in things of Nature at last is to be found approaching the dignity of a science, and after that it rapidly develops. Secondly, in taking this course, the endeavour has been made, as far as possible, to piece together a sort of narrative, less by grouping collected facts together, than by adhering to a chronological arrangement. This certainly seems the best mode of proceeding, for although it may break up the connection of the story, and necessitate a few rather unconnected paragraphs, it preserves the order of dates in their sequence. There are practically no materials with which to begin this narrative before the time of the Romans. It is true that bird-remains, which were assigned to the Grey

Goose, Barnacle Goose, Duck, Crow, Jackdaw, Kestrel, Crane, Capercaillie, Blackbird and Pigeon, were exhumed from a cave dwelling in Somersetshire* considered to be late-Celtic, but Roman coins were found as well.

Setting aside the Father of Natural History, that is, Aristotle, we must begin with the labours of the celebrated Pliny, who died A.D. 79, leaving to posterity a work of encyclopædic magnitude, and very discursive—the "Historia Naturalis." "Pliny," writes Professor Newton, quoting from his first translator, Holland, "relying wholly [in the case of birds] on characters taken from the feet, limits himself to three groups—without assigning names to them—those which have hooked talons, as Hawks; or round long claws, as Hens; or else they be broad, flat, and whole footed, as Geese and all the sort in manner of water-fowl."†

It is not to be expected that there should be any bird in Pliny's Natural History answerable to the Solan Goose, although he does name a species which appears to be the Cormorant.‡ Nor is there much in that first century work which has reference to England, or its Natural History, except where, as Professor Bensly points out, Pliny makes this observation, that "of the Goose kind there are Penelopes and also Chenalopeces, the latter generally smaller than a Goose; and Britain knows no richer feast than these." The "Chenalopeces" were possibly what we in England now call the Sheld-Duck.§

We therefore commence with the Roman occupation of England, which lasted from 52 B.C. to A.D. 410, during which time many permanent settlements were formed by the conquerors. The excavations undertaken at the Roman town of *Calleva* (now Silchester) in Hampshire, by Sir William St. John Hope and his colleagues, have done much and helped to reveal to us the then fauna of England. But, previously to this, remains of the Horse, Stag, Fox, Boar, Hare, Rabbit, Mouse, Cat, Polecat, Goat, Pig, Sheep, Duck, Fowl, Rook, and some smaller birds had been disinterred

* "Archaeologia," 1911, p. 590.
† "Dictionary of Birds," Introduction, p. 3.
‡ Book I., ch. 69, and Book XI., ch. 41.
§ *See* Turner "Avium Praecipuarum" (Evans's edn., p. 25).

by the exertions of an antiquary at a Roman villa in Gloucestershire.*

From the settlement of Calleva, we are in possession of sufficiently identified remains of the domestic fowl, the Duck, Goose, Swan, Crane, Raven and Crow.† The Thrush, Woodcock, Plover, Teal, Pheasant and Jay are also to be included with some doubt.

"The most common birds' bones [at Silchester]," writes Mr. H. Jones, "after those of the domestic fowl, have been identified as those of the Raven. . . . The numerous bones found amongst the Roman remains would almost point to its having formerly lived there in a semi-domestic state. Considerable remains of the Wild Swan, all apparently from one bird, were recovered. The numerous bones of the domestic fowl, especially the spurs of cocks, seem to show the presence of at least two varieties. . . ."‡

Again, in another place, it is stated : "The Raven and the Crow, especially the former, seem to have been very plentiful, and gave the largest number of identifiable bones. §

The abundance of the Raven is curious, but it may be it was hung in a cage at the entrance, as the Magpie was in Rome, to help keep guard against intruders or to salute those who came invited to a villa.||

The only other discovery was the leg bone of a Guinea Fowl, if the identification be correct, encircled by a metal ring, probably an imported pet to Silchester, for a knowledge of which I am indebted to Mr. H. M. Wallis.

But Hampshire and Gloucester are not the only counties where birds' bones have been found, for from Mr. James Ritchie I learn that Haddington has yielded remains of the Buzzard. To this species some bones from Roman debris at Folkestone may also have belonged.¶

With regard to other Roman birds we have surmises in plenty, as well as sundry facts. An Eagle served as a

* "Antiquities of Richborough," by C. Roach Smith, 1850, p. 109.
† "Archaeologia," 1892, p. 288 ; 1902, p. 20 ; 1905, p. 369 ; 1906, p. 167. For these references I am indebted to Mr. J. Quinton.
‡ "Archaeologia," 1892, p. 288.
§ "Archaeologia," 1893, p. 573.
|| Fosbroke, "Encyclopædia of Antiquities," I., p. 54.
¶ "Archaeologia," XLVII., pp. 450, 455.

standard to the Roman legions and they had Owls on their
coins.   Unquestionably they had aviaries in England, were
breeders of poultry, and kept more than one sort of fowl.   It is
an open question whether they brought the Peacock, which
was not likely to have been introduced by the Saxons.   That
they brought the Pheasant there can be little doubt, as
Professor Dawkins has long ago suggested.*   Knowing their
fondness for Geese, we may assume that they tried domesti-
cating the Grey-lag Goose, which, being a resident in English
fens, was not hard to come by.   According to Horace, the
liver of a white Goose fed upon figs was a dainty among
the Romans, and Ovid tells of their being kept in lieu of
house-dogs.   Fosbroke,† the industrious antiquary, informs
us that flocks of Geese were driven to the markets at Rome,
even from Picardy and Flanders,—that Magpies were kept
in barbers' shops,—that Ostriches were made to fight with
gladiators,—that the Romans imported Parrots, but apparently
had only green ones,—that their epicures esteemed the tongue
of the Flamingo, and still more Thrushes which had grown fat
on figs (of which Italy can produce such abundant crops),
a circumstance borne out by their own poets.   "Obeso nil
melius turdo," says one of them, the practical Horace, when
enumerating the good things of the land.‡   Even in those
days white Blackbirds were not unknown and excited curiosity
in the towns, where they were sold for the aviary rather than
for eating.   That the Romans had large aviaries cannot be
doubted, and plenty of domestic Fowls, both in England and
Italy ; indeed the method of fattening cocks by castration is
supposed to have been introduced by them.   They sometimes
varied the bloody scenes of the amphitheatre by indulging
in cock fights, but, unlike the Greeks, they were not greatly
addicted to this form of sport, being more concerned with
Quails for combat.§

* "Ibis," 1860, p. 358.

† "Encyclopædia of Antiquities and Elements of Archaeology," by
T. D. Fosbroke (1825).

‡ Lib. I., Ep. XV., line 40.   It is an opinion shared by all Italians to the
present day, see the accounts of their *Roccoli*, given in the "History of
Fowling," by H. A. Macpherson (pp. 101–106).

§ "Archaeologia," 1786, p. 144.

Turning to animals other than birds, we have the best proof that the Romans had the Fallow Deer in this country, which they are credited with having introduced. They were not great hunters by nature, but there is evidence of their chasing the wild Red Deer with dogs. According to Cæsar's Commentaries there were Hares in England, but the natives did not eat them, and they had the same prejudice about the Cock and the Goose.* Both Romans and Britons were well acquainted with the Wild Boar, which they chased and brought to bay, but a Boar in his lair was a dangerous beast for a man armed with nothing better than a sword and a spear. About 1740–48 there was found in a garden in Weardale, Durham, a Roman altar of great significance of the hunter's peril in the chase. It was dedicated to the God of the Forests in gratitude by one Tetius Veturius Micianus, a prefect of soldiers, who had slain — maybe single-handed — a great Wild Boar which had set all previous hunters at defiance. This singular relic is recorded by Dr. Taylor in " The Philosophical Transactions."†

The inscription, which is repeated by Mr. T. Birch in the " Gentleman's Magazine " for 1749,‡ has been looked upon as one of much importance and has attracted great attention. This sculptured stone is generally referred to by archæologists as The Weardale Altar, see Harting " British Animals Extinct within Historic Times " (p. 78), where an excellent account of the Wild Boar is given.

Sixth and Seventh Centuries.

References in Saxon Poetry to Birds.—It was not until Anno Domini 571 that the Saxons came in force over the North Sea, and one of their number assumed the title of King. They had with them scribes and minstrels, no doubt diligent in their office, whose duty it was to write poems, perpetuating in some cases real history, in others acceptable legends. It is from this source that we get very early mention of British birds.

* " De Bell. Gall." (Lib. V., c. 12), " Archaeologia," 1792, p. 164.
† No. 486, p. 173.
‡ Vol. XIX., p. 449.

What must needs be the first mention 'of the Solan Goose is discoverable in the Anglo-Saxon poetry here referred to, in what is known as the romance or poem of Beowulf. Here the most noticeable bird of the ocean, the Gannet, at once becomes emblematic, and the sea was figuratively referred to as its bath. In this sense—

> . . . . Manig otherne
> godum gegrettan ofer ganotes bæð
> sceal hring-naca ofer hea-thu bringan
> lac *and* luf-tacen. . .

(*Translation*) : . . . Many a one shall greet the other with benefits, over the Gannet's bath ; the ringed ship shall bring over the deeps offerings and tokens of love.

It is difficult to fix the date of the writing of this poem, which, thanks to the Early English Text Society, is accessible in autotype, but it was subsequent and possibly long subsequent to A.D. 597. The margins of the MS. are unfortunately sadly worn, and the word " ganotes " scarcely legible.

The next mention of the Gannet is to be found in the celebrated " Codex Exoniensis " in an Anglo-Saxon song " The Perils of The Seafarer," which will be quoted from Mr. Benjamin Thorpe's translation :—

Translation.

> " At times *the* swan's song
> I made to me for pastime,
> *the* ganet's cry,
> and *the* ' hu-ilpe's ' note ;
> for men's laughter,
> *the* men singing ;
> for mead-drinking,
> storms there *the* stone-cliffs beat ;
> there them *the* starling answer'd,
> icy of wings.
> Full oft the eagle scream'd,
> dewy of wings.
>
> . . . . . .
>
> So also *the* cuckoo exhorts *
> with mournful voice."

* The Cuckoo also comes into " The Legend of Saint Guthlac ' (Bk. VI.).

This is an exceedingly interesting passage, for it gives us the names of four birds, all mentioned for the first time as British. If the *Huilpe* could be identified, it would make five : Professor W. Skeat considered it agreed that it was a bird of some sort.*

Possibly it was the Whaup or Curlew, but what was meant by the *stearn* or Starling is obscure. It is hardly likely to have been the bird which we call a Starling now.†

A third mention of the Gannet occurs in the Anglo-Saxon Chronicle, and a fourth in an Anglo-Saxon rune :

> " Oak is on earth
> to the sons of men
> food of the flesh,
> often he goeth
> over the ganet's bath." ‡

In an A.S. metrical psalm there is a fifth allusion— " fuglas comon of garseoge, ganetes fleogan "—" there came birds of the ocean, Gannets flew."

.   .   .   .

The only other item which calls for quotation, is a vague one, coming as before from the Saxon Chronicle : " A.D. 671. This year happened that great destruction among the fowls " —how, or from what cause, the writer does not tell us.

Here I may be pardoned for observing that the earliest printed translation of the Saxon Chronicle was undertaken by a member of my family—Anna Gurney, of Northrepps, and completed in 1819.§

Eighth and Ninth Centuries.

Birds known to the Later Saxons.—Two hundred years of residence in England could not be altogether without

* " Notes on English Etymology," 1907, p. 6.

† *See* Ælfric's Glossary in Somner's A.S. Dictionary. The Rev. F. C. R. Jourdain thinks it was the Tern, a suggestion which has been before made. The Saxon word in the orginal is *Stærn*, and that is very similar to *Starn*, which is a provincialism still in use for Terns : *Stær* is given for a Starling in Bosworth's A.S. Dictionary.

‡ " Archaeologia," 1840, p. 344, J. M. Kemble.

§ The collection of Teutonic and etymological books formed by this learned lady is preserved in the Norfolk and Norwich Library : an obituary of her by Mrs. Austin appeared in the " Gentleman's Magazine " for September 1857.

effect on the civilisation of the Saxon population. It was too early for a love of letters to manifest itself among a

ENGLAND IN THE NINTH CENTURY.

people whose chief notion of right was brute force, but ideas began to circulate, and learned thoughts to permeate; not many of these were committed to writing, but the

Saxon Chronicle went on, continued by other hands. There were plenty of domesticated animals. Food of all kinds, flesh of swine especially, was plentiful, and those by the sea could, in addition, maintain themselves by fishing. Already had begun what was destined to be one of Britain's greatest industries, the catching of herrings, as indicated by a reference to it in 709 in the Chronicles of Evesham, an important monastery (67 monks) in Worcestershire. This early Saxon herring fishery, which showed enterprise in the population not to have been expected at that date, must have developed rapidly. We judge that it did so, from what it was at the Conquest, see " Introduction to Domesday," by Sir H. Ellis.*

The names of four more birds are now to be met with in the Saxon Chronicle : the Kite, Goshawk, Vulture (?) and Raven. These are believed to be correctly identified ; indeed the Raven would have been familiar to the invaders. It was consecrated by the Scandinavians to the god Odin, and was a bird always invested with superstition.

Earliest Annals of Falconry.—The only other facts about Saxon birds, on which complete reliance can be placed, are to be sought for in the early annals of Falconry, a sport which may claim to be the first form of the chase known. Mr. J. E. Harting, who has elucidated this subject with his usual erudition, and written some charming chapters about it, considers that the date of the introduction of Hawking into England cannot now be ascertained.† It must, however, have been of Saxon origin, as the Romans have never been suspected of introducing it when they came to Britain. That it had been practised in some parts of Europe is certain, and that the sport was already in vogue in France is also known ; this much being proved, *inter alia*, by a singular table of seventh century rates obtained from the *Lex Ripuar* and *Lex Alaman* by Mr. John Whitaker,‡ among which we

* 1833, Vol. I., p. 141.   Ellis indicates a great spread.   In the eleventh century Beccles near Yarmouth had to pay the abbey of St. Edmunds thirty thousand herrings.   In 1195 it had still further prospered, so much so that the fishery at Dunwich in Suffolk, the greater part of which port is now under the sea, was able to furnish Henry II. with twenty-four thousand herrings.

† " Essays on Sport and Natural History," 1883, pp. 67-68.

‡ Taken from that author's " History of Manchester," 1771 (Vol. II., p. 347).

discover some of the prices for hawks, and in particular the value set on a falcon of one year,

			s.	d.
C. 37 *Lex*	An untamed Hawk	.. .. ..	3	0
Rip.	A Hawk a year old	.. .. ..	12	0
C. 84 *Lex*	A Hawk that flies at Cranes	.. ..	6	0
Alam.	A Goshawk	.. ..	3	0
	A Crane	.. ..	3	0

In Persia there was Hawking 1700 years B.C., and in China before that, and even in Europe Mr. Harting thinks that it was practised three centuries before the Christian era,[*] which shows the extraordinary antiquity of this sport.

Pennant[†] and Strutt—who devotes an elaborate chapter to the early history of Hawking in Great Britain in his "Sports and Pastimes of the People of England" (1801)— would seem to be the first authors to relate the following, which is somewhat differently told by Mr. Harting, and the original of which is to be sought in "Epistolæ Sancti Bonifacii."[‡]

About the middle of the eighth century (prior to 755) Boniface, Archbishop of Mons in Belgium [§] himself a native of England, presented to Ethelbert II., the Saxon King of Kent, one Hawk and two Falcons, the latter probably Gyrfalcons. A King of Mercia, which was a part of England farther north, also requested the same Archbishop to send to him two Falcons which had been trained to kill Cranes.

This is an early notice of the Crane, and here, no doubt, the real Crane was meant. There must have been Cranes—for which the Saxon name was *Cræn* or *Cornoch*—on the marshes of the west and north of England, or Falcons would not have been needed in Mercia to fly at them. The passage further shows that to be an ecclesiastic was no bar to the enjoyment of the pursuit of Hawking. But the Kings of Kent and Mercia were not the only monarchs who took delight in Falconry, as will appear presently. Their sports were imitated by that

---

[*] *T.c.*, p. 68.

[†] "Arctic Zoology," 1784, by Thomas Pennant (Vol. II., p. 219).

[‡] *See* edn. Würdtwein, Ep. 84, or edn. Duemmler (Mon. Hist. Germ.), Ep. 106.

[§] According to one account, Boniface, who was murdered in 752, was Archbishop not of Mons, but of Mentz in Germany.

somewhat mysterious royalty of the ninth century, Alfred the Great (A.D. 849–901).

King Alfred.—Alfred's gifts in respect of " falconarios, accipitrarios, canicularios quoque," are alluded to in the ancient chronicle of Florentius Wigorniensis. Alfred is even supposed to have himself penned, or to have had written, a treatise on the subject of Hawking, so great was his delight in this occupation, a treatise which, did it now exist, would take precedence of all that has been written in this country.

Birds eaten in Scotland by the Picts.—If the few Saxon documents which survive afford us very little information about Natural History, there is another way in which we may glean something, and this is by the use of the spade. Already in several cases the bones of birds, mostly large ones, which have been used as food by early dwellers in the land, showing little signs of decay, have been exhumed.

Especially has this been the case in Scotland, in the vicinity of ancient earth-forts and dwellings, where the half-eaten remains of animals were likely to be thrown away by the Picts or Caledonians. These were the inhabitants of North Britain a thousand years ago, and they have left their marks behind them.

In the course of some excavations in an ancient earthwork of this sort, in the Orkney Islands, assigned to the Picts, recognisable remains of the Solan Goose, Cormorant, Shag, Great Northern Diver, Whooper Swan, Gull, Manx Shearwater and Great Auk were dug up.* But these are not the only remains of the Solan Goose which have been disinterred, for in Caithness similar bones were discovered,† as well as in the North of Ireland,‡ and in Ayrshire,§ and in the kitchen-middens of Denmark.

Mr. James Ritchie has been good enough to inform me that a large collection from Dunagoil Cave in Bute, a likely locality for Solan Goose bones, being only thirty-five miles from Ailsa Craig, contained none, nor were there any with the abundant remains of the Shag in three caves examined in East Fife, in which were also found remains of the Goose, Gull and Diver.

* N. F. Ticehurst, " British Birds," 1907-8, Vol. I, p. 309.
† In 1864. *See* " Prehistoric Remains of Caithness."
‡ " Irish Naturalist," 1899, p. 5.
§ " Zoologist," 1915, p. 406.

CHAPTER III.

TENTH AND ELEVENTH CENTURIES.

The Tenth Century: The Laws of Howel. Athelstan, King of the West
Saxons. Edward the Confessor.—*Legends about Birds :* A Fowl of Value
A New Zealand Legend. The Barnacle Shell. The Raven.—*The Eleventh
Century :* Falconry, the Sport of the Normans. Domesday Book.

*England in the Tenth Century. The Laws of Howel
relating to animals.*—Much has been written about the manners
of the Middle Ages in England, but bird-life in the time of
the Anglo-Normans, for want of facts, never can be properly
described. We might expect the recital of their feasts to shed
some light upon it, and we do get a few brief items from the
chronicles of William of Malmesbury, while the later writings
of Holinshed and Speed, Camden, Joseph Strutt and Wright
describe the enormous quantity of provisions which were
consumed. But none of these writers relate all we should
like to know about the different kinds of birds which were eaten.
With the beasts of the forest it is rather different, for there
is more about hunting. and various materials are to hand
which tell of the Wild Boars and Wolves which were only
too numerous for the welfare of the people. A good many
of these anecdotes and references are gathered together in
Harting's " British Animals Extinct within Historic Times "
(1880), and afford very suggestive reading, as well as valuable
matter for reference.

To the tenth century probably belong the Welsh laws of
Howel, King of Cambria, which have been translated by
William Probert. From these we learn that there were three
Common Hunts in Wales—namely, the hunting of a Stag, of
a swarm of Bees, and of a Salmon. There were also three
" barking hunts," so called because the game was " treed "
or brought to bay by dogs, viz., the hunting of the Bear, the
Squirrel, and the Pheasant ; and three Clamorous Hunts in

pursuit of the Fox, the Hare and the Roe-buck. These terms are easily understood and imply that Bears, Squirrels and Pheasants were in existence to be hunted. Howel also alludes to Hawking, which must have been introduced by the Saxons into the less mountainous parts of Wales. There are, he says, three animals whose feet are of the same value as their lives, that is to say, without them they would be worthless—a Horse, a Hawk, and a Greyhound.

Athelstan and Edward the Confessor.—When Athelstan, the Saxon, defeated the King of Wales in 937, he imposed upon him for tribute, among other things, the providing of " birds trained to make prey of others in the air." This is related in the " Gesta Regum Anglorum " of William of Malmesbury, who died in 1143.* No doubt these birds which preyed on others were, as Mr. Harting supposes, Hawks for hunting : the expression is very applicable.

The same historian says of Edward the Confessor, who died in 1066, that his greatest enjoyment was in hounds, and in " the pouncing of birds, whose nature it is to prey on their kindred species."† These " pouncing " birds must also have been Hawks, trained for the chase like the others which were rendered to Athelstan.

Joseph Strutt thinks that the Confessor wrote, or commanded to be written, a treatise on hawking,‡ which would be a valuable book, if we possessed it, showing the growth of the sport. It is related of him that every day after divine service was over he spent the rest of his leisure in hunting or hawking. " It was his chiefest delight," says Mr. Harting, quoting the historian, " to follow a pack of swift hounds in pursuit of their game."§

There is one very interesting and ancient illustration of hawking which is given in Strutt's work, and which is also referred to by Mr. Harting, taken from a manuscript of the tenth century.

It is a painting in six colours, representing a Saxon nobleman on horseback, with a Gyr falcon on his right hand,

* English Trans., edn. 1815, p. 154.
† *T.c.*, p. 283.
‡ " Sports and Pastimes," 1801, p. 25.
§ " Essays on Sport," pp. 71, 72.

SAXON FALCONRY.

while his man has another which he is about to cast off at some Wild Ducks on a lake or river, beside which an unmistakable Crane, in adult plumage as shown by its elevated tertials, is stooping to feed, unconscious of any danger.

Names of Animals.—No account of the tenth century would be complete without a reference to certain Saxon lists of animals' names.* The principal one is known to Saxon scholars as Archbishop Ælfric's Vocabulary, and was probably compiled for educational purposes. This singular list, and another Vocabulary of slightly later date, perhaps in part drawn up from the first, contain the names of nearly one hundred birds. But it is not stated or implied by their compilers that they are all British species : nor can they be, for the Ostrich, Vulture, and Pelican are included. These catalogues, giving the Latin and Saxon names, are by no means valueless, but at the same time the identity of some of the species is obscure.

The following are some of those named—

Cignus, ylfetc.	Mergus, scealfr.
Pauo, pawe.	Mergulus, fugeldoppe.
Aquila, earn.	Auca, gos.
Beacita, stearn.	Aucarius, goshafuc.
Cornix, crawe.	Anser, ganra.
Olor, swan.	Anas, ened.
Ardea, hragra.	Ciconia, storc.
Ficedula, swertling.	Rubisca, rudduc.
Strix, ule.	Auricinctus, goldfinc.
Lucinia, nightegale.	Alauda, laucrce.

The Colloquy of Ælfric.—What is called The Colloquy of Ælfric is a series of dialogues for educational purposes, between a master and his pupils, which after being privately printed from Cottonian MSS., was published by Mr. T. Wright in " Anglo-Saxon and Old English Vocabularies."† From this dialogue a passage about hawking, which was partly translated by the late Professor Newton for my father, may be appropriately extracted.‡

* Edited and collated by T. Wright in 1857, second edition 1884.
† P. 88.
‡ This hawking dialogue is also given in " A Perfect Booke for Kepinge of Sparhawkes or Goshawkes," edited by J. E. Harting.

MAGISTER : What say you, Auceps ? How do you beguile birds ?

AUCEPS : I beguile birds in many ways; sometimes with nets, sometimes with snares, sometimes with bird-lime, sometimes with a call, sometimes with a hawk, sometimes with a decoy.

MAGISTER : Have you a hawk ?

AUCEPS : I have.

MAGISTER : Do you know how to tame them ?

AUCEPS : I do know. What use would they be to me if I did not know how to tame them ?

VENATOR : Give me a hawk.

AUCEPS : I will willingly give you one, if you will give me a swift dog. What hawk do you desire to have, a larger or a smaller one ?

VENATOR : Give me a larger one.

MAGISTER : How do you feed your hawks ?

AUCEPS : They feed themselves and me in winter, and in spring I let them fly away to the wood, and I take the young in autumn and tame them.

MAGISTER : And why do you let your tamed hawks fly away ?

AUCEPS : Because I do not wish to feed them in summer, for they eat too much.

MAGISTER : Yet many people feed their tamed hawks through the summer, that they may have them ready again.

AUCEPS : They do so, but I do not wish to take so much trouble about them, for I know how to catch others, not one only but more.

As indicated by Professor Newton, one of the points of this dialogue is that the letting loose of a Goshawk or Sparrow-hawk to tend for itself and breed, mentioned in at least one instance in the fifteenth century—see "Hawking in Norfolk," by A. Newton (Lubbock's " Fauna of Norfolk ")—was no exceptional practice at a much earlier date. Another point, as Mr. Harting observes (*in litt.*), is the describing of the various methods of bird-catching adopted in Anglo-Saxon times, which is not without interest.

Legends of Birds. A Færöese Legend of a Fowl of Value. —Undoubtedly some of the legends of the North are of antiquity ; and a history of the early annals of ornithology would hardly be complete without a reference to them, for there are many which have an important bearing upon birds : a book, for instance, might be written on the folk-lore of the Raven, and very curious it would be. It was not until the seventeenth century that the Legendary or Credulous Period of Natural History, as one writer aptly terms it, was laid to rest, and finally disappeared. Then with the spread of printing, it gave place to a better era—an era of investigation at first hand, which elicited facts, and scattered idle beliefs about birds and other animals. Although the legend about the Solan Goose does not refer to the British Isles, it is worth giving because of its age, and we shall probably not be wrong in assigning it to the tenth century.

A certain sorcerer in the Færöes—a group of islands between Iceland and the Shetlands—who flourished many centuries ago, seeking peace after many fights from one who was a giant, bribed the foe with the yearly promise of " a sort of Whales and Fowl in the Land, which were not gotten in other places of *Feroe*." This priceless Fowl was the " Sule," or Solan Goose, which was then and there bestowed by the sorcerer on the island of Myggenaës, where they breed to this day. This strange story, which is another evidence to the antiquity of the name " Sule," or Solan, is related by Lucas Jacobus Debes in the " Færöe and Færoa Reserata," 1673.

A New Zealand Legend.—Sir Walter Buller tells us that the Australian Gannet (*Sula serrator*) has a place in an ancient fable of New Zealand, in which one of the Maori legends recounts a trial of strength which is supposed to take place between the birds of the sea and the birds of the land.*

The Legend of the Barnacle.—Although we have no documentary evidence of the famous legend of the Barnacle before the twelfth century, yet we may surmise that it existed in England before that. There is no mention of the fable in classical authors, yet Sir Ray Lankester tells of an unmistakable drawing of a ship's barnacle producing a young Goose, which occurs on a Mycenæan vase dug up in Crete. From what origin the story sprang it is not easy to comprehend.

* " Birds of New Zealand " (1888), II., p. 148.

All we know is that widely spread was the belief that certain birds called Barnicle or Barnacle Geese, which one would think were not common enough to be familiar, owed their origin to an aberrant crustacean *Lepas anatifera*, from which they were generated.

Even as late as the sixteenth century, a naturalist of so high repute as William Turner could not shake himself free from the accumulated evidence of this absurd story, the truth of which had been solemnly vouched for by one Octavian, an Irish ecclesiastic of his acquaintance.

Legends of the Raven.—Anglo-Saxon *Hræfen*, from its cry. *Hrefnes-fot*, raven-foot. Proverbs respecting the Raven are many. An interesting account is given by the Rev. C. Swainson of this bird in " Provincial Names and Folk-lore " (1885), under the headings of :—

Folk-lore of the Raven.

The Raven in Northern Mythology.

The Raven as prognosticating Death.

The Raven Stone.

The Swallow-Stone —The legend of the Swallow-stone ran as follows. It was supposed by the peasantry of France that the Swallow knew how and where to find a certain small round pebble, or as some say, the polished operculum of a shell from the shore. This talisman had the marvellous power of giving sight to its young ones when applied to their still unopened eyes, and it was soon discovered that it was efficacious also for human ophthalmia. The legend, which is told at greater length in " La Normandie Romanesque," by Amélie Bosquet, flourished most in Brittany, but it had a standing elsewhere, with some variation of detail.*

Eleventh Century.

FALCONRY AND DOMESDAY BOOK.

England in the Eleventh Century. The Pastime of Falconry.—Falconry seems to have grown in favour with each succeeding generation. History abundantly proves that in the estimation both of the Saxons and their conquerors the Normans, to be the bearer of a Hawk was one of the chief

---

* 1845, p. 217. For an excellent account of this legend *see* Harting's " Essays on Sport and Natural History," p. 277.

privileges of nobility. No one of inferior rank was permitted
to appear in public with his Goshawk, even if he possessed
one, so distinctive was it considered to be. It will be observed
that two of the figures in the cut are ladies, but there was
nothing unusual in this : women sometimes accompanied men
in the diversion of hawking, and sometimes went out alone.
If, says Strutt, we may believe John of Salisbury, who died
in 1180 (Lib. I., cap. 4), some even excelled the men in knowledge and exercise of the art. That hawking should be
forbidden to clerics was to be expected, but as the case of
Bishop Boniface proves, the prohibition was not always
enough to restrain the more ardent ecclesiastics, in spite of
the law which said : " si clericus venationes exercuerit, I
annum pœnitent."

In the celebrated Bayeux tapestry, Harold, King of
England is represented approaching William, Duke of
Normandy, mounted, and bearing upon his hand a Hawk.
It is commonly supposed to have been a Sparrow-Hawk, but
in the tapestry it is almost large enough to be an Eagle.
The Duke also has his Hawk, and hounds are not wanting.
This King and also William II., and their Courts, were
greatly addicted to hunting and hawking, which led to much
overbearance. So lightly was life valued that it was less
criminal to slay a man than to purloin a Tiercel. It was the
same with game. Terrible penalties, such as the loss of both
eyes, were meted out to peasants or villeins who killed
game reserved for William and his nobles. As he forbade
the slaying of Harts, so also did he of Wild Boars, but
not of Hares.

In order to keep the New Forest solely for hunting,
William I. is accused of laying waste a large tract, expelling
the inhabitants of Hampshire. The chronicler Malmesbury
draws a melancholy picture of the forest, as a spot appropriated for the nurture and refuge of wild beasts, where
before had existed human intercourse, and the worship of God,
a place where Deer, Goats, and other animals, which were not
for the general service of mankind, now ranged unrestrained.*
Such was this monarch's passion for the chase that nothing
could stay his impetuosity.

* " De Gestis Regum," 1125. Lib. III.

LADIES HAWKING. (After Strutt.)

D

As an example of the violence of William's temper, it is related by Dugdale that when Fitz-Osberne, the Steward of the Household, set before him the flesh of a Crane scarce half roasted, the King took such offence that he lifted up his fist and would have struck him fiercely, but that his dapifer Eudo warded off the blow.*

Domesday Book.—In 1080 or 1085 William ordered the commencement of a General Survey of England—*Liber Censualis Angliæ*—known as the Dome's-day or Doom's-day Book. This great document was intended to be a register whereby to determine the right in the tenure of estates, and for the proper making of it Commissioners were sent into every county and shire, except the four most northern ones. These Commissioners associated themselves with leading persons in each shire, and their duty was to elicit information on various points, including the number of "*Servi*," Freemen, and Tenants in each Manor, the number of oxen, swine and sheep, the quantity of wood, meadow and pasture, with particulars of any fish-ponds, or river fisheries ; even the eyries of Hawks were recorded, and the number of eels which a particular mill and its stream might afford to the proprietor.

Sir Henry Ellis states that besides the New Forest, four other forests are noticed in the Domesday Survey, viz., Windsor Forest, Gravelinges in Wilts, Wimburne in Dorset, and Wychwood in Oxfordshire.† *Silva* and *Nemus* are the usual terms in the Survey for wood, and in a few entries *Silvula*. On account of the running and feeding of numerous herds of hogs, acorns and beechmast had a degree of importance of which we can form a very inadequate idea at this time.‡ These pigs were the sustenance on which the country folk principally depended, and which the King's severity might cause them to lose.

The eyries of Hawks in William's time were thought of no small value, for it was these which principally contributed to the sport of falconry. The word "eyrie or "acrie" is perhaps capable of two meanings. Sir Henry Ellis, in his

* " Baronage of England." 1675, p. 109.
† " General Introduction to Domesday Book." 1833, Vol. I., p. 103.
‡ *l.c.*, pp. 96, 97.

" General Introduction to Domesday Book,"* quotes authority for thinking that it meant not only the nest or brood, but the place destined for the breeding or training of Hawks, in evidence of which he cites a charter granted by Henry III. in the thirteenth century to the Church of York.†

There are frequent mentions of Hawks' "aeries" in Domesday, sometimes in conjunction with manorial or other rights, which Sir H. Ellis has been at the pains of collecting.‡ One of the instances of a Hawks' breeding-place in the south of England cited by Ellis was in Sussex, on land belonging to Battle Abbey, which was founded by William I., where were " iii nidi accipitr' in silua." These nests may have belonged to Peregrines, or more probably to Goshawks if they were in woods, for the nest of a Sparrow-Hawk would hardly have been of sufficient consequence to specify.§ Eyries of Hawks are also noticed in Domesday in Bucks, Gloucester, Worcester, Hereford, Shropshire, and, more frequently than in other counties, in Cheshire,‖ as well as among the lands between the Ribble and the Mersey.

The Great Fen District of East Anglia.—This is all the information about birds to be extracted from Domesday Book, but there are still a few other sources which can be tapped. The natural features of England in the eleventh and twelfth centuries differed less from those of the twentieth than is commonly supposed, but there was much more woodland. In 1217 Henry III. granted a Charter of the Forests, which perhaps reached their greatest extent in Lancashire and Yorkshire ; there were also large untouched tracts in Staffordshire, Derbyshire, Leicestershire, and Notts ; while in the south and east of England there was more water and marsh. Especially must this have been so in what was known as the Fen Country of east England, where the Romans

* Vol. I., p. 341.

† For a good exposition of the various forms of this word, and its earliest use by authors *see* Swann's " Dictionary of English and Folk-names of British Birds," p. 2.

‡ *T.c.*, p. 340.

§ The Rev. F. C. R. Jourdain reminds me that, although British Peregrines. and Buzzards, also, now nest upon cliffs, yet they breed freely upon trees elsewhere, and no doubt used to do so in England.

‖ *See* " The Birds of Cheshire," by Coward and Oldham, p. 18.

had tried their hands at draining and not succeeded. What this wild tract, which comprised Cambridgeshire and Huntingdon, as well as a large part of Lincolnshire and West Norfolk, was like in the time of William the Conqueror, may be imagined by comparing it with the deltas of the Rhone or the Nile, as they exist at the present day. The eastern boundary of the Fen district, so far as Norfolk was concerned, commenced, says Henry Stevenson, " immediately below the town of Brandon, in the low ground, through which the Little Ouse winds its way, and rounding the uplands of Hockwold, turns northwards towards Methwold, then running up the course of the Wissey, nearly as far as Stoke Ferry, it bends to the westward in the direction of Denver, whence it pursues a comparatively straight course to King's Lynn, being, however, slightly diverted to the eastward up the valley of the Nar."*

The centre part of this great Fen area was little better than an inland sea of brackish water in winter, and a swamp in summer, suitable enough for aquatic birds, but noxious to human beings, who gave it up to the possession of the Bittern, the Godwit, and the Grey-lag Goose ; and maybe the Egret, the Stilt, the Night Heron, and the Ibis were there too. No Cornelius Vermuyden had as yet arisen, and Henry VII. had not sanctioned the general drainage of that part of his dominions, which must have been a wild birds' paradise, though there were no ornithologists then to enjoy it. Fortunately we possess the " Liber Eliensis" MS., which gives us some idea of the wilderness of reeds and their attendant water-fowl; when this brief chronicle, the labour of some unknown monk, was composed in the eleventh century, there could not have been less than two thousand square miles of marsh and fen. A good deal of it would have been literally teeming with wild-fowl, Ducks of many sorts and kinds in the open water, with Cranes, Bitterns, Spoonbills, and even Pelicans wherever the quaking bog afforded them standing room. " De avibus . . ." writes the author of the Liber, " Anseres innumeræ, fiscedulæ, felicæ, mergæ, corvæ aquaticæ, ardeæ et anetes, quarum copia maxima est brumali tempore vel cum aves pennas mutant, per eentum et tres centas captas vidi plus minusve : nonnunquam in laqueis et retibus ac glutine capi

* " The Birds of Norfolk," by Henry Stevenson (Vol. I., p. LIV.).

solent."[*] This list of birds is repeated with some slight alteration in the legendary narrative of some later monk, where one
Beda is made to say : " Of birds likewise there be innumerable :
So also of geese, bitterns, sea-fowl, water-crows, herons, and
ducks, abundance ; . . . "[†] Even more plentiful than birds
were the fish, and to the monasteries these were the most
valuable. Innumerable eels, the Liber tells us, were netted,
great pike, pickerels, perch, roach, barbel, lampreys (which
were called water-snakes), and sometimes shad, and a royal
fish, the turbot, was taken.[‡]

Besides the testimony of the Liber, we have that of
that grand old chronicler, William of Malmesbury, before
quoted, who had heard of the character of the fens, if he had
not personally been there. Writing in 1125 he says, " Here is
such plenty of fish as to cause astonishment in strangers, while
the natives laugh at their surprise. Water-fowl are as plentiful ;
so that five persons may not only assuage their hunger with
both sorts of food, but eat to satiety for a penny."[§] Such was
the character which these wild wastes of water bore, the home
of monastic institutions, as well as a haven of security.

Hugh Albus, or Candidus. — Of beasts there were not
many. The stagnant water of the fens would have been too
sluggish to please the Beaver, yet its bones have been found
in a semi-fossilised condition, as well as those of the Wild
Boar.[||] Of Polecats there would have been plenty, and of
Otters any number with so much fish to prey on.

None of these creatures are alluded to by another author
not often quoted. Hugh Albus or Candidus, who, writing about
1150, has left a scanty sketch of Fenland. " From the flooding
of the rivers, or from their overflow," he says, " the water
standing on unlevel ground makes a deep marsh and so renders
the land uninhabitable, save on some raised spots of ground.
. . . There are found wood and twigs for fires, hay for the

* " Historia Eliensis " (Bk. II., ch. 105) ; I am indebted to Prof. Bensly for
verifying the reference, and spelling.

† " The History of Imbanking and Draining," by Sir William Dugdale,
p. 187.

‡ *See* notes communicated by the translator, the Rev. D. J. Stewart,
editor of the Liber, to " The Fenland Past and Present " (p. 355).

§ " Gesta Pontificum," translation.

|| " On the Zoology of Ancient Europe," by Alfred Newton (p. 24).

fodder of cattle, thatch for covering houses, and many other
useful things. It is moreover productive of birds and fishes.
For there are various rivers, and very many waters and ponds
abounding in fish." Besides the "Anseres innumeræ" of the
" Liber Eliensis, " the Bitterns, the Mallards, the Coots and
Herons, which were all food for a scanty population, and which
Hugh the White probably had in mind, there were many other
birds, could we but know their names. Also there were eels,
which formed a staple article of food. By a very early Saxon
Charter we learn that " I Eadgar, King . . . added to the
former gift, every year, for those monks [of the Abbey of
Ely] ten thousand Eel fishes . . . ." Four thousand eels were
a yearly present from the monks of Ramsey to those of
Peterborough.* " In Wisbece abb de Ramesi viii piscatores,
redd v mil 7 cc. lx anguill " (Domesday),—a large contribution
for these fishermen to pay. Ely is even supposed to take its
name from the eels, and certainly the isle enjoyed great
advantages from its fresh-water fisheries. Domesday dis-
tinguishes the owners of fishing rights as *piscatores*, and no
doubt they were people of importance, and not at all confined
to the fens. In Norfolk there were thirty-two *piscatores*, and
Domesday allows as many as twenty-four for Suffolk.

The Keeping of Bees, Swine, and Fowls.—But it must not
be supposed that all England was like the Fen country.
Tillage was carried on by the Saxon population in wide
districts with a thrift and labour which brought in an
abundant yield, in spite of the oppression exercised by William
and his nobles. Coincident with the advance of agriculture,
the rearing of bees had been an important part of Saxon
industry, and was one which could be easily continued.
The *apium custos* was one of the assistants in husbandry
enumerated in Domesday.

Of the rights of Fisheries, by no means confined to fresh
water, we have already had evidence, and many traces which
still show their importance are extant. Swine were largely
bred, but can have been little more than semi-domesticated.
Much of the value of the forests consisted in the oak and
beech mast, which supplied food to the numerous herds, and,
according to the laws of King Ine (or Ini), the worth of a tree

* Dugdale's " Monasticon Anglicanum " (Vol. II., p. 546, and V., p. 144).

was reckoned by the number of swine which could stand under it.   *Porcarii* are frequently mentioned in Domesday, and these were not mere swineherds, but rich men who rented the privilege of feeding pigs in the woodlands : Sir Henry Ellis often alludes to them in his researches.*
Fowls seem to have been universally kept, although perhaps not in considerable numbers.   It was a practice, often quoted, to pay fowls in lieu of other rent, where coin was very scarce, as in the Fen district of Lincolnshire, known by the name of Holland, or hay-land.   Thus Pishey Thompson states that in 1279 sixty fowls were paid in lieu of five shillings, twelve in lieu of one shilling, and twenty-eight in lieu of two shillings and fourpence, which are entered in the extents of the Honour of Richmond.†   Such instances might be further multiplied.   These fowls were probably rather smaller than fowls at the present day, yet judging from the rough cuts of the twelfth and thirteenth centuries—in one of which an old hen is represented with a nestling on her back— they were such as could be matched now in many a farmyard.

The Abbey Church at Waltham.—We next come across the names of some birds in connection with the Abbey Church at Waltham, in Essex, which was founded in the time of Canute, viz., the Crane, Thrush, Partridge, Pheasant, Magpie, Goose, Fowl, and Falcon.‡   The Pheasant and the Magpie, which are quite sufficiently identified, are here mentioned especially.   These names occur in a bill of fare drawn up for monastic use in 1059, and preserved in a manuscript stated by Professor Dawkins to have been written about 1177.§

The Monks of Rochester in Kent.—In 1089 we find an assignment to the monks of Rochester from certain lands belonging to Bishop Randulfus, of sixteen Pheasants, thirty Geese, three hundred Hens, a thousand Lampreys, a thousand eggs, four Salmon, and sixty sheaves of finest wheat.||

* Ellis, " Introduction to Domesday," Vol. I., p. 88, *et seq.*
† " Boston and The Hundred of Skirbeck in the County of Lincoln," by P. Thompson, p. 169.
‡ *See* "The Foundation of Waltham Abbey," by W. Stubbs.
§ "Ibis," 1869, p. 358. The next mention of the Pheasant is in 1100, and again in 1179 and 1299. In Ireland we first hear of it in 1589, and in Scotland in 1594, when it comes into an Act passed by James VI. (14th Parl. Edin.) who had not then ascended the English throne.
|| Dugdale's " Monasticon Anglicanum " (Vol. I., additions).

Chapter IV.

TWELFTH CENTURY.

The Twelfth Century : Hawking, described by chroniclers. Fines Paid in Falcons. Giraldus Cambrensis.

Hawking in the Twelfth Century.—As has been already said, one leading feature in the lives of our Saxon and Norman ancestors was their vehement love of Falconry. There was something attractive in the art of training one bird to catch another, and then yield up its prey to its master. It was an ancient pursuit, far older than the Christian era, and so honourable an occupation was it considered that people carried a hawk on their fists when there was no intention whatever of hunting. This was so when Thomas à Becket went to France in 1158 ; on this occasion his retinue included hawks and hounds of different kinds. Yet probably neither Becket nor his numerous servants had thought of flying the hawks. It was the fashion to be accompanied by falcons and falconers as a mark of gentility, and this was carried on by the rich long after the twelfth century, a fact of which the later chronicles afford abundant evidence. Although among the manuscripts of the twelfth century there is no treatise on falconry extant in England, unless the Saxon colloquies are to be so termed, Mr. Harting has discovered laws on the subject in Spain.* The code in question consists of regulations, supposed to have been promulgated in A.D. 1180, by order of Sancho VI., King of Navarre. From these, observes Mr. Harting, it appears that the Hawks used in Navarre in 1180 were the Falcon, the Goshawk and the Sparrow-Hawk. They were taken young from the nest and reared in the hawk-house, fed upon meal paste, mixed with the flesh of birds, such as Pigeons, Partridges or Water-Hens, cut up small, less paste being given as the Hawk grew older until at length it was strong enough to be fed twice a day on beef or mutton. When

---

* " Bibliotheca Accipitraria," by J. E. Harting, 1891, p. 111.

a month old, the training commenced, and for this directions are given.

In England, as in France, Goshawks and Falcons were flown in the open country, but the keeping of them was not confined to country establishments; on the contrary it extended to towns and even to the city of London. "Many citizens," says William Fitz-Stephen, who wrote a tract in the twelfth century relating to the metropolis, "take delight in Sparrow-hawks, Goss-hawks, and such like and in Dogs to hunt in the woody ground." From the context he is here alluding more particularly to forests on the north side of London, where, according to this author, there lurked Bucks and Does, Wild Boars, and Bulls, the latter probably in a semi-wild state.

Mews for Hawks and Falcons in London.—The practice of keeping Hawks in London, which may have been partly for use in processions, was not discontinued, for in the fourteenth century we learn that Richard II. still had them in mews at Charing Cross. This fact is related by John Stow, who wrote a Survey of London in 1598 (republished 1754).* Yet, as Mr. Mullens remarks, there was clear country within easy reach of London, as at Mortlake and Richmond, where hawking could be practised if desired. Another early allusion to Falcons being used for the chase is cited in the "History and Antiquities of Furness Abbey" by T. A. Beck, and Mitchell's "Birds of Lancashire" (p. xiv.). The reference is to an eyrie of hawks which was reserved on certain mortgaged lands at the time of the second Crusade, *i.e.*, between 1135 and 1153.

---

* Stow is not the only writer who mentions them, for John Norden, writing five years earlier (1593), has the following about the rebuilding of the Royal Mews. "King Henry VIII caused it most especially to be erected for a place wherein to preserve his haukes, and therein to mew them ; and placed in the middle of the court or yard a Dovehouse for feeding them, which is now decayed. It serveth now for a most stately stable for Her Majesty's [Q. Elizabeth] horses and palphrayes" ("Speculi Britanniæ Pars" printed for The Camden Soc., p. xviii). It is said to have been this and similar con-versions which account for the present meaning which the word "mews" bears, viz. a stable or place for the housing of horses. These Charing Cross Hawk-Mews were about where the National Gallery now stands. Their fate was that of so many other old houses—to be eventually burnt, with, the historian tells us, many great horses and much hay, *see* Stow's "Survey of London and Westminster" (Vol. II., p. 576). I find the name retained in a map as recent as 1761.

Fines Paid in Falcons.—This was a period when " fines," as they were called, were levied in kind. The word " fine " did not bear the meaning which it has now ; in most cases it was not inflicted as a punishment, but as a tax, and these receipts formed a large part of the Crown revenue. In this connection it will be proper to cite what Thomas Madox has to say about the collecting of these fines in King Stephen's reign (1097-1154), in his " History and Antiquities of the Exchequer " (1711). The law did not insist on their being collected in coin, which was only to be found in the coffers of the barons, and in which the lesser gentry could not pay. We find that the Crown payment was more often rendered in such kind as Palfreys, with gilt spurs and other appurtenances, Destriers (war-horses), Chasours (hunting-horses), Leveriers (grey-hounds), Brachets (scent-hounds), Gupilerets * (fox-hounds), Hawks and Girfals (Gyr Falcons). Of this we have many instances.

In the year 1139 one Outi, a gentleman of Lincolnshire, had to render to the Exchequer under the name of a fine, " one Hundred *Norway* Hawks and one Hundred Girfals : Four of the Hawks and Six of the Girfals were to be *White* ones ; if he could not get Four White Hawks, he was to give Four White Girfals instead of them."†

It is to be presumed the " White Gyrfals " were what we now know as Greenland Falcons, and the " White Hawks " perhaps were what we call Iceland Falcons.

Either in the same reign, or in the reign of Henry II. (1153-1189), Ralf son of Drogo, and four other defaulters, were made to supply good hunting hawks, and the much prized Gyr Falcons in lieu of marks of silver. Others were made to meet their liabilities by rendering up such home produce as bulls and mares. One Ernald de Aclent had to produce no fewer than a hundred and forty palfreys, and Robert de Ellestede six bald (*i.e.,* smooth) Vulperets or fox-dogs.

These instances are taken from Madox's " History," chapter IX. " Of the species wherein the ancient Crown

---

* Mr. Harting reminds me that Golpileret is from the Norman Golpil or Goupil, a fox, *see* Kelham's Norman Dictionary. " Girfals " is a not infrequent contraction for Girfalcons.

† *T.c.,* p. 186.

Revenue was usually paid," but more of the same kind are given in chapter XIII., " Fines of Divers Sorts."

Thus (page 318) the Earl of Warenne is fined one Palfrey and one Sore * (*i.e.*, young) Hawk.

P. 324. Nicholas the Dane was to give the King a Hawk every time he came into England.

P. 325. Geoffrey Fitz-Pierre was fined in two good Norway Hawks. that Walter le Madine might have leave to export a hundredweight of cheese.

P. 350. The Bishop of Norwich was fined in two palfreys for a Crane (*pro quadam grue*)—the meaning here is not very evident, unless it indicates, as suggested by Mr. Harting (*in litt.*) that he had killed a Crane on Crown land without license.

P. 352. William de Cyrinton was fined in one good " hautein falcon," literally one of proud bearing, but meaning here in high condition.

And so on, these old payments are certainly very curious, as throwing light on the manners of the times. Moreover, Mr. Harting has pointed out that not only were all these " fines " or taxes paid in kind, as Madox here describes, but that prisoners were sometimes ransomed by a payment of Hawks.†

Under the heading of " Nota rem inauditam," the following strange relation of what appears to be a true incident is to be found in the Chronicle of Roger of Wendover :— " In the same year [1191] a young man of the bishop of London's household taught a hawk [*nisum*] especially to hunt teals ; and once at the sound of the instrument called a tabor

---

* " Sore " is an adjective, meaning red or reddish, coming, like a good many other hawking terms, from the old Norman language, and was generally applied to a Sparrow-Hawk of the first year. Originally spelled *Sor*, the word now stands in modern French, slightly altered, as *Saure*, with exactly the same meaning. Prof. Newton in his Dictionary finds the word akin to *Sorrel*, as applied to a horse of a reddish-brown colour.

The term continued in use for some centuries, of which we find an instance in the famous Paston correspondence. In September 1472 John Paston writes from Norwich to his elder brother : " I pray God send you all your desyrs, and me my mwyd [mewed, *i.e.* moulted] gosshawk in hast, or rather than fayle, a sowyr hawke."

A " Sore Sparrow-Hawk " is well figured under that name in Rowley's " Ornithological Miscellany " (Vol. I., p. 51).

† It was on these terms that a Welsh bishop captured by King John was allowed his liberty in 1212 (" Essays on Sport," p. 73).

by those who dwelt on the river's bank, a teal suddenly flew quickly away ; but the hawk baffled of his booty intercepted a pike swimming in the water, seized him, and carried him apparently forty feet on dry land. . . ."

This is the same story rather differently referred to in " Hints on the Management of Hawks," p. 171, where the author suggests that the bird may have been an Osprey ; the word stands in the original as *nisus*. The use of a tabor or drum for rousing water-fowl was not unusual, *see* Wright's " History of Domestic Manners," p. 308.

Giraldus Cambrensis, his references to Hawks.—We next turn to the writings of Gerald de Barri, called Cambrensis, and here again there is something about Falconry. In his " Topographica Hibernica " (1183-1186), Giraldus treats first of Hawks and Falcons, noticing that the female was larger than the male, and making other observations which Mr. Harting finds to be exact at the present day.* " Eagles are as numerous here [in Ireland] as Kites are in other countries," he says (ch. IX.). Giraldus was probably familiar with the Kites in English towns, inclusive of London. In another place he says (ch. VIII.) :—

" This country produces in greater number than any other hawks, falcons, and sparrow-hawks [*nisos*], a class of birds which nature has endowed with courageous instincts and armed with curved and powerful beaks and sharp talons to fit them as birds of prey." This looks as if he did not write altogether from hearsay, but from observation. Then comes a curious story, but it is one which might hold good of other countries besides Ireland. " It is, however," he says (I follow Forrester's translation), " a remarkable fact in the history of this tribe of birds, that their nests are not more numerous than they were many centuries ago ; and although they have broods every year, their numbers do not increase."

This is exactly what has struck many a modern naturalist not only in regard to birds of prey, but about many other species as well. The explanation of it must be that a certain extent of land is meant to hold a certain number of birds, and the rest either migrate or die. There would not be food

* " Zoologist," 1881, p 436.

enough for all, and if the young (or most of them) did not disappear the balance of nature would soon be upset somewhere.

Giraldus winds up with some pertinent remarks on falconry, which he cannot but have witnessed himself, in which he describes the hawk soaring high in wide circles, and then the velocity of its stoop, and the endeavours of the hardpressed quarry to escape, as it "flits from side to side, now high, now low, while all the spectators are filled with delight."

One might imagine oneself in the company of an enthusiastic modern falconer. Falcons he considers more pertinacious than Sparrow-hawks, and at the same time he knows them to be "more ready to return to their keeper when he raises his hand, or even at his call."

CRANES IN IRELAND.

In chapter XIII. Giraldus alludes to the exportation of Gyrfalcons and Goshawks from Iceland, but the latter species is not known to inhabit Iceland. Harting, however, states the Gyrfalcon was sometimes called Gos-falcon,* which is a sufficient explanation of what would otherwise be an error.

In his Welsh Itinerary (ch. XII.) Giraldus favours us with a singular story of a Kite which seized a weasel, and, flying into the air with it, was presently bitten by the little animal, and so fell dead. This is quite credible, for similar instances have been recorded of other rapacious birds in modern times. In 1188 Giraldus travelled with Archbishop Baldwin through Wales, which was his native country. In the itinerary of this journey mention is made of Deer, Wild Boars and Beavers, of Falcons of a generous kind, and of a bird called the *Aureolus*, possibly the Green Woodpecker which, seen from

* "Essays on Sport," p 80.

above, looks very yellow, and which would be likely to attract notice by its loud cry.

Another chapter of the " Topographica Hibernica " treats of the Crane, said to be so common in Ireland that " uno in grege centum, et circiter hunc numerum frequenter invenias." These may have been only Herons, but the statement is backed by two pictures of Cranes in the Giraldus MS. preserved in the British Museum.

Other birds enumerated by Giraldus are the Merlin, Hobby, Kingfisher (*aviculæ quas martinetas vocant*), Shrike, Raven, Hooded- and Carrion-Crows, Grouse, Capercaillie (?), Quail, Woodcock, Snipe, Land-Rail and Wild Swan.

Giraldus further describes a white Goose called a " Gante," which was wont to come to Ireland " in multitudine magna." Probably he only meant a migratory species of Grey Goose, but the passage is obscure, and puzzled Mr. J. F. Dimock.

In this sense Gante is employed by Venatius Fortunatus—

" Aut Mosa dulce sonans quo grus, ganta, anser, olorque ;
  Triplice merce ferax, alite, pisce, rate."—*Lib*. 7, *Poem* 4

—and by other writers quoted in the " Glossarium ad scriptores " (1733), of Du Cange, the French historian. " Gante " was used in the " Rolls of Normandy " of the twelfth century for the domestic Goose, from which it has descended to families of that name at the present day.

Saint Cuthbert's Birds. —Before quitting the twelfth century a word must be bestowed on the Farne Islands, a rich nursery of birds upon the Northumbrian coast, and doubtless a breeding-place of great antiquity. Such a resort of Gulls and Guillemots might be expected to have bequeathed us some early legends about its sea-fowl, yet only one has been preserved. A monk who lived in the twelfth century, and was known as Reginald of Durham (*d*. 1173), has left an historical chronicle—printed in Vol. I. of the Surtees Society's Publications*—wherein is described a miracle in connection with certain birds on the Farne Islands, one of which, presumably an Eider Duck, was killed and eaten by a manservant named Leving. After commencing

* 1835, I., p. 60, Cap. XXVII.

with a pretty good description of that species, and describing
the subsequent miracle, the monk goes on to speak of " Lomes,"
with which he appears to have confounded the Eider Duck.
" Aves illæ Beati Cuthberti specialiter nominantur; ab
anglis vero Lomes vocantur; ab Saxonibus autem et qui
Frisiam incolunt Eires dicuntur." Loon or Loom is understood
to mean a bird which is awkward on land, and deficient in
walking powers. Both these names have been applied to
the Divers, but the reference here is most likely to the
Guillemot, which no doubt was then, as now, very abundant
on the Farne Islands.

The word " Eires " is not so plain, but is perhaps synonymous with Alk = an auk. Professor Skeat has pointed out
that it can hardly mean Eider Ducks in this passage,* as
the editor of Reginald's Chronicle supposes,† abundant as
is that species on the coast of Northumberland. It may be
remarked also that Aron or Arron, a word which might be
latinised as Eire, for it is very similar, is found, as has been
indicated by Mr. O. V. Aplin, to be a local name for the
Guillemot in parts of Wales (" Zoologist," 1902, p. 109).
Mr. Aplin, who is no doubt right in thinking that it is
taken from the bird's cry, also draws attention (*in litt.*) to
the use of Arrie for the Guillemot in Russia, and Airo, which
is nearly identical, in Portugal—*see* note by A. C. Smith,
" Ibis," 1868, p. 457.

---

* " Notes and Queries," 1912, p. 115.
† *T.c.*, p. 332.

CHAPTER V.

THIRTEENTH CENTURY.

The Thirteenth Century: King John. Edward I. Decoys. Household Accounts. The Crossbill. The Solan Goose.

As we enter another century we become a little better acquainted with the English people and begin to know something of their sports from the pages of Strutt, as well as of viands on their dinner-table, the animals which they chased, and even a few of the birds. Of all their pastimes, none continued to be in greater vogue than the chase with Falcons and Goshawks, even ladies and church dignitaries excelled in it. The Hawk, its head covered with a hood which effectually prevented it from seeing anything prematurely, was carried on its master's wrist, protected by a thick glove, while straps of leather were put on its legs for holding purposes, and small bells which would reveal its whereabouts if lost. All our earlier English monarchs were addicted to hawking, both Edward II. and Edward III. evinced a taste for this kind of sport, and where royalty led the way nobles and squires would not be slow to follow. The panegyric of Bartholomew de Glanville on the Goshawk is very character-istic of the times when a feat of falconry rivalled a noble deed of arms. The Franciscan friar dilates on its merits with enthusiastic ardour, a royal fowl is the only name worthy to be applied to the favourite of the chase, which he quaintly describes as " armed more with boldness than with claws." He deemed his brave Goshawk to be one of a disdainful sort, " for if," says he, " she fail by any hap of the prey that she reseth [riseth] to that day unneth [scarcely] she cometh unto her lord's hand."* The falconer's favourite sport was to fly Hawks at Cranes, if he could find them. Cranes are continually mentioned in connection with hawking, but the

* " De Proprietatibus Rerum," ch. II., in Berthelet's translation: to Mr. Mullens I am indebted for the passage.

question is, were not these so-called Cranes in some cases only Herons ? There is no reason why the geographical distribution of the Crane should have altered; on the other hand, the extensive morasses and immunity from firearms are in favour of its having once been much more abundant in England, and undoubtedly it has given its name to places in the eastern counties.* King John appears to have been of the number of those who took delight in hawking. In 1209 this King, disappointed at finding so little game wherewith to exercise his Falcons, issued a proclamation forbidding the taking of wild-fowl in his domains, a step which would ensure in a few years a better supply for the sport of hawking. Three years later he feasted, Mr. Harting tells us, a certain number of the poor for every Crane taken by his Hawks, a liberality which would encourage them to leave his game alone, and it was probably done with that object. At another time, having taken the field with his Falcons, and again been satisfied with the sport obtained, King John commanded his retainers to feed a hundred paupers with a dinner of bread, meat and ale, which was a luxury to the common people. In 1212 King John is stated to have flown his Hawks at Cranes in Cambridgeshire, and to have killed seven. Either the same year, or in 1213, he flew his Gyr Falcons in Lincolnshire and took nine more Cranes.†

So great was his love of falconry that when his army entered Wales, and captured Rotpert of Shrewsbury, the ransom fixed by John was two hundred Hawks, that being preferred to a fine in money (Lhoyd's " Historie of Cambria," 1584). A recent writer has hazarded an opinion that these were Peregrines from Stackpole, but for this there is no authority ; indeed, so many could not have been obtained from one locality.

Again, we learn from " Manners and Household Expenses of England " that in 1218 Henry III. sent Geoffrey de Hauville with four Gyr Falcons and seven grey-hounds into Bedfordshire and Cambridgeshire for the purpose of catching Cranes.‡

* Also it must not be forgotten that not longer ago than 1544 William Turner, who will be fully quoted in another chapter, said he had very often seen their young ones.

† " Rotulus Misæ Anno Regis Johannis, 1212-13," as quoted in " Essays on Sport," p. 77.

‡ P. xlvi., quoted from Rot. Claus., 2 Hen. III.

Perhaps it was a captured Crane brought home by some falconer to which a rather singular allusion occurs in 1265 in " The Household Roll of the Countess of Leicester."* Here a payment is made to a boy for seeking a Crane in a well, or more likely, as Mr. Evans suggests, in some wet place or marsh.† In 1282 Edward I. sent to Spain for the King of Castille four grey Gyr-falcons for Crane and Heron hawking.‡ In 1298 falconers took Cranes in Cambridgeshire, which were presented to the King.§ The passage having reference to them, as quoted by Mr. Harting from the King's Wardrobe accounts, runs :—

" Jan. 5. To Alexander Coo, The King's falconer, for presenting to the King 3 Cranes taken in Cambridgeshire by the Ger-falcons of Sir Geoffrey de Hauville . . . 6s. 8d. (half a mark)."

These Ger-falcons may have been from Iceland, forwarded to England via Norway. Mr. H. Slater cites very early instances of Falcons being sent from that country, in one instance even to Tunis.||

The Price of Hawks.¶—Mr. Harting, in his admirable " Ornithology of Shakespeare," has collected (p. 77) various prices paid for Hawks and Falcons, which, as they were trained birds, ran into high figures, one " cast " alone costing as much as £23. These large prices are very different from the small sums given for wild Hawks in the thirteenth century, which

---

* Shakespeare Press, 1841. " Manners and Household Expenses of England," edited for the Roxburghe Club by B. Botfield, p. 57.

† Capons, Fowls and Geese are also named in the Countess's Roll, and the editor points out that " pullagium." a term which is made use of, may have comprehended other species. Eggs, which seem to have been an important item in the *ménage*, cost the Countess about fourpence per hundred : on Easter Sunday upwards of 1200 were purchased at Wallingford, the greater part of which the editor supposes to have been stained and given away as Pasque eggs.

‡ " Mittimus vobis quatuor Girofalcones grisos, quorum duo apti sunt & instructi ad grues & heruncellos " (" Foedera conventiones," ed. 1705, p. 1087).

§ " Essays on Sport," p. 78.

|| " Manual of the Birds of Iceland," p. 32.

¶ Mr. Harting has been at the pains to search out several early statutes relating to hawks and hawking, but finds nothing earlier than 1217, when Henry III., then in the first year of his reign, and anxious to adopt a conciliatory policy, granted by a *Carta de Foresta* (cap. XI.) the right to every man to have eyries of hawks, sparrow-hawks, falcons and eagles in his own woods (" The Management of Hawks," p. 243).

are cited by Professor Rogers in his "History of Agriculture and Prices in England" (1866, Vol. II., p. 566).

In 1268, this author tells, us twelve Hawks at Framlingham cost /1½, and sixteen at Hoo /1½, while at Staverton nine cost /2, eleven /1½ and two nets /3. In 1271 thirty-four Hawks at Framlingham, which I suppose was the town of that name in Suffolk, cost /2½, and in 1272 twenty-three at Saham or Soham /2 + /3½.

Some of these Hawks' prices are taken from the records of the earldom of Bigod, from lands held in Norfolk and Suffolk, and Professor Rogers thinks (*t.c.*, I., p. 164) the bailiffs of the various manors encouraged the bringing of young hawks from nests. There are also other items of interest. In 1273 a Peacock's tail at Wytchurch is priced /4¾, and another in 1277 at Halvergate in Norfolk at /1½. The Peacock was a bird on which our forefathers set great store, chiefly because of its resplendence when served in its feathers at banquets. Professor Rogers considers the pig to have been the most important article of food in the thirteenth and fourteenth centuries. The low price of poultry suggests to him that they were kept by the poorest classes in the land. Fowls, Geese and Ducks were universally eaten, Peafowl and Swans more rarely; on some manors a large number of tame Pigeons were kept. Hens' eggs were exceedingly abundant, with no great variation of price. Rats and Moles were considered nuisances, and payments were made for destroying them. Rabbits do not seem to have been plentiful, and the Professor remarks that he has not met with any entry of the sale of Hares (*t.c.*, Vol. I., p. 32). For taking Conies and Partridges with hawk, dog and ferret at Waleton in 1272 4/6 was paid, while for taking five Crows and five Pies and thirty-four rats at Weston, in 1297, 1/2 was charged.

Edward's Falconers.—Edward I., like his predecessors on the English throne, John and Henry III., found plenty of time for falconry. He had no fewer than eleven falconers with two horses, and six falconers with one horse apiece. *See* preface with notes to the "Roll of the Household Expenses of Richard de Swinfield."[*] This prelate was bishop of Hereford,

---

[*] Camden Soc., 1855. For a reference to this Roll, which was edited by Mr. J. Webb, I am indebted to the Rev. T. S. Cogswell.

and his expenses during 1289 and 1290, which have come down to posterity, have been made accessible to antiquarians by Mr. J. Webb. The Bishop's falconer was one Adam Harpin, whose doings can be followed in several places. One of his principal occupations was catching Partridges, with which it was his duty to keep the episcopal table supplied. As we find him provided with additional twine for his nets, it is evident that he netted them, either at night, or possibly, as Mr. Webb suggests, by means of a trained Hawk which caused them to lie close.

How many Falcons he had under his care we are not told, but perhaps several. At the beginning of March 1290 the Bishop sent a favourite Falcon to Hereford Cathedral for cure. In June of that year Harpin is employed in watching young Falcons at some eyrie, in order to keep off thieves, and catch them when sufficiently fledged, in which occupation he seems to have had the assistance of John the huntsman, another time the same duty is entrusted to the woodward of Cradley, who has a reward for his services—sixpence. To these men was entrusted the sole care of the Tiercels and Falcons, a task of no slight responsibility. If a Hawk was ill, or experienced some difficulty in getting through its moult, all sorts of strange remedies were tried, and finally, if none of these were effective, an offering was made at some shrine for its recovery.

This offering might take the form of a waxen image of the bird, of which an instance is cited by Thomas Rymer, at Hereford,* where such a propitiation was placed on the tomb of St. Thomas de Cantelupe, with what success we are not told.

It appears from Rymer's " Foedera " that Edward I. received Gyr Falcons from the King of Norway on more than one occasion, and in 1282, we are told, he sent as a royal gift to the King of Castille in Spain " quatuor Girofalcones grisos."† From this passage some further particulars are given in the fourth edition of Yarrell's " British Birds."‡

Blount's " Fragmenta Antiquitatis."—Thomas Blount, in his " Fragmenta Antiquitatis, or Ancient Tenures of Land "

* *T.c.*, Pref. 1.

† " Foedera," 1705. p. 1037.

‡ Vol. I., p 44.

(1679), cites many instances of the granting of lordships and manors for the rent of a Hawk, to be rendered yearly. *See* Section XI., entitled " Of Petit Serjeanties *performed by keeping for and delivering* Hawks etc. *to the* King."

Thus we hear of a mewed Sparhawk to be delivered to the King's Exchequer, of a Sore (*i.e.*, young) Sparhawk to be rendered at Lammas (August 1st), and of the mewing and keeping of a Goshawk or a " Girefalcon " for " our Lord the King." This was Henry III., and probably none of the grants are later than the thirteenth century. One Petit Serjeanty was held in Cumberland by keeping the King's aeries of Goshawks (*aerias austurcorum*). A manor in Bucks was held by the service of being Marshal of the King's Falcons and other Hawks.

A manor in Notts was held by the service of carrying one Gyr Falcon from the Feast of Saint Michael the Archangel until Lent. Another manor in Bucks was held by the service of keeping one Falcon until it could fly, and for the keeping of it, when he took it to the King, Reginald de Grey was to have the King's horse, etc.

Lands were held in Northampton by the service of finding dogs for the destruction of wolves, martens, cats and other vermin. John de Bellovent was to have fifty-six shillings and seven pence for maintaining seven greyhounds, three Falcons, and a Lever [Lanner ?] hawk, and for the wages of a huntsman. For the lordship of Sheffield two white hares were to be rendered. Some further information on this subject will be found in an article by Mr. Harting, entitled " Of Hawks and Hounds in Essex in the Olden Time."*

Falconry in Europe.—" On looking into the history of Falconry in Europe," writes Mr. Harting, " one figure of a great falconer in the Middle Ages stands out prominently—namely, the Emperor Frederick II. of Germany, who died in 1250. He had seen something of Hawking in the East, and in 1239, on his return from a Crusade which he had undertaken the year before, when he was crowned King of Jerusalem and Sicily, he brought with him

* " The Essex Naturalist," 1889, Vol. III., p. 189

from Syria and Arabia several expert falconers with their hawks.

*   *   *   *   *

In the Middle Ages the Germans were great falconers ; so also were the French and the natives of Brabant, of whom a celebrated Spanish falconer in 1325 wrote that they were the best falconers in the world. To a less extent the art was practised in Spain and Italy during many centuries."*

Wild-Fowl Decoys in England.—So far nothing has been said about decoys, but they were already in use, with many other clever devices for netting birds, which were mostly superseded when guns came to be employed. The word decoy is one of antiquity, and is probably an abbreviation of the Dutch words eende-kooi or coy (Middle Dutch *koye*), that is a cage or trapping-place for Ducks, *see* Skeat's " Etymological Dictionary " (1901). Eend or Eende, which is Dutch for a duck, also comes very close to the Anglo-Saxon word Ened. In the " Promptorium Parvulorum " (fifteenth century) we find it spelled Ende, and the equivalent *dooke byrde*—Duck bird.

The word *enede* is stated by the learned editor, Mr. Albert Way, to occur in the glosses on Gautier de Bibelesworth :

" En marreis ane iaroille (enede queketh) "
" In marshes the Duck quacketh " ; and in another passage :

" . . . . il ane (enede) et plounczoun (douke) "
" The Duck and the ? Grebe."

There can be no doubt that in the thirteenth and fourteenth centuries, and much later than that, Lincolnshire, where so many decoys were afterwards constructed, was a paradise for wild-fowl, though few of the early writers not excepting even William Camden (1586) bear any testimony to it. Here were situated Crowland, and its famous monastery, a place so encompassed with deep bogs and marshy pools that there was only access to it by two narrow causeways.†

---

* " Bibliotheca Accipitraria," by J. E. Harting, Intro. XIII., XIV
† "Britannia," Vol. I., p. 553.

Doubtless the Abbot of Crowland, and his sixty-two or more monks, were entirely dependent on the supply of fish and wild-fowl, which were to them as cornfields.*

In a very interesting communication to the "Field" of April 27th, 1878, on the subject of "Decoys Past and Present," Mr. J. Hoare states that decoys for catching Wild Ducks "were common in England in the reign of King John [1199-1216], when they were looked upon as an adjunct of the King's forest, and as they appertained to the royal prerogative, no one dare draw them without license. There were some celebrated decoys in Holland and Kesteven in Lincolnshire, which, being a subject of litigation about the year 1280, we find the importance attached to them in those days duly set forth in the Rolls of Parliament."

Mr. Hoare's researches show at what an early period these decoys were commenced, yet they must not be understood as having been decoys on the Dutch plan. The system of enticing Ducks into a tunnel net (which gradually curved and lessened in size) by means of a trained dog, which curiosity prompted the birds to follow, was not introduced until later. The operation in all probability consisted, as Mr. T. Southwell supposed,† in the simpler but much less efficacious plan of driving the Ducks into hoop nets and then catching them by hand. There was another method of catching the fowl, which was by the driving of " flappers " in July, when no doubt a good many old Ducks with shed primaries were caught too. It will always be with the eastern counties that the early decoys are associated, and much of very great interest might be written on this head.

Household Accounts, Feasts, and Prices.—Very few Privy-purse or Household Accounts were kept in the thirteenth and fourteenth centuries; in fact there were not many

---

* In Cordeaux's " Birds of the Humber " (p. 146) a quotation is given from William of Malmesbury, who lived in the twelfth century, to the effect that the Lincolnshire fens were so covered with Coots and Ducks, and the flashes (pools) with Fowl, that in moulting time, when they could not fly, the natives could take two or three thousand at a draught with their nets.

This passage, if it be Malmesbury's, which is very doubtful, is certainly not in the " De Gestis Regum " (1125), nor in the " De Gestis Pontificum " (1125), although in the latter work there is an allusion to young water-fowl in the account of Thorney, which is in Lincolnshire, *see* note by Professor E. Bensly in " Notes and Queries " (Sept. 23rd, 1916).

† " Norwich Nat. Tr.," II., p. 538.

educated enough to know how to write them. Whale and porpoise were commonly eaten at feasts, and many birds. In Lent, 1246, Henry III. ordered the Sheriffs of London to purchase a hundred pieces of the best whale, and two porpoises.* We learn from the "Rotulus Hospitii Comitissæ Leicestriæ" that two hundred pieces, or two cwt., of whale were bought for the Countess of Leicester and the King of the Romans, previously to Palm Sunday, 1265, besides which grampus or porpoise and sea-wolves † are mentioned several times in the Roll during Lent.‡

For long after this the appearance of the porpoise in bills of fare is frequent, and it was dressed in a variety of ways. Sometimes it was prepared with a sauce made of fine bread-crumbs, mixed with vinegar and sugar. On the occasion of a City banquet, the porpoise was to be brought whole into the banqueting hall, and then carved or "undertraunched" by the officer in attendance.§

In 1251 Henry III. held a great feast at York, and in the "Rotulos Familiæ" of Edward I. there are items of scullery expenditure as early as 1292.‖ It cannot be said that they convey much information, but they are perhaps the earliest of the kind in which birds are noticed. Here we learn that sevenpence was paid by the larderer for a Goose, two shillings for six Geese, a penny for some corn for the Geese, the same (?) for a Falcon, for a Hen, and for some parsley. A wild buck cost eightpence, two sticks of eels were elevenpence, and a lamprey a shilling.

The editor, the Rev. J. Brand, remarks that the items of diet in the Roll evince how rigidly Lent was kept. Of the shellfish and other fish mentioned, such as herrings, congers, eels, pike, lampreys, gurnards, trout, whiting, plaice, salmon, all except one (the lamprey) are eaten at the present day; yet one cannot help wondering how minnows (if by *menums* these little fish are meant) could have obtained a place at the royal board.

* "Manners and Household Expenses of England," 1841, p. xlii.
† Seals.
‡ *T.c.*, p. xlii.
§ Bidwell, "Norwich Nat. Tr.," IV., p. 594.
‖ "Archaeologia," 1806, p. 362.

Mr. H. Saunders states that tame Swans are particularly mentioned in England, in a manuscript of 1272,* which I have not seen. The passage referred to, as I learn from Mr. Harting, who was Saunders' informant, is to be found in the Wardrobe Accounts of Edward I. published by "The Society of Antiquaries." In 1275 a table of permitted poulterers' prices was issued by order of Edward I. in which the Crane was priced at three shillings, and the Bittern and Heron at sixpence, the Teal (Cercel) at sixpence, and the Curlew at threepence.† In the time of Edward I. oaths were sworn on the Swan, Peacock and Pheasant, which were looked on in the light of royal birds.‡

In 1289 we learn from the "Household Expenses of Richard de Swinfield"§ that Pheasants were to be had in the London market, which may have been tame bred ones; in any case it is certain that they could not have been common. For this and other references of archæological interest, I am indebted to the Rev. T. S. Cogswell.

Heronries in Kent and Norfolk.—Turning now to another subject, there is good reason for believing that some of our British Heronries are exceedingly ancient, that is to say, that though the birds may have changed from one wood to another as trees died and fresh ones grew up, the same river valley has from time immemorial held its heronry, or two heronries. This appears to be the case in Kent, for, from an "Inquisition" which Dr. N. F. Ticehurst has cited in his "Birds of Kent," (1909) we learn the undoubted fact of a heronry having existed at Chilham, in that county, before 1280–93.

The same love of its old haunts is shown by the Heron in the valley of the Yare and other rivers of Norfolk. Here,

* Yarrell, "B.B.," IV., p. 327.

† As quoted by Stow and Maitland from the "Statuta de Poletria."

‡ In 1306 Edward I. vowed upon the Swan that he would take vengeance upon Robert Bruce, while in 1483 Philip, Duke of Burgundy, vowed on the Pheasant to go to the deliverance of Constantinople. A correspondent of "Notes and Queries" conjectures that the oath by the Peacock and that by the Pheasant were one and the same ("N. & Q.," 4th ser., III., p. 565). The Peacock was evidently a fairly plentiful bird in the thirteenth century. Among other entries which prove this, Mr. Cogswell draws attention to a passage wherein five of these birds are stated to have been sent to Lopham in Norfolk in 1277, just after Michaelmas, on the occasion of a visit from Edward I. to the Earl of Norfolk (*see* "A Norfolk Manor, 1086–1565," by F. G. Davenport, 1906).

§ Printed for the Camden Society, 1855 (p. 40).

judging from the Patent Rolls of Edward I.,* there can be no doubt of there having been heronries more than six hundred years ago, that is to say A.D. 1300 or earlier. They had their value, and it appears from this document that protection was needed for them in certain parishes, viz., Whinburgh, Cantley on the Yare, and Wormegay on the Nar.† Moreover, these parishes contained, if the preamble is to be taken literally, eyries of Sparrow-hawks, Spoonbills and Bitterns, in addition to the Herons.

Blackborough Nunnery.—Another Norfolk record, although it does not touch Herons, to which Mr. J. C. Tingey has drawn attention, is an entry of the twelfth or early thirteenth century, in the unpublished Cartulary of Blackborough Nunnery, near King's Lynn. In this William de Warren, who Mr. Tingey has reason to believe died in 1208, the lord of Wirmegay or Wormegay—the site of one of the heronries just mentioned —concedes certain holdings. The concession is made for the annual payment by Thurchetel of Lynn of " duas curleus vel iiij^{or} aves vel octo cerceles vel viij hulvestres [silvestres, *i.e.*, wild-fowl] " in lieu of money. The " cerceles " were probably Teal : the word is used in the same sense in the Middleton accounts, to be quoted in the next chapter, and has its equivalent in the French " Sarcelle." According to Dugdale this Nunnery was entitled to an annual gift of four hundred eels from the fishery of Emma de Bellofago at Wilton (" Monasticon Anglicanum," IV., p. 204) ; perhaps it should read " sticks of els," as four hundred would be a very small number : a bundle of ten sticks was two hundred and fifty eels.

The Monk of St. Albans.—It was in this century that England was visited by flocks of Crossbills. This fact is vouched for by the Monk of St. Albans, Matthew Paris, who would have thought such a circumstance beneath his notice if the birds had not attacked the apple orchards, which in the thirteenth century had already assumed a considerable importance in the western counties where cider was made.

---

* " Calendar of Patent Rolls," pp. 546 and 621. In the second passage the names of the birds are erroneously entered as Herons, Bustards and Buzzards, the right reading being heyronum, poplorum, (spoonbills) bittorum.

† Professor Newton, " Norwich Naturalists' Tr.," VI., p. 159.

The visits of the Crossbill to England have always been somewhat mysterious and are not regulated by the laws which govern the majority of migratory birds. Sometimes for many years they are rare or altogether unseen, and then comes a large invasion, which lasts or dies away, according to the food supply to be found. Seeds of the Scotch fir are their natural diet, but occasionally apples are attacked, chiefly for the sake of the pip.

"In the course of this year" [1251], writes the chronicler, "about the fruit-season there appeared, in the orchards chiefly, some remarkable birds which had never before been seen in England, somewhat larger than Larks, which ate the kernel of the fruit and nothing else, whereby the trees were fruitless, to the loss of many. The beaks of these birds were crossed. . . ." The original manuscript, which contains a rude drawing of the Crossbill, was examined by Professor Newton at Corpus Christi College, Cambridge, where it is preserved.

Matthew Paris was not a naturalist, but incidentally he gives us three or four other items of zoology of about this date —Woods were to be kept free from wolves, which were far from being extinct in England—Buffaloes (?) were brought to England in 1252—a Sea-Monster, not of the Whale kind, was washed up in the diocese of Norwich in 1255—in the same year the first Elephant was brought to England, having been presented to Henry III. by Lewis, King of France. About the same time also the King had a White Bear sent him from Norway.

Other marvels of the thirteenth century were hailstones "as gret as an ey"* which fell in 1203, in which year were also seen fowls flying in the air, bringing in their bills burning coals, which burned many houses in London.† This story possibly has its origin in the mischievous habits of the Jackdaw.

The Solan Goose. Translation of an Extent or Inventory of Produce in the Reign of Edward I. (1274).—Turning now to the Solan Goose, it is to Sir T. Duffus Hardy that we are indebted for disinterring a thirteenth-century record of a

---

* Professor Bensly, to whose assistance I am much indebted, suggests that " ey " should read " egg."

† " A Chronicle of London from 1089 to 1483," p. 5.

breeding-place at Lundy Island, off the north coast of Devon.* In 1274 certain appointed Jurors (whose names are given) reported to the Crown, to whom Lundy Island belonged, that : " There may be there twenty acres of arable land, which may be sown with barley or oats. . . . Also the taking of rabbits is estimated at 2000, worth £5 10s. and the estimate is at 5s. 6d. each hundred skins, because the flesh is not sold.   Also the rock of gannets [*petra ganetorum*] is worth 5s. ; there are other birds, but they are not sold.   There is also one eyrie of lanner falcons [*Falco peregrinus*],† which have sometimes three young ones, sometimes four, sometimes more, and sometimes less.   This eyrie the jury knew not how to estimate, and they build their nests in a place in which they cannot be taken."

A perusal of this document leads us to infer that the Lundy Gannets—the occupants of the " petra ganetorum," doubtless the isolated rock which is to be seen at the northeast end of the island—were not very numerous.   If they had been, their value would surely have been reckoned as greater than a hundred rabbit-skins.   Evidently the " lanner falcons," although building in almost inaccessible cliffs, were highly esteemed.

* " Collectanea Topographica et Genealogica," Vol. IV. (1837). pp. 313–330.   It is also printed, with slight alterations, in the " Calendar of Inquisitions preserved in the Public Record Office " (1916, Vol. I., p. 298).

† The words are : Una ayeria falconum lanerium.   The falcons from this eyrie had been already bestowed in 1243 by Henry III. " dilecto clerico suo Ade de Eston " (" Close Rolls," 1242-1247, p. 95).   Modern falconers have considered Lundy Peregrines to be of the best. *cf.* " Birds of Devon," 1892 p. 161.

CHAPTER VI.

FOURTEENTH CENTURY.

The Fourteenth Century : Lundy Island, North Devon. Ranulph Higden Household Accounts. Geoffrey Chaucer

Lundy Island.—Reverting again to Lundy Island and the Solan Geese, we learn from Sir T. Duffus Hardy's investigations that in 1321, during the reign of Edward II., a second " Inquisition " into the products of the island was ordered.

Translation of the Second " Extent " of Lundy made in the Reign of Edward II., 1321.—" Sir John [de Wyllynton] held the island of Lunday. . . . There is also a rabbit warren worth in ordinary years 100s. but this year destroyed in great part by the men of John de Wyllyngton and the Scots. Also a certain rock, called the Gannets' stone, with two places near it where the Gannets settle and breed, worth in ordinary years 66s. 8d. but this year destroyed in part by the Scots. Also eight tenants who hold their land and tenements by a certain charter of Herbert de Mareis, granted to them for the term of their lives, who pay 15s. yearly. Also one tenant who should keep the said gannets during the whole season of their breeding [aereacionis] thereon, for which service he will be quit of his rent of 2s."

Here it is clearly implied that the Gannets bred in three places, and it is also evident that, in the forty-seven years since the previous " extent " was made, their value had increased, for they are valued at 66s. and 8d. instead of at 5s., and have a special guardian appointed to protect them.

In 1325 or 1326, some twelve months before he was brutally murdered, Edward II., in order to avoid his rebellious barons, thought to take refuge on Lundy Island, and with a view to the King's coming there a third "extent" was made, which mentions Gannets among the products of the island.

Stow's Translation of the Third " Extent" of Lundy.— "The Isle of Lundy, which is in the mouth of the river Severne, two miles in length every way, abounding with pasture grounds, and oats, very pleasant. It bringeth forth Conies very plentifully, it hath Pigeons, and other foules, which Alexander Necham calls Ganimedes Birdes, having great nests. Also it minestreth to the inhabitants fresh springing waters. . . ."

The " Ganimedes Birdes" were Solan Geese. It is a play on the word Gannet, referring to Ganymedes, son of Tros, who was carried off by one of Jove's eagles. The Necham here alluded to was Abbot of Cirencester and a somewhat prolific writer. Here it may be remarked that the antiquary John Leland mentions Lundy Island twice in his " Itinerary "* and again once in the " Collectanea," but unfortunately in neither case is there any allusion to its birds.

The Puffin in 1337.—In these extracts the Puffin is not alluded to by name, although it must have been abundant, for the island of Lundy is supposed to take its name from *Lunde,* a Puffin. This is the Norwegian and Icelandic name for it, which has not, with this exception, found its way to England, where we call the bird a Puffin from its puffed-out appearance.†

It is a species which rejoices in a good many appellations, some of which, from the rounded shape of its beak, compare it to a Parrot. Assuredly one might have expected some mention of Puffins on Lundy Island, as well as of the Gannets, in these early documents, for Puffins have always been considered fit for food, which was never the case with the Guillemot. The Church of Rome, by a stretch of conscience, allowed Puffins to pass as fish during the fast, and it was this concession which has led to their finding a place in several manuscripts of a slightly later date.

Of these mentions the earliest seems to be in 1337 (Inquisitions P.M. IX. 100, 22 Edward III.). In 1337 the possession of the Scilly Islands (*caption of Seisin*), another

* Vol. III., p. 113 and Vol. V., p. 76.

† Prof. W. Skeat.

GANNET ROCK, LUNDY ISLAND.

place where these birds have always bred in great numbers, and where there are still thousands, as I can testify, was leased by the King, as Earl of Cornwall, to the Abbot Ranulphus of Blancminster for half a mark (= six and eightpence), or "c c c poffouns." No doubt they were intended for eating, and Professor Newton thinks they may have been young ones dried or salted.*

A rent of half a mark seems little more than nominal, but it was no doubt meant to fix the Earl of Cornwall's seigniory. Besides this record of Puffins at Scilly in 1337, there are one or two incidental allusions to them, in 1366 and 1367, as among the assets in Ministers' accounts. These latter, which are among the treasures of the Public Record Office, are cited in the " New English Dictionary."

Ignorance of Bird-life.—From a naturalist's point of view, the fourteenth century is chiefly remarkable for our extreme ignorance of the conditions of bird-life which then prevailed in the British Isles. Nor do we apparently know much of the ornithology of any part of Europe at this time, a circumstance which is to be regretted, but there is no help for it. There is the one exception of Falconry, a subject to which there are many references, this sport continuing as popular as ever, and, being the favourite pastime of princes and nobles, it continually comes into the MSS. of the time. When our Edward III. invaded France, in 1339, he took care that these insignia of royalty should not be wanting, having with him, as Jehan Froissart relates, thirty falconers. " Le Roi," says the old chronicler : " avoit bien, pour lui, trente fauconiers à cheval, chargés d'oiseaux, & bien soixante couples de forts chiens, & autant de levriers : . . . . ." (Vol. I., chap. ccx., p. 240). Yet we can hardly suppose that the rigours of war would have allowed him much time for hawking, or for coursing. It was in the reign of this king that an incident took place which shows the estimation in which a trained falcon was held, and not by the laity only. The Bishop of Ely attended the service of the church at Bermondsey, Southwark, leaving his hawk in the cloister, which in the meantime was stolen, whereupon the Bishop, discovering his loss, promptly pro-

* " Dictionary of Birds," p. 751.

nounced excommunication on the thieves who had taken it.
" Persons of high rank," says Strutt, who so well describes
the manners of this period, " rarely appeared without their
dogs and their hawks ; the latter they carried with them when
they journeyed from one country to another, and sometimes
even when they went to battle, and would not part with them
to procure their own liberty, when taken prisoners. These
birds were considered as ensigns of nobility, and no action
could be reckoned more dishonourable to a man of rank than
to give up his hawk."* But other birds besides hawks appear
to have been frequently kept, not for the sake of sport, nor
for beauty of plumage, but as watch-guards, or in some cases
for eating. We are told that two favourite birds in English
baronial mansions were the imported Parrot, and the Magpie,
the former for its drollery, while the Magpie had a place in the
poultry yard, because from its watchfulness against depredators
and the noise it made on the approach of fowl-stealers, it
was considered a useful safeguard. It was a time when the
middle classes were making some considerable advance both
in independence and wealth, and when consequently we may
suppose they had more leisure for the animals which lived
around them ; but, if they had, they have left us few records,
except as to falconry and trifling details of their housekeeping.
This may be in part due to a certain degree of stagnation
which overspread the land, following upon the depopulation
of counties which took place in 1348-9.

Animals Destroyed by Plague.—These were the years
of the Great Plague, which ravaged not England only but a
great part of Europe. So virulent was the epidemic that
even animals, such as dogs and cats, perished in the infected
houses, and cocks and hens also died.† In one pasture
there lay five thousand sheep, and they were so putrid that
neither beast nor bird would touch them.‡

Professor Rogers speaks of the great change which is
known to have taken place in the relations of labour and
capital from this cause. Meanwhile, minor matters had to be
content with a place in the background, and agriculture, for

* " Sports and Pastimes," p. 18.
† Baluze, " Vitæ Paparum."
‡ Roger Twysden, " Hist. Angl. Script."

F

want of labour, must have suffered severely. But although the poor suffered, the pursuits of royalty were not to be abandoned. In Thomas Rymer's "Foedera," there is a tract entitled "De Pardonatione Venationis" in which the author enumerates a list of the animals killed in 1356 by one of the Kings of Scotland.* No birds are named, but of fish the King got ninety-five pike, a hundred and nine perch and six bream, as well as roach, tench and chub. Fresh-water fish, pike more particularly, were always held to be an important article of food, trout were in less demand, but the larger salmon were appreciated. Before alluding again to Lundy and its Solans, it is desirable, in order to preserve a chronological

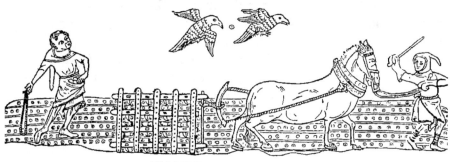

HARROWING, c. A.D. 1340.
Loutrell Psalter.

sequence, that some reference should be made to Lord Middleton's manuscripts, which are preserved at Wollaton Hall, Notts.† In the large selection printed by the Historical MSS. Commission there are only a few brief references to birds in the fourteenth century, but these few extend as far back as 1304–5. They make mention of fowls bought for the Falcons, which were no doubt an important part of the establishment, also pork for them. They also mention Wild Geese, Wild and tame Ducks, Teal (cercell), Plovers and small birds, which were purchases made for the kitchen. At that early date it was not the custom to keep elaborate accounts, or if it were, they have been lost.

* "Foedera, Conventiones, Literæ," edn. 1708, Tom. V., p. 870.
† For references to which I am indebted to the Rev. T. S. Cogswell, and have since inspected some of them.

Ranulph Higden.—Next in order of date come Higden's notes, chronicled some time between 1330 and 1360. A Chester Benedictine, Ranulph Higden, has bequeathed a good deal about Irish birds in what is known as the "Polychronicon," but he was an extensive borrower from Giraldus. Describing the natural productions of Ireland, Higden (translation in Rolls series) says—"That londe is more habudaunte in kye [kine] than in oxen, in pasture than in corne. Nevertheless, hit habundethe in salmones, eles, lawmpreis, and in other fysche of the see; in egles, cranes, pokokkes [? capercaillie], curlewes [?], sparrehowke, ffawken [Falcons] and gentille gossehawke; hauenge wulphes [wolves] and moste nyous myse [noxious mice] and weselles lytelle in body, but bolde in herte. Also there be bryddes which thei calle bernacles, lyke to wylde gese, whom nature producethe ageyne nature from firre trees. . ."

Further on, taking his cue from Giraldus, Higden says, as if the remark was original, that Ireland does not possess " a kynde of hawkes that be callede lanerettes and grete-fawkones [gyro falcones], partricehe and fesaunte, pyes, nyghtegales, bucke and doo, wontes [moles] and other bestes of venom." This last fortunate immunity, he goes on to say, is attributed by some men to the prayers of St. Patrick.

The absence of the Magpie—at the present day a bird so common in Ireland—is remarkable, but on this subject see a paper by the late Mr. G. E. Barrett-Hamilton in the "Zoologist,"* where a great deal of evidence about the former status of this species is adduced.

Both Giraldus and Higden include " Pavones " among the birds of Ireland, and, although the evidence of the latter counts for nothing, this is generally accepted as meaning the Capercaillie, an opinion in which Mr. J. F. Dimock, who edited Giraldus' Chronicle, shared.† Giraldus' words are: "Pavones silvestres hic abundant." Higden says : " Abundat . . . pavonibus, coturnicibus, niso, falcone et accipitre generoso." It is possible that both authors meant not the Capercaillie but the Peacock; yet the expression Wood Peacock implies a wild haunter of the forest. When the Capercaillie became

* "Zool.," 1891, p. 247.

† Edition of 1867.

extinct in Ireland is not certainly known, but it seems from
Ware's " History and Antiquities of Ireland " that there were
none left when Harris's edition of that work was published in
1764 (see Vol. II., p. 172), in spite of what Thomas Pennant
says to the contrary.

It may be that in the fourteenth century this fine bird
was an inhabitant of Ireland, as well as of the tracts of
forests in Gallowedia, Argyle and Scotia. On this subject
see Mr. J. A. Harvie-Brown's monograph on " The Capercaillie in Scotland " (1879), where matter relevant to the
question is brought together.

Mr. J. E. Harting, in a review of Mr. Harvie-
Brown's labours in the " Zoologist,"* further mentions
fourteenth-century grants of land in Durham (circa 134–361)
held by the tenure of paying " one wode-henne." But
the question is, were these Wood Hens Capercaillie or
Black Grouse ?

Household Accounts in the Fourteenth Century.—Mr.
Harting, who has dug more deeply than most into the
annals of the past, quotes a case of several persons
being fined in May, 1318, at a Court Baron of the
Bishop of Ely, for collecting Bitterns' eggs (*ova botorum*).†
The Bittern was a regular inhabitant of the Fen country,
and in many places, owing to the absence of trees, it may
have been a more plentiful species than the Heron.‡ It
must have been in considerable favour for the table, for
Bitterns are named in nearly every Dietary. They were
perhaps less fishy than Herons, but both were in request ;
the former were recommended to be eaten with no sauce,
but only with salt.§

Of Household Accounts and Charges at Feasts there are
but few. Mr. Harting has given extracts from a dinner at

* 1879. p. 468.

† " Handbook of British Birds," Revised edition, p. 217.

‡ The Rev. F. C. R. Jourdain, to whose assistance I am greatly indebted,
thinks this does not follow, for the Heron will breed on the ground in the
absence of trees. In Holland Mr. Jourdain has found their nests among reeds
in shallow water, and at Aqualate, in Staffordshire, a few nests have been
found in reeds, although there are large trees at hand. The Heron, in Mr.
Jourdain's experience, is commoner in Holland, even where trees are absent,
than the Bittern.

§ " Norwich Nat. Tr.." IV., p. 592.

Oxford in 1395,* which seems to have been an ornithological occasion.†

Attention has been drawn by Mr. Walter Rye to the "Deeds and Records of the Borough of King's Lynn" (1874), by H. Harrod, wherein are quoted three entries from the Chamberlain's Rolls, of Bustards and Herons provided for corporation dinners in 1338, 1370 and 1401.‡

But Mr. Rye has also pointed out that in the eleventh Report of the Historical Manuscripts Commission§ the second of these entries is rendered "botores [bitterns], herouns et avenis [oats]," which an examination of the original passage by Mr. E. M. Beloe confirms. There can, therefore, be little doubt that, in the other two entries also, the correct reading should be Bitterns, and not Bustards.

Prices of Provisions. —The following prices of provisions are given by Joseph Strutt as current in this century.‖ No poulterer to charge more than :—

		sh.	d.
For a Swan		4	0
,, ,, Teal			2
,, ,, river Mallard			5
,, ,, fen Mallard			3
,, ,, Snipe			1
,, 4 Larks			1
,, a Woodcock			3
,, ,, Partridge			5

* "Zoologist," 1879, p. 337. Some doubt has arisen as to the meaning here of the word "upupa," which, translated literally, would be a Hoopoe, in the passage : "Et in vij upupis emptis pretium capitis ij d. xiiij d," but probably, as suggested by my father ("Zool.," 1879, p. 379), the birds really were Lapwings. On the spelling of Hoopoe, *see* Swann's "English and Folk-names of British Birds," p. 125.

The whole passage is printed under the heading of "Empcio poltriæ, et volatilium" in Professor Rogers' most useful "Agriculture and Prices in England" (1866, ii., p. 644).

† There exists a Roll of Ancient Cookery, "The Forme of Cury," compiled in this century (but not printed until 1780) which gives many curious recipes.

‡ Pp. 74, 80, 84.

§ 1887, part iii., p. 220.

‖ "Manners, Customs, Arms, Habits, etc." (1776), Vol. III., p. 113. Reign of Edward III., E. Libro MS. in Bib. R. B. Cotton. The difference in the value of the shilling between then and now has to be remembered.

	sh.	d.
For a Plover		3
,, ,, Pheasant	1	4
,, ,, Curlew		10
,, 13 Thrushes		6
,, 13 Small birds		1*

Mute Swans must have been appreciated in Edward III.'s reign to be priced so highly; on the other hand, Teal and Snipe do not seem to have been thought much of. In 1357 Edward III. was moved to concede to private persons a grant of all unmarked Swans—that is, cygnets which could not be caught—on the Thames between Oxford and London for seven years, while in 1393 his successor on the throne made a similar concession in respect of rivers in the County of Cambridge. This alone proves the value which was placed upon these large birds.

* *The price of Fish in Norfolk.*—Mr. Hamon le Strange has obliged me with the following prices of fish, extracted from the Household Accounts of the le Straunges of Hunstanton Hall, in Norfolk, from 1340 to 1346.

Anguillæ (Eels)	of store.
Grindling or Grinling (Qy. Groundling).	
Cheling (Cod)	to the value of a few pence.
Doggedrove (Dogfish)	100 bought for 40s.
Haddock	one penny.
Hanon (Qy. Whiting)	one halfpenny or one farthing.
Herring White or fresh } ,, Salt }	200 cost 10d.
Lucea (Pike)	one farthing.
Ling.	
Makerell	2d., but number not given.
Mulvell (Qy. Mullet; *cf.* Higden's " Polychronicon," *t.c.,* p. 423)	one penny.
Playce	from ½d. to 2½d.
Porpoise	twenty pence.
Salmon	1¼d., weight not stated.
Sole	twopence, number not given.
Stookfish	sixty cost 2/2.
Sprotts (Sprats).	
Trotta (Trout)	one halfpenny.
Turbut.	
Verdiyng (unidentified)	to the value of a farthing.
Crabbys	
Cravose (Lobster)	two cost three halfpence.
Muscula (Mussel)	to the value of a farthing.
Ostrea (Oyster)	,, penny.
Welks	,, xixd.

Birds, with the exception of the Mallard, hardly come into these accounts, Mr. le Strange finds the price of a Goose was threepence, of a Mallard or a Capon twopence, of a Hen three halfpence.

A little later (*circa* 1384) when Richard II. had come to the throne, it appears from the " Liber Albus "* an emended list of prices was issued, for the control of poulterers, in which cygnets rank at a much lower figure :—

A best	cygnet was to be	..			fourpence
,, ,,	purcel (little pig) was to be				six ,,
,, ,,	teal	,, ,,			two ,,
,, ,,	river mallard	.. .,			three ,,
,, ,,	snipe	,, ,.			one penny
,, ,,	woodcock	,, .,			threepence
,, ,,	partridge	,, ,,			four ,,
,, ,,	plover	,, .,			three ,,
,, ,,	pheasant	,, ,,			twelve ,,
,, ,,	curlew	,, ,,			six ,,
,, ,,	bittern	,, ,,			eighteen ,,
,, ,,	heron	,, ,,			sixteen ,,
,, ,,	brewe (? whimbrel)	,, ,,			eighteen ,,
Four	larks	,, ,,			one penny
Twelve	thrushes	., ,,			sixpence
,,	finches	,, .,			one penny

MARKING THE BEAK AND FEET OF A SWAN.

These prices were assessed by the Mayor, and proclaimed from time to time to the people, who were informed that any person selling unsound birds was liable to be set on the pillory.

This is also a memorable century as marking the gradual rise of letters, and especially as being the period in which

* " The White Book of the City of London, compiled A.D. 1419," translated by H. T. Riley, 1861, p. 401.

Geoffrey Chaucer the poet flourished, who, like the observant Shakespeare, evidently had a fondness for animals. In " The Assemble of Fowls " (or " Parlement of Briddis "), where an Eagle, being beloved of three Tereels, makes her choice upon trial, we meet with no less than thirty-six kinds of birds, amongst which are the Merlion. Kite, Sparow, Ruddocke [Robin], Swallowe, Feldefare, Starling, Chough, Popingeie [Green Woodpecker], Lapwing, Storke and Cormeraunt. The epithets employed by Chaucer are shrewdly characteristic of the habits of the birds. Thus the Fieldfare, in allusion to its being a winter visitant, is described as frosty, the Cormorant full of gluttony, the Goose wakeful, the Heron the eel's foe, the Turtle Dove is wedded, and the Chough a thief, while the false Lapwing is full of treachery. Chaucer's Tereels are meant to be male Eagles, but this is a very unusual use of the term, which, spelled in many ways, has been always applied to a male Hawk of some kind. In modern falconry Tiercel (the derivation of which is uncertain) is restricted to the male of the Peregrine Falcon, which in Shakespeare's day was termed a Tercel-gentle to distinguish it from a Goshawk.*

The Peregrine Falcon figures in " The Squire's Tale " (Part II., line 448), but is not named by Chaucer in " The Assemble of Fowls."

---

* " The Ornithology of Shakespeare," p. 53.

Chapter VII.

FIFTEENTH CENTURY.

The Fifteenth Century: Sir Richard Holland. Decoys. William Botouer. Birds in the Fifteenth Century. Feasting in the Fifteenth Century. Nevile and Warham.

Most of the old English poets show themselves to be fond of nature by their allusions to the names and habits of animals. Chaucer's frequent mentions of birds are very apposite, and in this century we have Sir Richard Holland.

In Holland's poem of " The Howlat " (*i.e.*, Owl or Owlet), supposed to have been written in 1453, several birds are introduced by name—as the Solan Goose (spelled Soland), the Bittern (spelled Baytown), the Stork, the Starling, the Corncrake, the Gowk (Cuckoo), the Tuquheit (Lapwing), and the Swallow. This curious old allegory was intended to be a satire on James II. of Scotland, whose face was somewhat deformed and who is here likened to an Owl. It is a literary curiosity, not without some meaning for the naturalist. The names in " The Howlat " may be compared with somewhat similar ones in " Nomina avium fferorum," part of a Pictorial Vocabulary of about this date, published by Mr. T. Wright.* Here we meet with a few specimens of phonetic spelling past puzzling out, but the following birds' names are intelligible :—

A rodok (ruddock=Redbreast).
A donek (dunnock=Hedge Accentor).
A potok (puttock=Kite).
A mawys (mavis=Thrush).
A schevelard (shovelard=Spoonbill).
A thyrstyllecok (throstle-cock=Mistle Thrush).
A wodake (wood-hack=Woodpecker).
A howylle (Owl).
A roke (Rook).
A rewyn (Raven).
A cote (? Coot).
A wagstyrt (Wagtail).
A schryche (Shrike or Screech-Owl).†

* " Anglo-Saxon and Old English Vocabularies," 1884, ed. Wülcker, I., p. 761.
† J. E. Harting.

Another and shorter list in the same vocabulary is entitled " Nomina avium domesticarum," and in this we find the stokdowe (Stockdove), and the names of Hawks used in falconry. These lists have their value in a century where there is so much dearth of exact information.

It still seems best to adhere to a chronological order rather than attempt an arrangement of these early records under subjects. Although this method has a tendency to result in a string of more or less unconnected quotations, it best displays what can be said of the early history of ornithology in the British Isles. Readers will, I think, admit that the alternative plan, namely, that of grouping the matter to hand under the names of species, or under subjects, such as Feasts, Household Accounts, Hawking, etc., is outweighed by the chronological method. The student of natural history in investigating this period cannot but heave a sigh at the lack of available information. As in the fourteenth century, so now, the notices of birds are singularly few and far between, and what we do get are imperfect, and of a very fragmentary character. Guns were practically unknown things in the fifteenth century, but, in default, the fowler knew how to use the net and the crossbow with a dexterity which would nowadays astonish us. Decoys as a means of taking Wild Ducks, which visited England five hundred years ago in far greater numbers than they do now, had come into use, but were possibly confined to the eastern counties. In his account of " Decoys Past and Present " before alluded to, Mr. J. Hoare informs us that the old Deeping Decoy at Croyland (or Crowland), in South Lincolnshire, was a sub-ject of dispute between the Lord of Liddel and the monastery in 1455. Also that on May 12th, 1432, a mob came armed with swords, sticks, bows and arrows, and took six hundred wild Geese (anches, query aucœ) out of the Abbot's decoy and did other damage to the amount of £100. The amount of wild-fowl taken in the East Anglian decoys must have been very large, if it is to be judged by more recent statistics, when the marshes had become less. They were probably not worked with a dog, but were what are described in Payne-Gallwey's " Book of Duck Decoys " (1886, p. 195) as Trap decoys, with doors at the end of the pipes which could be lowered with a wire from some concealed hut. In this case the arbitrary regulations imposed by one of the great abbeys had become too onerous to be borne, and the peasantry rose in revolt and slew the Abbot's wild-fowl, either when they were too young to fly, or when they were moulting. A special

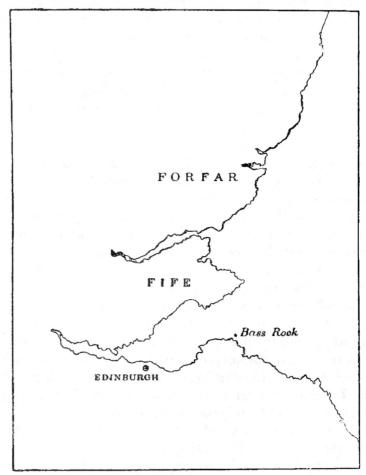

jury was summoned the following year, and the sheriff had orders to fine the delinquents.

Solan Geese at the Bass Rock.—The earliest intimation which we have of Solan Geese at the Bass Rock in Scotland is contained in the still preserved "Codex" of the Cistercian Abbey of Cupar. This Codex is considered to have been written about 1447 by Walter Bower, the Abbot of Inchcolm, an island in the Firth of Forth.

The passage about Solan Geese, tantalising in its brevity, for it merely tells us that Solan Geese breed there in great abundance, is as follows :—

" Insula de Bass, ubi solendæ nidificant in magna copia : cujus protector exstat Sanctus Baldredus, Sancti Kentigerni olim suffraganus ; qui eam ab insultu mirifice protegit Anglicorum."

We hear no more of them after that until 1493, and then only indirectly as wild-birds, or wild-fowl producing grease, which had a great value in the eyes of the Prioress of North Berwick, who was so wronged about the Gannets by one Robert Lauder that she applied to the Pope.

William Botoner. Solan Geese at Pentybers.—It seems probable that there was a small Gannetry at this time on the north coast of Cornwall, if the " Itinerarium " of William

Botoner is to be credited.* In August 1478, Botoner visited several islands, of one of which he writes : " Pentybers rock, a very great crag, situated on the western side of the Severn water, four miles distant from the harbour of Padstow, and the castle of Tintagel, and one mile from the shore, and there nest birds called ganets, gulls, sea-mews, and other sea birds" (*Translation*).

Although there is no evidence of a change of name, and the words " very great crag " are hardly applicable, it seems almost certain that this Pentybers can be none other than a rock which now goes by the name of Gulland, which lies at no great distance from Pentyr Point. In both cases the meaning of " Pen " is a head or headland. Botoner has not much to say of animal life on other islands, but he alludes to the Puffins at Scilly, where they seem to have been an article of food ; to the snakes on Priestholm in North Wales ; and to Cormorants and Seamews on " Lastydenale in Wallia." Mr. O. V. Aplin, in writing of Botoner† has identified this last named with St. Tudwal's Island on the Carnarvon coast, and no doubt rightly.

British Birds in the Fifteenth Century.—Leaving poets and Solan Geese for the present, let us see what there is available, which is beyond mere conjecture, about British birds generally, to which we can turn for information. As a matter of fact there is very little; it would be much easier to collect information about the sixteenth century than about the fifteenth, where only some scattered items bearing directly on Natural History are discoverable. What there is, has been to some extent sifted by Mr. W. Denton in his " England in the Fifteenth Century," where this author cites various curious passages, one of which referring to some old Trevelyan Papers‡ may be worth quoting as a fair sample of the times. In 1532 a certain tenant of Nettlecomb in Somerset was indicted by one John Trevelyan for sundry infractions of his covenant in respect of the holding of the estate and manor : several things were alleged against him, viz., that he

* " Itinerarium sive Liber Rerum Memorabilium." In another place Botoner alludes to the island of Grasholm, but says nothing about any Gannets being there.
† "Zoologist," 1915, p. 68.
‡ Which have been printed for the Camden Society (1857).

and " hys folkes " killed the swine [perhaps semi-wild ones]
and kept greyhounds which hunted the deer, also " he and
hys company kylled sum by nyght,"—made " harepypes "
[snares] and destroyed conies,—had young herons out of
their nests,—set up " a rode nette " in the woods to take
woodcocks,—stole " coulvers " [pigeons] out of the barn,—
" fyssyd " in the park—and went " by nyght a byrdbattyn
[bird-catching] dyvers tymes,"—all of which acts were
contrary to privilege.

The allusion here is to tame Pigeons in a barn, but they
were more generally kept in substantial brick towers.   Fowls
were also largely bred at farms and homesteads, and not
always for their owners, as many went to supply the religious
houses, which were by no means entirely dependent upon
eels and pike ! Mr. Denton observes that among other
services, the cotter had to render poultry, when the lord's
table or the lord's falcons required them, but in that case they
were supplied as part of the tenant's rent.   Occasionally in
household accounts we come across such an entry as " In
X. gallinis pro falconibus emptis, xvd.," or "in gallina empta
pro falcon Domini Ricardi,"*   The guardian of a large rabbit
warren was an important man, and like gamekeepers of the
present day, he did not forget to have a " gallows-tree " for
vermin.   Such an one was James Radcliff of Byllinforth
[Billingford near Dereham] in 1490 or thereabouts, who was
in the habit of suspending all " mysdoers and forfaytours
[offenders] as wesellis, lobsters [stoats] polkattys, bosartys
[buzzards] and mayne currys [great curs]," and no doubt
any large hawks or Owls.†   In the fifteenth century,
as now, severe winters from time to time decimated the
smaller birds by starving them, of which an instance, from
the " Chronicon Angliæ " of Thomas Walsingham, which refers
to 1408, is quoted by the Rev. F. C. R. Jourdain in " British
Birds."‡   Doubtless the oversea migration went on in the
east of England in much the same way as described by Sir
Thomas Browne two hundred years later (about 1662), and
in fact as it does now.   But were there then the hundreds

* " Manuscripts of Lord Middleton," pp, 324, 326.
† See " Norwich Naturalists' Trans.," V., p. 523.
‡ Vol. XI., p. 267.

of thousands of Rooks, Starlings and Skylarks that there
are at the present day ? This is greatly to be doubted,
indeed it is improbable, considering the changed conditions of the country : some species which are now very
plentiful may then have been very scarce. Throughout
England there must have been a considerable difference
among the resident birds. In the county of Norfolk alone
at least thirteen sorts of birds could be named which have
now ceased to nest there, all of them species which there
is every reason to assert bred and were unmolested in the
fifteenth century. It may well be that the number is far
more than thirteen. Five hundred years ago the agricultural
conditions so favourable for the Chaffinch did not exist ;
trimmed Thorns and Privet hedges, dear to the Greenfinch
and the Linnet, were few and far between. Some few Box
bushes for the Bullfinch to nest in were to be found, but,
assuredly, congenial ricks and stack-yards for the House
Sparrow were not so plentiful as they are now, while in those
remote times there would have been no Laurel shrubberies
for the Thrush and no large planted fruit-gardens for the
Blackbird. The Bunting and the sprightly Yellow Hammer
would have had less grain to live upon than now ; but, on the
other hand, the handsome Reed Bunting, with the greater
extent of marsh, might have been more plentiful than it
is. The confiding Robin, so long known by its Saxon
appellation of *ruddock*, which is still the surname of some
families, would hardly have been at every humble door, as
nowadays. It is likely, although incapable of proof, that
Swallows and Martins were far less abundant then than at
the present day, for in Great Britain they appear to have
thriven with house-building. The multiplication of nesting
sites tends to increase a species, just as does the tilling of
land favourably affect those game birds which seek their food
upon its surface. The Jackdaw, perhaps less common than
at the present day, appears to have been none the less troublesome.—" Pro exclusione nodularum ab ecclesia " we read in
1410 in the ancient account-rolls of the Abbey of Durham.*

They often found their way into churches and cathedrals,
which led to such entries as the above. Small birds were not

* Publications of the Surtees Society," Vol. C. (1899).

considered friends by tillers of the soil in England, and it was
the custom for boys to be sent into the fields with bows and
arrows, which with the help of shouting, were expected to scare
all such thieves away. Then, as now, the parasitical House
Sparrow, whether a native or not, knew well how to thrive
upon man's labour. No one can prove from where the Sparrow
originally sprung, but a robber of grain it has been from the
earliest times, and in proof of this indictment may be cited
an illustration in the "Hortus Sanitatis." This "Hortus,"
which was a medical treatise of the fifteenth century (printed
1485 and 1491) sometimes with coloured pictures, depicts four
Sparrows attacking a field of ripe corn, probably real Sparrows,
but it has to be remembered that the term was used in a
generic sense. Another very quaint delineation of street life
occurs in the later editions of "Hortus," in which Kites and
other birds form a prominent feature. One of the Kites is
sitting on a man's head, a plain testimony to the tameness of
these privileged city cleaners. Everywhere they were tolerated,
and especially in hot countries, because of their utility in
clearing up garbage, and animal matter which would infallibly
spread disease, if left to rot. In England, where they had not
lost their Anglo-Saxon name of Glead—(*glida* or *cyta* from
their gliding flight), they must have been quite common, and
very serviceable, in spite of eating a few young fowls at times.
In the same picture are to be seen Storks attending to
their nests on chimneys. The Stork appears never to have
been an English bird, yet it once bred in Scotland, as Dr. Eagle
Clarke has pointed out; this was in 1416, when a pair nested
on the top of St. Giles's Church, in the heart of Edinburgh,
according to the old chronicler Bower.*

On the other hand, granivorous birds would have been
less plentiful. Partridges, though commonly eaten, and
Pheasants also, as bills of fare testify, would have been few
compared with the multitudes of to-day. Yet the Pheasant
seems to have been common in Ireland, and Professor Newton
states, on the authority of Nicholas Upton (whose work was
written in the fifteenth century and to whom we owe the first
mention of Choughs in Cornwall), that Pheasants were occasionally reared and fattened in England, which indicates that they

* Abbot Bower, *see* "Scottish Naturalist," 1919, p. 25.

were birds of the aviary as well as found wild. This rearing by hand was regularly practised at a somewhat later date, and in the reign of Henry VIII. would seem to have been a customary proceeding. We know that this King's servants of whom one at least was French, reared Pheasants, at the King's country palace at Eltham in Kent, keeping them in aviaries until they were wanted for eating. In a very entertaining volume, entitled " The Privy Purse Expenses of King Henry the Eighth,"* Sir N. H. Nicolas quotes many entries about them. Here we twice read of as much as two crowns, which would be nine shillings and fourpence, being paid to a French priest, who was the Pheasant breeder.

Turtle Doves were only seen occasionally, maybe, and cultivators of the soil would not have had to complain of their plots being devastated by armies of omnivorous Wood Pigeons. The House Sparrow was establishing itself, and was already honoured with a nickname,† Rooks were being seriously complained of, and an Act was passed in Scotland in 1424 (I James 1, cap. 19) to keep them in check, which, put into modern English, ran as follows :—" Item. Therefore as men consider that Rooks building in church-yards, orchards, or trees do great damage upon corn, it is ordained that they whom such trees pertain to, do let them build, and suffer on no wise that their young ones fly away, and where it be proved that they build and the young be flown, and the nests be found in the trees at May-day, the trees shall forfeit to the King." In 1457 this was followed by a second Act (II James 14, cap. 31) which also proscribed Eagles, Buzzards, Kites, and some Hawk called " Mittales " (elsewhere spelled Mittaine and Myttaine).‡ From 1457 until the present time it has been a moot question whether Rooks do more harm than good, but the balance of evidence is against them in the twentieth century as it was in the fifteenth, and many farmers would like to see these obsolete Acts revived, and the increasing Rooks greatly lessened.

In the fifteenth century the larger sorts of birds of prey were no doubt abundant : the Buzzard, a common

* See pp. 10, 181, 265, 266, 271, 276.
† Phyllyp Sparrowe.
‡ Probably from Mittle, to hurt or wound (see Jamieson's Scot. Dict.).

G

breeder throughout the land, as it is in some parts of Europe still, and the Goshawk nesting in small numbers, while the Osprey would have been no rare sight, and Harriers much too common to call for remark.

One very interesting fact regarding the Kite, which was first brought to the notice of naturalists by the late Professor A. Newton, is that the Bohemian Schaschek—who in the capacity of guide and Latin Secretary accompanied the Baron Leo von Rozmital on his tour in England, between 1465 and 1467 and kept a diary in Latin—after mentioning London Bridge and the houses that stood upon it, goes on to say that nowhere had he seen so great a number of Kites as there. They were protected as useful scavengers, and probably there was not a large town in England without them. The Kites and Ravens in our towns also excited the wonder of the Venetian Ambassador Capello, an Italian who spent the winter of 1496–7 in England. In his Journal, printed in the Camden Society's " Transactions " (1847), his Secretary, writing for him, says :—" Common fowls, pea-fowls, partridges, pheasants, and other small birds abound here above measure, and it is truly a beautiful thing to behold one or two thousand tame Swans upon the river Thames, as I, and also your Magnificence have seen, which are eaten by the English like ducks and geese. Nor do they dislike what we so much abominate, i.e., crows, rooks, and jackdaws ; and the raven may croak at his pleasure, for no one cares for the omen ; there is even a penalty attached to destroying them, as they say that they keep the streets of the towns free from all filth.

" It is the same case with the Kites, which are so tame, that they often take out of the hands of little children, the bread smeared with butter, in the Flemish fashion, given to them by their mothers." This gives a curious picture of what London was like in the fifteenth century, when the city was built of wood, and its streets were not yet paved.

Swans on the Thames.—The swans on the Thames were no doubt protected, or there would not have been so large a number as two thousand. They had already been the subject of legislation under Edward III. in 1357, and in 1482 or 1483 there was again an enactment passed in their favour, which recites that no person other than the son of the King, or a substantial freeholder, could possess a swan-mark. As this was the case, perhaps these Thames swans were mostly Crown property. That they were maintained in full strength until the succeeding century is shown by the observations of a traveller, the Duke de Najera, who visited England in 1543-4, who, referring to the Thames, says : "Never did I see a river so thickly covered with swans as this."* Another writer, who was an Italian bishop, Paul Jovius, about the same time also alludes to them in his description of Britain. That the King was accustomed to maintain swan-herds, who were responsible for the birds, on other rivers besides the Thames, is certain, and he had also the prerogative right of seizing his subject's swans, if they were not marked.

Birds seen by Vergil.—Another Italian, Polydore Vergil,† who visited England four years later, also remarks on the Swans upon lakes and rivers, but says nothing about Kites. What Vergil seems to have been most struck with were the Kentish hens and the delicacy of young grass-fed Geese.

"Of wilde burdes these are most delicate, partriches, phesaunts, quayles, owsels, thrusshes, and larckes." Of the Skylark he remarks, "This laste burde in winter season, the wether not being to owtragios, dothe waxe wonderus fatte, at which time a wonderfull nombre of them is caughte. . . ." Like Capello, Vergil marvelled at the Crows, Rooks and Jackdaws, which he had not been accustomed to see so numerous in Italy : "Crowes and chowghes [Jackdaws] are everie daye in the morning earlie harde clattering in theire kinde. In noe cuntrie is there a greater multitude of crowse ; being soe harmefull a kinde of birdes, yet are thie spared in that lande, bie cause thei eate woormes and other vermin . . ."

He also gives another reason why Crows and Rooks were spared, and that was because Herons were wont to build in their old and disused nests, and Herons were of prime importance for Hawking.‡

* "Archaeologia," XXIII., p. 355 (*trans.*).

† "Polydore Vergil's English History," translation, printed for the Camden Society, 1846, p. 23.

‡ This supposed habit of the Heron, on which Ray cast doubts ("The Ornithology," p. 278), has met with no confirmation by modern observers, nor does it seem likely that it is founded on fact.

Hawking in England.—What Hawking was like in the
fifteenth century is to some extent a matter of conjecture,

but there is a good deal about it which may be gathered
from the correspondence of the Norfolk family of Paston.
The Paston Letters, which were written by different members

of a distinguished family during the reigns of Henry VI., Edward IV. and Richard III., have formed the text of an article by Professor Newton in the second edition of Lubbock's "Fauna of Norfolk"* where the references to Hawking are discussed, and extracts given.

That the high estate of Falconry had lost none of its prestige is very possible, for in the fifteenth century it was still a usual out-of-door exercise with the English nobility, and so it remained until firearms were invented. Important personages still showed a preference for being painted in hawking costume, or holding a Hawk, the taste for this species of dress implied love of the chase, which was universal and ardently followed. All this may be inferred from the literature of the time, as well as from the pages of the " Bibliotheca Accipitraria," in which Mr. Harting gives a portrait—here reproduced by permission—of one of the Kings of Scotland as a young man, holding a Sparrow-Hawk on his wrist. As the use of guns superseded the chasing of birds by trained Hawks, so did it at a later date supersede the employment of the Decoy for catching Ducks. That Norfolk, with its large extent of flat country, some of it comparatively treeless, was well suited for falconry is easily understood, and the pursuit of it was probably general among the rich. Early as is the Paston correspondence, it does not contain the first reference to Hawking in Norfolk, for, as pointed out by the Rev. T. S. Cogswell, there are three incidental allusions to it in the Domesday Book.

Feasting and Food.—There was not a little gluttony displayed in the heavy carousals of the Middle Ages, but they have the merit of having bequeathed to us some particulars about a good many birds which perhaps we should not otherwise have had. On great occasions a Boar's head "enarmede," that is larded, was brought in, or a Peacock "endored," i.e., with its head gilt, enveloped in its own skin after roasting, formed the principal course, and being lifted high by the bearers, was ceremoniously placed on the board. Thus garnished it was a "Pecok enhakyll," that is to say, a Peacock dressed. Fosbroke says the Pheasant sometimes divided the honours with the Peacock, and was decorated not only with

* Southwell's edn., 1879, p. 224.

its own prismatic feathers, but with a collar of gold, to enhance its gaudy appearance. Greatly did the good things shine forth at British festivals, when

> " O'er capon, heron-shaw and crane,
> And princely peacock's gilded train,
> And o'er the boar's head garnished brave,
> And cygnets from St. Mary's wave ;
> O'er ptarmigan and venison,
> The priest had spoke his benison."
>
> —Sir Walter Scott.

The price of a Peacock was about one shilling, and we may judge how plentiful they were from George Neville's banquet, to be mentioned immediately. But the Peacock was not the only bird in favour ; there was the Swan, and at Henry V.'s Coronation dinner (1413) a chief ornament of the royal table, at which he and Katherine his consort were to be seated, was a Pelican. This ornithological centre piece was seated upon her nest, with her young birds round her, probably modelled in sugar and paste. A dish of this kind was termed a " sutiltie," a device our forefathers were very fond of at banquets. If this Pelican was a real bird it must have come from the south, as such a rarity would hardly have been procurable in England. Samuel Pegge's " Forme of Cury " (cookery) compiled by the master cooks of Richard II. explains the composition of many unusual dishes.

Bishops Neville and Warham.—Of all the public feasts of which we have any record, the most extravagant as regards consumption of provisions were in September, 1465, when Neville, the Chancellor of England, was made Archbishop of York,* and a few years later, when Warham was enthroned at Canterbury. The quantity of porpoises, seals, and fish of all descriptions, fresh or salted, on the second occasion, is even in excess of the goodly provision of birds on the first, but the numbers given probably represent what were ordered, not what were actually brought to table.

* For the precise date, Sept. 22nd and 23rd, 1465, I am indebted to Mr. W. H. Mullens.

The following list of what was commanded for Neville's banquet is taken from the " Appendicis [*sic*] ad Joannis Lelandi antiquarii collectanea."

Wild Bulls	... ...	6
Swans	... ...	400
Geese ...	... ...	2000
Capons ...	... ...	1000
Plovers	... ...	400
Quayles	... ...	1200
The Foules called Rees	... ...	2400
Peacocks	... ...	104
Mallards and Teal	... ...	4000
Cranes ...	... ...	204
Rabbits...	... ...	4000
Bittors	... ...	204
Heronshawes ...	... ...	400
Fessauntes	... ...	200
Partridges	... ...	500
Woodcocks	... ...	400
Curlews	... ...	100
Egrittes	... ...	1000
Stags ...	... ...	500
Pike and Bream	... ...	608
Porpoises and Seals ...	... ...	12

Besides the birds in the above list, there are named in the particulars of the courses Redshanks, Styntes, Larks and Martynettes, but what these last were is not clear, probably Swallows.*

Egrets and " Rees."—It has been thought that Neville's Egrets were Lapwings, and to this theory Newton lent his support, but this can hardly be maintained, because in many later instances, some of which are cited by Mr. F. J. Stubbs,† both are mentioned. On the other hand, that the Egret was ever in any sense abundant in England would be difficult to establish, nor is it conceivable that a thousand could be obtained at one time.

* A quite different list of the birds and other viands at Neville's feast—including even the " Ganetz "—is given in " A Noble Boke Off Cookry " (15th cent.), edited from the Holkham MSS. by Mrs. A. Napier in 1882 (p. 7).

† " Zoologist," 1910, pp. 150, 380.

The Egret of these old lists was a name taken from the French *Aigrette*, to which possibly not much meaning was attached by the writers, beyond that it was something of the Heron tribe, which claimed that name.   It is likely MS.

MARSHLANDS DRAINED BY THE GREAT BEDFORD LEVEL.   (*The shaded area.*)

cookery books based on French and Italian sources, similar to the Forme of Cury, were in existence, from which many terms and even the names of birds were borrowed, and the name of Egret must have been found in them.   Yet such a bird as the Egret may at that time have had a more northern breeding-range, attracted by the fen lands of Cambridgeshire and South Lincoln; for Vermuyden, the Dutchman, had not yet drained the "Great Level." Even long after drainage had been begun, there still extended from Ely to the Wash some 300,000 acres of marsh land, very tempting to aquatic birds.

The Fowls called Rees.—The Fowls called Rees, which the larderer was evidently doubtful about, and which Pennant imagined to be to be Land-rails, are now known to have been Ruffs and Reeves, but where could they have expected to get 2400 head of a species which was little more than a summer-migrant? Evidently Neville's figures must not be accepted too literally, but must be taken in the sense of a general estimate.

Identity of the bird called a Brewe.—At a great feast held in London in honour of King Richard II., in September 1387, among "The pultry" enumerated in "the purviaunce," we meet with "x dosen Curlewes, xij dosen Brewes."* The Brewe also comes into sundry documents of the fifteenth century, *e.g.*, Russell's "Boke of Nurture" (1452), and of the sixteenth century, *e.g.*, on the occasion of the visit of Charles V. to England in 1522.† At a later date there is some change in the name, which in 1605 is spelled Brue.‡ It has generally been supposed that this bird was the Whimbrel, but names were used somewhat indiscriminately in those days, and very likely it sometimes served for the Godwit, as Mr. F. J. Stubbs has suggested.§ In the reign of Edward I. a brewe was valued at eighteen pence, and a Curlew at six-pence in 1275 and the same prices held good in 1384,‖ which implies a decided culinary inferiority for the Curlew, which was either commoner or less appreciated. The name brewe may be synonymous with breve, *i.e.*, small or short.

One of the receipts given in Cookery-books of the fifteenth century is for "Brew rost," of which the following version may be taken from "A noble boke off cookry ffor a prynce houssolde."¶—*Brew rost.*—A Brewe, sley him in the mouthe

* "Fifteenth-Century Cookery-Books" (Early English Text Society, 1848, p. 67).
† "Rutland Papers," p. 76. Camden Soc. Publications, 1842.
‡ "Archaeologia," 1800, p. 341.
§ "Zoologist," 1910, p. 154.
‖ *Supra*, p. 71.
¶ Edited by Mrs. A. Napier, 1882, p. 63.

as a curlewe, skeld hym and drawe hym as a henne, then brek
his leggs at the kne and tak away the bone from the kne to the
foot, as a heron cut of the nek, by the bodye, then rost hym and
raise his winges and his legges as a heron, and no sauce but salt.

The opening sentence " sley him in the mouthe," with
a knife or other instrument, seems to imply that the
" Brues " were netted, and kept in pens until wanted.

Henry IV.—Interesting also are the birds served up
on other festive occasions, as at the nuptials of Henry IV.
in 1403, and at the coronation of Henry VI. in 1422.*
Again there is the document known as Russell's " Boke
of Nurture " (1452) which contains the names of birds,
of which one is the Stockdove, but both here and in
" The Boke of Keruynge " (1513), we may take it that the
appellation of Stockdove is meant to apply to tame Pigeons,
now kept in large numbers. The birds served at Henry VI.'s
dinner included the mysterious Egrettes, Curlew, Cocks, Plover,
Quails, Snipe, Larks, Swan, Heron, Crane, Partridge, Bittern,
Peacock.† One might have expected that Spoonbills would
have been mentioned in all these Dietaries, but they are not.
Yet as " shovelards " they come into one of the vocabularies
of this century, and under the same name we find them twice
alluded to in John Russell's quaint book of recipes, and once
in "The Boke of Keruynge." That they made a show at some
principal feasts is evident, as at Oxford, where under the
equivalent name of Poplars we meet with them in 1452.‡
Perhaps it is worth remarking that in a very different way
they come into the will of Richard Le Scrop, dated 1400.§

* And at the Duke of Buckingham's wedding in 1480 ("Archaeologia,"
1834, p. 311).

† *See* " A Chronicle of London from 1089 to 1483, written in the Fifteenth
Century " (1827), Notes, p. 169, and comments in " Norfolk Archaeology,"
I., p. 276, where the Egret is held by Mr. Dashwood to be the young of the
Heron. This coronation feast took place on the 6th day of November, 1429.

‡ Episcopal Feasting described in " Historia et Antiquitatis Universi-
tatis Oxoniensis " (1674, lib. 1, p. 219).

§ Here among many other things the scribe has put down : " . . aulam
meam cum poplars textam, et lectum meum integrum cum costeris de rubeo
cum poplars et armis meis hroudatum . . " ("Testamenta Eboracensia"
part I., p. 276). Where designs of birds were used, Spoonbills would be
a favourite decoration. Examples of this occur more often abroad, but
as " Popelers " on tapestry they form an item in the Roll of the effects of
Sir J. Fastolfe of Norfolk in 1459 ("Archaeologia," 1827, p. 332, and *see*
Gairdner's edition of the Paston Letters, Vol. I., pp. 479, 483).

CHAPTER VIII.

SIXTEENTH CENTURY (1ST PART).

The Sixteenth Century (1st part): Solan Geese of Canada. John Major. Hector Boece. The name Brissel.

The Boke of Phyllyp Sparrowe, compiled by Master [John] Skelton (1508).—The awakening of western Europe at the end of the fifteenth century and beginning of the sixteenth, led to an increasing search for knowledge, obtained by means of personal observation and actual experiment. Hitherto the attitude of learned men towards animals and plants had not had much relation to real knowledge, but improvement slowly began to manifest itself. The position of those who claimed to be scientific teachers was still rather vague, such men were rather to be called explainers. Theirs was what a learned writer has termed an elaborate doctrine of symbolism which comprised all nature. This is demonstrated in more ways than one; it is shown not only by the importance attached to the medical properties of herbs, but also by the anatomical schools which began to be founded, in which the study of animals was recommended not to be neglected. Nevertheless, zoology, as we now understand the word, moved at a very slow pace, and it certainly is remarkable how little there is about birds in the literature of any country before the middle of the sixteenth century. Birds were regarded as things which could or could not, be eaten, and no further interest was taken in them; they did not possess the virtue which was supposed to lie in herbs, and there were very few medical secrets which physicians could hope to extract from them. "The Boke of Phyllyp Sparrowe," written by a native of Norfolk, is some exception to this rule, for the poem brings in the names of sixty-nine birds. They are all recognisable, except the "Rouse" and the "Kowgh," which latter may be "Chough." Route or

Rout is also a Scotch provincialism, and Jamieson thinks it was a name intended for the Brent Goose.*

Meaning of Brent Goose.—The Brent is a bird which I have often heard called Rode or Road Goose on the estuary of the river Tees in Durham, where in winter it is rather common, and this is an appellation not very dissimilar from the spelling adopted by the poet Skelton. On the coast of Durham the name Road Goose has probably been in use for centuries, judging from Willughby's mention in " The Ornithology " (1678, p. 361) of the Rat-Goose or Road Goose, as coming in packs to the Tees. It is curious that neither Willughby nor Ray realised that the Road Goose was the same as the Brent Goose—an error in which they were followed by Ray's friend, Samuel Dale.

In connection with Scotland, the word " Routs " also occurs in Gordon's " Earldom of Sutherland " (1630), as well as the name Ringouse, which latter is similar to the German Ringel-Gans, and is probably another name for the Brent. From Mr. J. E. Harting's observations it would appear to be very likely that both these names, as well as Rut-goys (1530),† Rot-gans of the Dutch, and Radde-Guss of the Heligolanders are traceable to the same root, and have been earned by this species from its habit of feeding upon grass-wrack, submerged at high, and exposed at low, tide.‡

The Solan Goose, 1511–1529. — Information about the Solan Goose is still scanty, but it is now that we first hear, and from four different sources, of the famous Gannetry on Ailsa Craig, as well as of the equally important one at Sulisgeir on the north-west coast of Scotland. Royalty was not averse from partaking of the Solan Goose, as appears from the Privy-purse accounts of James IV. of Scotland, some items from which have been communicated by Mr. J. Anderson, who

---

* *See* " Dictionary of the Scottish Language " (1825, Suppt.).

† Item, 3 Februarii [1533] 1 rutgoys, 3d.—1 mawlert [mallard], 2d. —6 dunlyngs, 2d.—1 seepye, 1d. (" Liber Bursarii Ecclesiæ Dunelmensis, p. 327). On another page of this " Liber " it is amusing to read of " 3 pisces vocatos puffynes " being brought to the Prior (p. 54). On pages 46 and 129 the Whympernell is mentioned, no doubt the Whimbrel.

‡ *See* " Handbook of British Birds," 1901, p. 238. " Rodge," as applied to the Gadwall, probably has the same origin. Rotington, in Cumberland, is thought to derive its name from Rotgoose (" Fauna of Lakeland," p. 244).

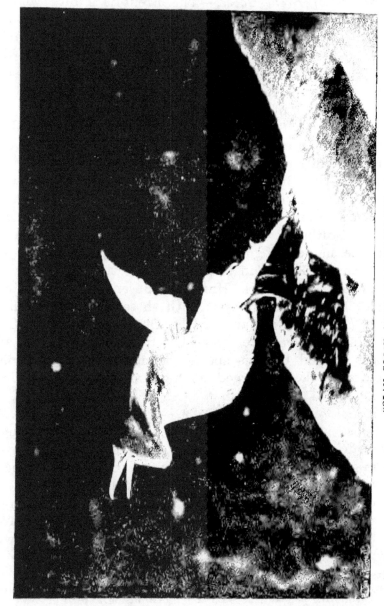

SOLAN GOOSE ABOUT TO TAKE FLIGHT.

observes that the prices are in Scotch money. On September 11th, 1511, there was bought " i sollane "——*, on the 14th, " ij sollanis ijs," on the 15th, "ij sollanis ijs," and on the 22nd " ij sollanis ijs."

The 6th August, 1512, when the accounts close, would have been rather too early for young Solans to be on sale, and after that Mr. Anderson finds a long gap of nineteen years in the series—namely, until September, 1531.

In the " Libri emptorum " of the next King, James V.— printed by the Bannatyne Club †—among many purchases for the furnishing the royal larder, such as Moorfowls, Partridges, Wild Geese, Swans, Teal, Plovers, Herons, Cranes, Dotterel, Redshanks, Larks, etc., we find nine or ten references to Solan Geese. Thus we have an entry of : " ij porcelli ij auce solares," probably a clerk's slip for " solanes." These were served to the King on September 4th, 1525, at Edinburgh. And again on August 17th, 1529, there is " Empt' vj auce solares."   Auca is a well-recognised Latin name for the Goose, and one adopted by many authors.   In the preface, the editor of these " Excerpta E Libris," Professor John Fleming, has some interesting notes about the birds which were eaten, in the course of which he says : " The Turkey, Guineafowl and Pheasant appear to be wanting, though the Peacock holds a place. . . . . The Quail is occasionally noticed as Qualye ; while a bird under the name of *Coturnix*, obtained from August to April, and which might have been suspected as similar, is probably the Water-Rail.   There is no reference to the Ptarmigan or the Capercaillie. . . . The Wood-Pigeon, under the name of *Turtur*, was occasionally purchased. With the exception of Larks, which are occasionally referred to, the list of land birds is thus limited.   Among the Waders, the Heron is occasionally recorded under the names of Herle,‡ Ardea and Ciconia."   The Crane is referred to, but I shall have more to say about this, and would now notice the

Meaning of the name Solan Goose.—All that can be said about the etymology of the obscure word Solan is admirably set forth in Professor W. Skeat's " Etymological Dictionary,"

* Price defaced, probably js.
† Proc., LIV., p. 14, and App. 3, 23.
‡ ? Herne.

as well as in " The New English Dictionary " (1912). Professor
Skeat could not accept the plausible explanation propounded
in Martin's " Voyage to St. Kilda,"* which was that the name
Solan was derivable from the Irish, *i.e.*, Gaelic, word *Sou'l-er*
—pronounced *Shulare*†—in allusion to the bird's sharp sight.

Some of the appellations employed for the Solan Goose
are rather curious, and the spelling varies considerably.
British authors alone afford us no less than seventeen
different spellings of Solan, but in the seventeenth century
every one was free to follow his fancy. The Swedish names
for the Solan Goose are *Sillebasse* and *Bergshammar*, see
Nilsson's " Skandinavisk Fauna."‡ Dr. Herluf Winge has
been good enough to inform me that the equivalent in
Danish of *Sillebas* would be *Sildebas* (or *Sildebasse*), and of
Bergshammar, *Bjerghammer* : *Sill* or *Sild* is a herring, and
Sild roget a red herring.

" *Bas* or *Basse*," continues Dr. Winge, " means a big
person, especially used for big children. *Sildebas* would
thus mean the big herring-bird, but possibly the *bas* in
Sillebas may be the same as the ' *bas* ' in *Bassgas*, which is
another Swedish name for the Gannet, implying the goose
from Bassrock." I am indebted to Professor Jagerskiöld for
further assistance in verifying these Swedish names.

Skinnernis (Icelandic) and *Skindernis* (Danish form), on
the authority of Dr. Winge, are very apposite appellations.
He observes that their equivalent in English would be skin-
sleeve, evidently from the loose manner in which the skin
adheres to the body in the Solan Goose.

Origin of the name Gannet.—The ancient appellation of
Gannet is still in favour on English coasts, as well as in Wales
and Ireland, but in Scotland it gives place to the more northern
name of Solan. As to the origin of Gannet, Dr. John Jamieson,
in his " Etymological Dictionary of the Scottish Language "
(1808), has " To Gant, Gaunt, *v.n.*, To yawn, by opening
the mouth." Whether applied to the Goose or the Gannet
it may be taken as meaning the opening of the mouth for
feeding, biting, crying out or gaping.

* " St. Kilda," p. 49.
† *See* " Irish Naturalist," 1015, p. 115.
‡ 3rd edn., 1858. "Foglarna," II., p. 510.

The Solan Geese of Canada.—Although these annals of
the past are chiefly confined to British birds, there is no
particular reason for thus limiting them, for the history
of ornithology in the Middle Ages in other countries is also
replete with openings for study—indeed, there is very much
which will repay investigation between about A.D. 1450 and
A.D. 1700, both in Europe and in the New World. In former
days the Solan Geese had breeding-places in North America,
which have long since become deserted. One of these, which
was on Funk Island, Newfoundland, is described as follows
in the quaint log-book of an adventurous French navigator
named Jacques Cartier.

*Translation after Richard Hakluyt, the geographer.**

" Upon the 21 of May [1534]," says Cartier, " the winde
being in the West, we hoised saile, and sailed toward North
and by East from the cape of Buona Vista [on the east of
Newfoundland] until we came to the Island of Birds, which
was environed about with a banke of ice, but broken and
crackt : notwithstanding the sayd banke, our two boats went
thither to take in some birds, whereof there is such plenty,
that unlesse a man did see them, he would thinke it an incredible
thing : for albeit the Island (which containeth about a league
in circuit) be so full of them, that they seeme to have been
brought thither, and sowed for the nonce, yet are there an
hundred folde as many hovering about it as within ; some of
the which are as big as jayes, blacke and white, with beaks
like unto crowes : they lie alwayes upon the sea ; they cannot
flie very high, because their wings are so little, and no bigger
than halfe ones hand, yet do they flie as swiftly as any birds
of the aire levell to the water ; they are also exceeding fat ;
we named them Aporath [? Razorbill (*Alca torda*)]. In lesse
than halfe an houre we filled two boats full of them, as if
they had bene with stones : so that besides them which we
did eat fresh, every ship did powder and salt five or six barrels
full of them. Besides these, there is another kinde of birds

* " The Principal Navigations, Voyages, Traffiques, and Discoveries
of the English Nation." By Richard Hakluyt (Edition 1904), pp. 184, 192
Hakluyt's translation is here slightly altered to bring it into line with the
" Relation Originale." For a knowledge of this " Relation " having been
recently published in English—*see* " A Memoir of Jacques Cartier," by J. P.
Baxter—I am indebted to Mr. Francis Jenkinson.

which hover in the aire, and over the sea, lesser than the others ; and these doe all gather themselves together in the Island, and put themselves under the wings of other birds that are greater : these we named Godetz [? Guillemot (*Uria troille*)]. There are also another sort of them bigger, that are white, which place themselves apart from the others in one part of the island, and which are very bad to attack, for they bite like dogs and are called *Margaulx*." These *Margaulx* were the Solan Geese. " And notwithstanding," continues the narrative, " the said island may be fourteen leagues from land, the bears pass thither by swimming from the mainland to eat of the said birds, of which our man found one of them [the bears] as big as a cow, and as white as a Swan, which leaped into the sea before them."

These " Margaulx " were Solan Geese, but it does not read as if they were very numerous. Cartier must have been mistaken in thinking that Guillemots put themselves under the wings of other birds, but perhaps it is the translation which is at fault here.

Shortly after another island was visited, in which again were " great store of Godetz, and crowes with red beakes and red feete : they make their nests in holes under the ground even as Conies." These so-called Crows must have been Puffins.

The Second Account of Jacques Cartier.—The second passage about Solan Geese in Cartier's journal is dated about a month later.

Translation after Hakluyt.

" The next day being the 25 of the moneth [June 1534] . . . wee went Southeast, about 15 leagues, and came to three Ilands, two of which are as steepe and upright as any wall, so that it was not possible to climbe them : and betweene them there is a little rocke. These Ilands were as full of birds, as any field or medow is of grasse, which there do make their nestes : and in the greatest of them, there was a great and infinite number of those that wee call Margaulx, that are white, and bigger than any geese, which were severed in one part. In the other were onely Godetz, but toward the shoare there were of those Godetz, and great Apponatz [Great Auk,

H

Alca impennis] like to those of that Iland that we above have
mentioned: we went downe to the lowest part of the least
Iland, where we killed above a thousand of those Godetz, and
Apponatz. We put into our boates so many of them as we
pleased, for in lesse than one houre we might have filled

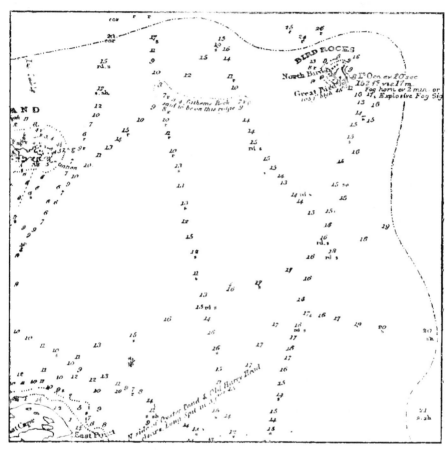

THE BIRD ROCKS, CANADA.

thirtie such boats of them : we named them The Ilands of
Margaulx."

The identity of these three islands with Bird Rocks is
sufficiently established, and it is evident that in 1534 Cartier
found Gannets in greater plenty there than at Funk Island,
As to the signification of the Indian names, *Aporath* or *Aponath*
meant Razorbill, *Great Apponatz* the Garefowl, and *Godetz*
or *Godets* probably the Guillemot.

That " Margot," of which " Margaulx " is intended for the plural, meant Gannet is clear; indeed, it is a French fisherman's name for that species applied to this day in the English Channel and Pas-de-Calais. Equivalent to Sea-fisher, from " mer," the sea, it was capable of having two meanings, for Cartier's sailors may not have been un-mindful of a black-and-white bird at home, the Magpie, commonly called " Margot " in France.

Here it may be observed that there are five Norman names for the Solan Goose, which are *Marga, Boubie, Harenguier, Margast* and *Sagan,** and of these *Marga* is the commonest.† *Margat* is the Picard spelling.‡ *Harenguier* means the herring-fisher, while *Sagan* is synonymous with the Gaelic *Sgadan,* and also stands for herring.

John Major and Hector Boece. —As we are partly treating in this chapter of the Solan Goose, it may be proper to quote some account of its celebrated Scotch home, the Bass Rock, which lies off the coast of Haddington. The first description of the Bass Rock Gannets is discoverable in the " De Gestis Scotorum," written by John Major (or Mair) in 1518, and printed in 1521 at Paris as " Historia majoris Britanniæ." Major was born at Glegharnie, rather less than four miles from the Bass, which explains the commencement of his narrative and his familiarity with the birds upon it.

Translation from the " De Gestis."

" In Lent and in summer, at the winter and the summer solstice, people go in early morning from my own Gleghornie and the neighbouring parts to the shore, drag out the poly-pods [lobsters] and crabs with hooks, and return at noon with well-filled sacks.

     *   *   *   *   *

" Near to Gleghornie, in the Ocean, at a distance of two leagues, is the Bass Rock, wherein is an impregnable stronghold. Round about it is seen a marvellous multitude of great ducks (which they call Sollends) that live on fish. These fowl are not

* " Faune de la Normandie, p. 399."
† " Bull. de la Soc. Nat. d'Accl.," 1915, p. 294.
‡ " Rev. Fr. d'Orn." II., p. 120.

of the very same species with the common wild duck or with
the domestic duck ; but inasmuch as they very nearly resemble
them in colour and in shape, they share with them the common
name, but for the sake of distinction are called solans. These
ducks then, or these geese, in the spring of every year return
from the south to the rock of the Bass in flocks, and for two
or three days, during which the dwellers on the rock are careful
to make no disturbing noise, the birds fly round the rock.
They then begin to build their nests, stay there throughout
the summer, living upon fish, and the inhabitants of the rock
eat the fish which are caught by them. The men climb to
the nests of the birds, and there get fish to their desire.

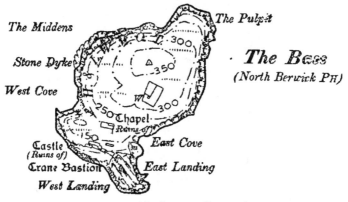

THE BASS ROCK (Ordnance Survey).

Marvellous is the skill of this bird in the catching of fish.
With lynx-like eye he spies the fish at the bottom of the sea,
precipitates himself upon it, as the hawk upon the heron, and
then with beak and claw drags it to the surface [*orig.:* quem
protinus ore & ungulis extrahit] ; and if at some distance
from the rock he sees another fish better than the first that
has caught his eye, he lets the first escape until he has made
sure of the one that was last seen ; and thus on the rock
throughout the summer the freshest fish are always to be had.
The ducklings, or goslings, are sold in the neighbouring
country ; if you will eat of them twice or thrice you will find
them very savoury. For these birds are extremely fat, and
the fat skilfully extracted is very serviceable in the preparation
of drugs ; and the lean part of the flesh they sell. At the end
of autumn the birds fly round about the rock for the space

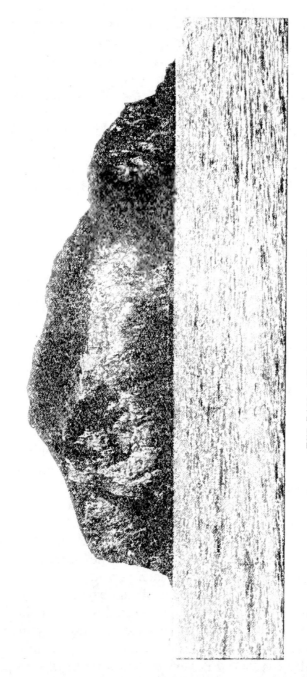

THE BASS, WEST SIDE FROM THE SEA.

of three days, and afterward, in flocks [*orig. :* agminatim] they take flight to southern parts for the whole winter, that there they may live, as it were, in summer ; because, when it is winter with us, it is summer with the people of the south. These birds are very long-lived, a fact which the inhabitants have judged by marks upon some of them [*orig. :* Diutissime hæ aves vivunt, quod per quasdam insuper signatas incolæ perpenderunt]. The produce of these birds supports thirty or forty men of the garrison upon the rock ; and some rent is paid by them to the lord of the rock."

It will be observed that it was only because the young Solans were of service to man as food, and because their fat could be utilised in making drugs, that Major admits them into his chronicle.

For any other reason birds would be regarded as too trivial to mention in a serious work of history : accordingly there is no allusion to the other species—Guillemot, Puffin, Kittiwake, etc.—which must have inhabited the Bass Rock in his day.

Boece's Cosmographe. —Hector Boece's description of the Solan Geese is taken from Major, but what he says of other birds in his famous " Cosmographe and Description of Albion " (1526) has been accepted as original, and is worth quoting. In Chapter XI., entitled " Of the gret plente of Haris, Hartis, and uthir wild Bestiall in Scotland. Of the mervellus nature of sindry Scottis Doggis . . . ," after speaking of these things, and of the noisome wolves, wild horses and foxes, and of hounds of marvellous wit, he continues :—

" Of fowls, such as live by plunder, there are sundry kinds in Scotland ; as Eagles, Falcons, Goshawks, Sparrow-Hawks, Merlins, and such-like fowls. Of water-fowls there is so great a number, that it is a wonder to hear. Many other fowls are in Scotland, which are seen in no other part of the world ; as Capercaillie, a fowl larger than a Raven, which lives always on the bark [? buds] of trees. In Scotland are many more cocks and hens which eat nothing but seed, or crops of heather. Such are great numbers of Blackcocks and hens, not unlike to a Pheasant, both in quantity and savour of their flesh ; but they have black feathers and red eyebrows.

" And besides these three uncouth kind of fowls is one
other kind of fowls in the Mers,* more uncouth, named Gustards
as big as a Swan ; but in the colour of their feathers, and
taste of their flesh, they are little different from a Partridge.
These last fowls are not frequent, but few in number ; and
so fairly hate the company of man, that if they find their
eggs breathed upon or touched by men, they leave them, and
lay eggs in another place. They lay their eggs on the bare
earth."†

An account of Boece or Boethius, born about 1465, died
about 1536, is to be found in the " Dictionary of National
Biography " (V., 297),‡ as also a notice of Major.§

The Earl of Atholl's Feast.—It was about this date apparently (1529) that the Earl of Atholl made lordly provision
for James V. when that king went to hunt in Perthshire.
No Solan Geese graced the table, but besides venison, no doubt
in plenty, the preparations for feasting included, as we learn
from the chronicler Robert Lindsay of Pitscottie, goose, gryse
[young pig], capon, cunning [rabbit], cran, swan, pairtrick
[partridge], plever, duik, drake, brissel, cock [*query* brissel-
cock = Guineafowl] and paunies [Peacocks], black-cock, and
muirfoull and capercailles.|| Robert Lindsay's " cunnings "
were rabbits, and his " paunies " presumably Peacocks,
which were always in request at great feasts, and were generally served in their feathers. Jamieson gives " pawn " and
" pawne " as alternative spellings for the Peacock. The next
author to mention the Capercaillie is John Lesley (or Leslie),
who refers to it in 1578 as a bird inhabiting Ross and Inverness.

Introduction of the Turkey. The Name Brissel.—The
meaning of the name Brissel-cock in the above passage is somewhat obscure, and gave rise to a notable discussion in
" Notes and Queries," in which Professor Newton and other
correspondents took part.¶ Brissel-cock was at first con-

* Mers, or Merse, that is the March or Border district of Berwickshire.
" Uncouth " is here used in the sense of " strange."

† " Cosmographe," ch. XI.

‡ And another by W. H. Mullens, in " A Bibliography of British Ornithology," 1916, p. 75.

§ XXXV., 386.

|| " Chronicles of Scotland," 1728.

¶ *See* " Notes and Queries," 1880 and 1881, pp. 22, 369.

sidered to mean the turkey, and there was nothing improbable in that supposition, for the name might have been bestowed in allusion to the hairy or bristly tuft which depends from its breast. That it was the Turkey was the view taken by that distinguished Scottish etymologist, Dr. Jamieson.* But this is a theory which on consideration cannot be upheld; the name Brissel is not to be accepted as meaning a Turkey, and this is partly because, as Professor Newton has pointed out, there is every reason for believing that no Turkeys had been brought to Britain at so early a date as 1529. The bird was not even described until after that.

What Newton considers to be the earliest description of the Turkey is found in the " Historia de las Indias " of Oviedo (1535), where there is a rather imaginative relation of a sort of Peacock with a bare neck, the skin of which changes into divers colours. It was reported also to have a horn on its forehead, and hairs upon its breast, no doubt in allusion to the pendulous bristles which are characteristic of these birds. On his return from Hayti, Oviedo had published the result of numerous enquiries into General and Natural History, and into the resources of the New World, then opening out enormous possibilities to merchants and mariners. That such a bird as the Turkey should excite great wonder was to be expected, and its introduction into Spain desired. In these reports he speaks of the Turkey as having been brought from Mexico, but that did not deter Barrington from erroneously, though with no small ability, maintaining in a skilful essay (" Miscellanies," 1781) that it was Asiatic. In this he was at issue with Count Buffon, who, some ten years before, had published the contrary, and we now know that Buffon was correct, and that John Ray† and other early naturalists were wrong.

In his " Whole Art and Trade of Husbandry " (1614), the poet Barnabe Googe says that no Turkeys were seen in England before 1530, but there is no documentary evidence of their being here even then. It was not until eleven years later that some directions laid down by Archbishop Cranmer

---

* *See* " Dictionary Scottish Language," 1808 and Suppl., 1825.

† " Ornithology," p. 160.

assure us of the fact of there being Turkeys in England, and that is the first certain date.

In 1541, in Cranmer's "A Dietarie," here alluded to, which was probably saved from destruction by the antiquary John Leland, and is printed in the posthumous "Collectanea" of that author, it is provided that for certain degrees of rank there should be served one Crane, Swan, Turkeycock, Haddock, Pike, or Tench, etc. Of lesser birds, such as Pheasants and Blackcocks, there might be two. Of Partridges an archbishop could have three, a bishop and other degrees under him only two. This is the first proof of there being any Turkeys in England.

It is true that we have a suggestion of their introduction afforded by certain lines in Sir Richard Baker's "Chronicles of the Kings of England,"* which run :—

> "*Turkeys, Carps, Hops, Piccarel* [Pike] *and Beer,*
> *Came into ENGLAND all in one year.*"

This is quoted in Barrington's Essay on the Turkey † with approval, and would be an earlier reference than Cranmer's, but unfortunately it is pronounced by Professor Newton to be untrustworthy.

The Guineafowl.—Another meaning must therefore be sought for Brissel-cock. If not intended for the Blackgrouse, which is separately specified, it may mean a Guineafowl, which is the signification favoured by Professor Newton, whose researches led him to conclude that in the sixteenth and seventeenth centuries the Guineafowl and Turkey were confounded by several of the mediæval zoologists. Chief of those who fell into this error were Belon, Aldrovandus and Sir Thomas Elyot, the latter of whom in 1542 says, " Meleagrides, byrdes which we doo call hennes of Genny, or Turkie hennes," supposing them to be the same. Sir Robert Sibbald was one who in this country did not help to clear the confusion by giving in 1684 the name of *meleagris* to the Turkey, among the birds of Scotland.‡ Thus the name Turkey Hen was, as Newton observes, at first and for a time synonymous with

---

* 1684, p. 298.

† " Miscellanies," by Hon. D. Barrington, 1781, p. 127.

‡ " Prodromus Historiæ Naturalis " (Pars sec., p. 16).

Guinea Hen, but as the birds became commoner and better known, the confusion was gradually cleared up.

Professor Newton also considers it to be the Guineafowl which is alluded to in " A description of Angus [Forfarshire]," by Robert Edward, a minister of Dundee, written in 1678, a translation of which appeared in 1793, from which he quotes *: " Angus is well stored with tame birds, and the great people possess hens of Brazil, peacocks, geese and ducks. Pigeon-houses are frequent."

In this passage, which differs from the translation supplied in Harvie-Brown's " The Capercaillie in Scotland,"† the word " Brissel " has become corrupted into Brazil. I suppose this arose from some idea that Guineafowls had come from the recently discovered country of Brazil (in French Brésil) in South America,‡ just as some consider the name Turkey to have been given because these North American birds were thought to have come from Turkey.§ It is also pointed out that the name *Brissel fowlis*, which is equivalent to Brissel-cock, occurs in a letter written by James VI. of Scotland, on the occasion of the baptism of his second son Charles I.‖ As regards the derivation of " Brissel," in Professor Newton's opinion it is simply a corruption of the French *Coq de broussaille*, that is, a cock of the brushwood, and he submits that the sixteenth century form of the word *broissaille* brings it even nearer to the Scottish pronunciation. That it has any connection with the old Scotch word for to broil, which was " brissel," as suggested by Mr. A. C. Jonas in " Notes and Queries,"¶ cannot for a moment be entertained.

* "Notes and Queries," 1881, p. 369.

† 1879, p. 20.

‡ On the other hand, Thomas Muffett ("Health's Improvement," p. 84) was hopelessly astray in his opinion that they came from North Africa.

§ *The name Turkey.* —This was John Ray's opinion, and perhaps Willughby's too. After quoting Peter Gyllius, a traveller who died in 1555, after writing a work on the Antiquities of Constantinople, these authors say about the bird : "In English they are called Turkeys, because they are thought to have been first brought to us out of Turkey " (" Ornithology," p. 160). But there is still another and very different theory as to the meaning of the name Turkey, which Professor Newton was one of the first to put forward, viz. that by its own note, resembling " turk," the bird had very likely named itself (*see* " Dictionary of Birds," p. 994).

‖ " Notes and Queries," 1880, p. 203.

¶ *T.c.*, 1881, p. 193.

Fowls and Capons.—Capons as distinguished from chickens, well fatted, were in constant demand, being a very favourite dish, and Thorold Rogers remarks that they were dearer during the fifteenth century than they were in the fourteenth, when the average price was threepence. In 1510 it was ninepence halfpenny, and in the following decade a shilling and a halfpenny. "Frequently," he observes, "these capons are purchased for royal and noble persons, or for banquets, when exceptional outlay was expected and incurred. A distinction is drawn towards the latter end of the period [*circa* 1582], between coarse capons and capons of grease [*i.e.*, well fatted], the latter being the choicest produce of the farm-yard. The latter quality is also described as Kent capons."*

The Peacock.—Peafowl continued to be in favour for civic feasts, and must have been rather generally kept, for William Harrison (1577), who has a good deal to say about domestic fowls, geese and ducks, makes no distinction in this respect between them and the "peacocks of Inde." Andrew Boorde (1562), the author of one of the earliest Dietaries, says: "Yonge peechyken of halfe a yere of age be praysed. Olde pecockes be harde of dygestyon." Archbishop Neville ordered a hundred and four for his great feast,† but we are not told if that number actually came up to table. The following is a recipe for cooking them :—

"A peacock flayed, parboiled, larded, and stuck thick with cloves ; then roasted, with his feet wrapped up to keep them from scorching ; then covered again with his own skin as soon as he is cold, and so underpropped that, as alive, he seems to stand on his legs." Thus prepared and placed on the table, and served in a large dish, the Peacock might with good reason be termed, as John Cotgrave has it, a gallant and dainty service—it was, in effect, a "peacock enhakyll," that is to say, a dressed Peacock ; hakyl or hakel being an old English word for clothing.‡ Other cookery books also commend the Peacock.

* "Agriculture and Prices in England," IV., p. 342. Polydore Vergil alludes to Kentish hens as being the largest, as does Dr. Muffett in 1595.

† *Supra*, p. 87.

‡ *Supra*, p. 85.

The Keeping of Tame Geese.—That domesticated Geese, originally the progeny of wild Grey-lag Geese, were a source of profit may be safely inferred, and that they were largely kept and pastured on the grass-lands of several counties, and particularly in Lincolnshire, Huntingdon, Cambridge and Norfolk. These Geese were most likely very close in the tints of their plumage to the original wild stock of *Anser cinereus*, from which they sprang, and so they continued to be for long afterwards.*

William Harrison (1577),† who has a good deal to say about tame Geese, chiefly from a utilitarian point of view, observes that in many places they were bred less for eating than for the sake of their valuable feathers. Large droves, he tells us, were attended by a gossard, no doubt packed together, and driven slowly along, as they continued to be in the eighteenth and nineteenth centuries, for custom is not likely to have changed much.‡ Harrison, who was a canon of Windsor, appears to have been much struck by the spectacle of Geese being led to a field like sheep, remarking that " their goose-herd carries a rattle of paper or parchment with him, when he goeth about in the morning to gather his goslings together, the noise whereof no sooner cometh to their ears than they fall to gagling, and hasten to go with him," obedient to the sound.

In the le Straunge accounts, which will be the subject of the next chapter, we find tame Geese named seven or eight times in connection with rabbits and wild-fowl, but the items may be worth giving.

To a wife of Yngaldesthorpe for vi gees xxd.
A Goos, iij Malards, ij Telys, and ij conyes of store.
A Goose and a coney of gist
A Goos vd.
A Goose, a cockerell, and ij coneys of store.
To Potter's daughter of Holme for bryngyng of a goose jd.

---

* In the early part of last century, when my father as a young man used to travel by road in Marshland and South Lincolnshire, he has told me that he was in the habit of passing many flocks of tame Geese being fed on the grass-lands, and that the large proportion of whole-coloured grey ones was very marked.

† A contributor to " Holinshed's Chronicles."

‡ *See* Rowley's pictures of Geese in " Ornithological Miscellany," III., pl. 105, *et seq*

Some of these were evidently Michaelmas Geese, which had been fatted on the stubbles on shelled-out grain. We have besides entries of :

ij grene geese [*i.e.*, off the grass in spring]	vd.
j dosen greengeese	xvd.
Warner's man for iij greengeese	ij
the vykers woman of Dokkynge for ij green geese and a hundrethe eggs	iiij

Origin of the Mute Swan (Cygnus olor).—Whether the Mute Swan—that is to say the silent Swan, as compared with the musical Whooper—is indigenous or not to the British Isles must be a matter of opinion. Professor Newton takes the view that so much early protection by law is indicative of its having been an introduced bird,* but Europe was its original habitat, so the theory of introduction is not necessitated. Newton also considers that it was once far more abundant in England than it is at the present time, and this seems to be justified by old records. Although wild Swans occasionally stay a while with tame ones, and have been even known to mate with them, they never produce any hybrid progeny, showing how distinct the two species are, which indeed their different carriage plainly proves.

Domestication of the Mute Swan.—We have seen what importance was attached to Swans in the fifteenth century, and also later than that, as clearly indicated by the rights and privileges appertaining to them.† Capello, de Najera, Jovius and Vergil in turn allude to the English Swans, but the last named notes that they were sometimes "not soe small a pleasure to the beeholder as a great greefe of minde."‡ Here he must mean that quarrels took place for possession, the ownership of cygnets being difficult to establish, but to remedy this state of things a system of marks was invented.

Swan-rights were by no means diminished during the sixteenth century ; whether emanating from the Crown, or on behalf of the religious houses, they had to be enforced, and the penalties for infringing them were exceedingly severe.

* "Dictionary of Birds," p. 929.

† *Supra*, pp. 70, 82.

‡ English History. ("Camden Soc. Tr.," 1846, Vol. I., p. 23.)

Abundant as were these birds upon the Thames, where Capello and de Najera saw them, there were plenty of other rivers which had them too, and very destructive they must have been to the fish, for Swans are great spawn eaters. The Swan continued to rise in favour in this country, and in Germany also, judging from the quotations given by a recent writer.* This was chiefly for its edible qualities, but the beauty of its white plumage was suggestive of purity of life, and heraldry claimed it for an emblem. The King's swanherd was a man of no little consequence, he was the *magister cygnorum*, holding jurisdiction over the whole kingdom, the supervisor of all Swans, more particularly those on the Thames. In course of time, tame Swans, at any rate those on the Thames, came to be regarded as a sort of appanage of kings. Certain flocks were to be called royal, but besides this the King was legally entitled to put in a claim to Swans on other rivers, so that the Swan was, in a sense, like the Sturgeon, dubbed a royal perquisite. This being so, no subject could legally have property in one, even on his own stream, except by special grant, or by getting a licence from the Master swanherd. Swan-marks, however, called in law Latin *Cygninota*— seem to have been freely granted, and these usually consisted of one or more indentations cut in the skin of the beak with a sharp knife.† These incisions or notches took a variety of shapes and forms—annulets, chevrons, crescents, swords or crosses—or, according to Yarrell, they might be some device produced from the heraldic arms of the owner.‡ There are said to have been nine hundred such marks, which I suppose included a hundred for Norfolk, for at least that number might be reckoned for that county alone. It must have been difficult to avoid having duplicates among so many, or always to identify marks possessing a general resemblance, even when helped by a few holes punched in the webs of the feet, but perhaps this was not important where Swans belonged to different streams.

The Swan as Food.—Attention has already been drawn (p. 109) to the estimation in which the Mute Swan was held

* " English and Folk-names of British Birds," p. 253.
† *See* Illustration given on p. 71.
‡ " British Birds," III., p. 123.

for its edible qualities, and further evidence might easily be produced of the demand for them on any great occasion. We have a notable instance of it in the feast of the Serjeants of the Inner Temple, which was a very elaborate occasion in London in 1532. The good things provided are enumerated in Stow's "Survey of London," and again in Sir William Dugdale's " Origines Judiciales," from which source we learn that the number of Swans served was a hundred and sixty-eight. More Serjeants' banquets took place in 1555, and at these also about ninety-five Swans were brought to table. A fattened Swan was occasionally spoken of as a franked Swan, the word " frank " signifying an inclosure in which animals were fed,* but the word does not seem to be met with in connection with the Norwich Swan-pit to be mentioned presently.

Lincolnshire and Norfolk Swan-rolls.—Although the largest swannery in England was at Abbotsbury, in Dorsetshire—and the oldest, for it was granted to an ancestor of the present Earl of Ilchester on the dissolution of the monasteries—there were probably nowhere a greater number of Swans maintained than in Lincolnshire. In this county the inhabitants of Crowland were exempted from the restrictions imposed in the reign of Edward IV., on their petition setting forth that their town stood " all in marsh and fen," and that they had great " games " of Swans, by which the greatest part of their relief and living was sustained.† It is easy to understand how valuable the big birds must have been in a district where neither corn nor cattle were too abundant.

The produce of meres and rivers was what the fenfolk of Lincolnshire had to rely on for their maintenance. Accordingly some very elaborate regulations were in force for the protection of Swans, of which the most important are to be found in a document concerning the river Witham, which bears date 1570.‡ This old deed or ordinance, proclaimed at a swan-herd's court, or a "swan-moote," which is stated to have been taken from a still older ordinance by one Matthew Nayler, who was perhaps bailiff of the rivers,

---

* As in the " Records of Lydd," p. 116 (N.F. Ticehurst).

† 6 Rot. Parl. 260, as given by Manning.

‡ For particulars of this ordinance *see* "Archaeologia," 1812 (XVI., p. 153).

contains eighteen clauses, and its composition is of a very stringent character. To begin with, it puts the penalty for destroying a Swan's nest, or killing a Swan as high as five pounds, nor was anyone to be allowed to set nets or snares, or shoot with a hand-gun or crossbow on the river in the summer, or even cut reeds within forty feet of a Swan's nest, so precious were they held to be. Another roll of about 1541 forbids any unauthorised person even to carry a swan-hook (which was a crook used for catching the cygnets)* ; while by a third ordinance it is enacted that any man, whosoever he be, that killeth any Swan with dog or spaniel shall forfeit to the King forty shillings.†

Norfolk institutions also possessed their Swans and swan-rolls, of which various curious particulars, collected by Stevenson, are given in that author's "Birds of Norfolk."‡ I have lately had an opportunity of examining one of these swan-rolls, which has long been in the family of Blofeld, of Hoveton Broad. It is on vellum and is in good condition. Together with another roll, of somewhat less interest, it was exhibited to the Society of Antiquaries by Mr. William Mint, in whose opinion its date may be approximately fixed at about 1530, which is earlier than the Witham roll.§ Mr. Mint finds fifty-seven distinct beak marks, clearly executed and with owner's names, and this is inclusive of five priories and two monasteries, viz., St. Olive's, Carrowe, Hyngham, Bromerton, Norwich, Langley and St. Bennet's. The Swan's heads are drawn as if looked at from above, as in the Witham roll.

Another parchment roll (or rolls) of 1566, with about three hundred Swan's heads depicted on them, each one with a distinctive mark, was knocked down at Dawson Turner's sale of MSS. for £2 5s., and is no doubt the same alluded to by Stevenson as containing swan-marks used on the rivers Waveney and Yare.‖ It is now in the British Museum.¶ A few other swan-rolls are mentioned by Stevenson, but these relics of antiquity appear in some cases to have been sold or stolen, or at any rate to be not forthcoming.

* " Archaeological Journal," 1850, p. 302.
† *Idem*, 1847, p. 428.
‡ Vol. III., pp. 102-111.
§ " Proc. Soc. Antiquaries, 1905," Vol. XX.
‖ " Birds of Norfolk," Vol. III., p. 110, note.
¶ Add. MS. 23732.

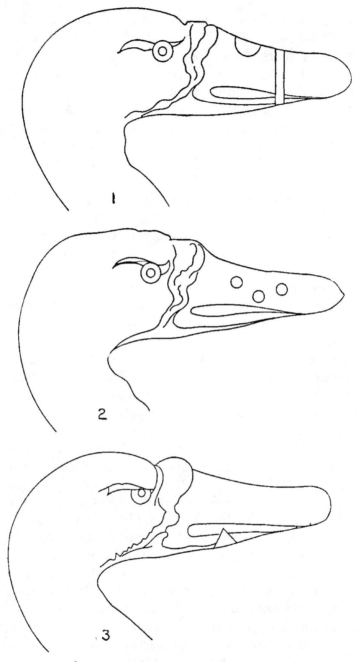

1. THE PRIORY OF NORWICH.
2. THE ABBEY OF ST. BENNETT'S.
3. THE PRIORY OF CARROW.

Norwich lies at the junction of two rivers, and its citizens of the fifteenth century had numerous Swans, and valued them highly. This we can gather from the pages of our famous local historian, Francis Blomefield, whose work is partly based on the collections of an earlier antiquary named Le Neve. Blomefield has a good deal to say on the subject; he tells us that in 1482 a statute for the qualification of swan-marks was made* " upon which statute an account of all the swan-marks in this county [of Norfolk] was taken and entered in a roll, which was renewed in the year 1598 . . . . . ."

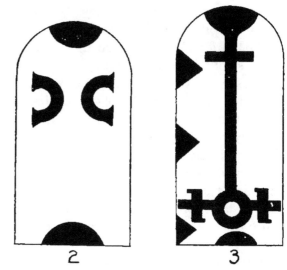

1. THE CANON'S MARK.   2. BINKNORTH'S MARK.   3. THE PRIORESS'S MARK.

Neither the original of 1482 nor that made in 1598 is any longer in existence, as far as Stevenson could make out, but I understand that a modern copy of the 1598 roll on paper is in the possession of Mr. J. E. Harting, who has quoted it in an article in the "Zoologist," where he treats of the old terms "Cob" and "Pen" formerly applied to the male and female Swans.† Also a modern swan-roll, beautifully executed in 1846, which may be in part a copy, is preserved in the Norwich Museum, and from this source the three heads shown on page 113 have been taken.

* By Edward IV., *supra*, p. 82.
† "Zoologist," 1895, p. 372.

The other illustration represents three ancient swan-marks figured in Thomas Martin's "History of Thetford" (1779), and known as the Canon's mark, Binknorth's mark, and the Prioress s mark, which are not without interest for Norfolk antiquaries.

The Swan-pit at Norwich.—There has been for a very great number of years a pit for fattening Swans at the back of some ancient almshouses in St. Helen's Parish at Norwich. The useful researches of Mr. J. C. Tingey among the muniments of the city of Norwich have proved that this pit or pond was in existence in 1487, in which year a payment was ordered to be made to one William Bylney " pro custodia cignorum" at St. Giles's Hospital, which was the name of these almshouses.*

Although there is little demand for Swans now, this pit is still supplied nearly every season by means of an August swan-upping expedition on the Yare, in which several boats sometimes take part, their object being to drive the cygnets into dykes and ditches, where they can be caught. The phrase "swan-upping," which sounds rather puzzling to the uninitiated, means the taking up of the young Swans ; thus, of the swan-herds of a certain river, it is fixed by an old ordinance that they " shall up no Swannes."

The ancient belief that Swans hatch best when there is thunder about has long held its own in Norfolk, and is probably not without some foundation. Dixon thought that the sultry weather which precedes a tempest would hasten the hatching of the eggs, and that may be so.†

Shakespeare's Swans.—The Swan is many times named in Shakespeare's plays, and the cygnet comes in for mention also. Mr. Harting has treated the subject very pleasantly in "The Ornithology of Shakespeare,"‡ showing how apposite are some of the poet's allusions.

For instance, to take a passage in " King Henry VI.," where Shakespeare's powers of observation are indicated in the lines :

> " So doth the swan her downy cygnets save,
> Keeping them prisoner underneath her wings."§

* " Norw. Naturalists' Tr.." VI., p. 388.
† " Ornamental and Domestic Poultry," by the Rev. E. S. Dixon, p. 28.
‡ *T.c.*, pp. 201-208.
§ Henry VI., Part 1, Act V., Sc. 3.

Chapter IX.

SIXTEENTH CENTURY (2nd Part).

The Sixteenth Century (2nd part): English Household Accounts of the Sixteenth Century. The le Straunge [*or* Lestrange] Accounts, 1519-1578.

The le Straunges of Hunstanton.—It has not been thought necessary to give up much space to Andrew Boorde's " Dyetary " (? 1542), curious as it is, extracts, with a good account of the author, being supplied in the " Bibliography of British Ornithology " (1916–17, p. 81) by Mr. W. H. Mullens. Boorde's work was intended to be a medical one, like Dr. Muffett's, which was written some fifty years afterwards, and there is but little about birds in it. Under the heading of " Wylde fowle " he gives his readers and patients some promiscuous information, instructing them that " . . . . . A Woodcock is a meat of good temperance. Quails and Plovers and Lapwings doth nourish but little, for they do engender melancholy humours. Young Turtle Doves do engender good blood. A young Heron is lighter of digestion than a Crane. A Bustard well killed and ordered is a nutritive meat. A Bittern is not so hard of digestion as is a Heron. A Shoveler [Spoonbill] is lighter of digestion than a Bittern. A Pheasant hen, a Moor-cock and a Moor-hen, except they be set abroad, they be nutritive . . . . ." Mr. Mullens gives 1562 as being the year of the first dated edition. Nor is it necessary to quote again the journal of Peter Swave, the Dane, who visited the Bass Rock in 1535,* nor the logs of the English navigators Hore, Parkhurst and Gilbert, who visited Newfoundland in the sixteenth century (A.D. 1556, 1578, 1583), all of which are printed at length in Hakluyt.† A naturalist can not but have a feeling of melan-

* Given in full in " The Gannet," p. 181.

† " Navigations, Voyages, Traffiques and Discoveries," by Richard Hakluyt.

choly in reading their description of the victualling of ships with Penguins, *i.e.*, Great Auks, which were in great plenty on one or two islands.

Havoc was soon made among them, and one early voyager, André Thavet (1555), tells how these simple birds could be driven into boats " ainsi que moutons à la boucherie," with the natural result that they were speedily wiped out of existence.

Let us therefore turn to the wider subject of Household Accounts, which were generally kept by the stewards of large establishments,* but unfortunately most of them have perished. Among those which by a lucky chance have not

* Of this a good sample is a curious " Breviate " of directions for the ordering of a nobleman's house in the sixteenth century, printed in the thirteenth volume of " Archaeologia " (1800, pp. 315–389). The author, whoever he was, names sixty-three birds, of which a few of the more mysterious are—
Cudberduce or Cutburduk (St. Cuthbert's Duck, *i.e.*, the Eider).
Indecoke (probably for Judecocke, elsewhere given as Jedcoke, *i.e.*, the Jack Snipe).
Mullet (possibly a mistranscription for Pullet, but these latter are included as well, from the context it appears to be a bird). At Scarborough this name was given to the Puffin (Willughby's " Ornithology," p 325).
Bayninge (this name has already proved a puzzle to Mr. Stubbs (" Zoologist," 1910, p. 154). It cannot be the Bittern, occasionally termed Baytour, because that bird is separately included.) It is perhaps a diminutive, meaning the little bay or red bird.
Kennices (also spelled Kenneces and Kennecis). Probably Chickens. In " Richard the Redeles," written in 1399, a poem, part of which (pass. iii.) is in praise of the Partridge, we meet with " Kenne " in the sense of *generate*, *come to life*, or *kindle*.
Blankett (also spelled Blonkett). This is another puzzle : it cannot be the Coot, called Blishöne in Denmark, or the Avocet, called Brogeb-lit in Denmark. Possibly the name Blankett means some small bird of a grey colour, in which sense the adjective " bloncket " is used by Spenser. In the thirteenth century *blanchettum* was a white woollen cloth (Swinfield, *t.c.*, p. 244), and we have the word *blonket* with that meaning in the Account Rolls of the Abbey of Durham (printed for the Surtees Society). Mr. Jourdain observes that Blankhane is a Swedish name for the Golden-eye Duck.
Martine (perhaps the House Martin).
Ree (Reeve, the Ruff is mentioned separately).
Petterell (the Kittiwake Gull, *see* Nelson's " Birds of Yorkshire," II., p. 692).
Cullver (Dove).
Chitte (equivalent, as Mr. Harting suggests, to May Chitt, a Sanderling).
Didaper (Grebe).
Churre (? Dunlin).
Tearne (probably Tern : in the Naworth accounts the Sea Swallow is entered as eatable).
Golney (also spelled Goldne and Golne, probably a contraction of Golden-eye). In Jamieson's " Scottish Dictionary " (1808, suppl. 1825) we have Goldeine, in 1555, and Golding, in 1600, as old Scotch names.

been lost are the Books of the le Straunges.* The le Straunges
or Lestranges, by whom Hunstanton lordship has been held
since 1100, were people of no small distinction. living at
Hunstanton, on the north coast of Norfolk, about a mile
from the sea. The original mansion of the le Straunges is
known to have been built at the latter end of the fifteenth
century, but very little of what must have been a noble

edifice exists now. In 1834 it was more perfect, Mr. D.
Gurney being able to describe it as surrounded by a moat,
with stew-ponds for fish, and entered by an imposing gateway.
A picture, drawn by Robert Blake some time prior to 1823,
shows what it was like. Unfortunately, in 1853 this venerable
structure was much injured by fire, when the ancient
banqueting hall and eighteen other rooms were destroyed.
The cut gives the eastern front as it is now, and the bridge

* The spelling of le Straunge in preference to Lestrange has been
adopted, by Mr. Hamon le Strange's advice, as being the form in most general
use at the time when these sixteenth-century Accounts were penned.

HUNSTANTON HALL, NORFOLK.

across the moat; the central portion as shown contains what, in the sixteenth century, was the Guard room, with the Priest's chamber above it. The Accounts, which are really house-keeping books, run from 1519, two years after Sir Thomas le Straunge* had succeeded his cousin, to 1578, when Hamon le Straunge was in possession. It is now eighty-four years since a part were printed in the " Archaeologia "† by Mr. D. Gurney, who supposes some of them to have been written by the steward, some by Sir Thomas's personal servant (who in 1549 was Eustace Rolfe), and one or two by Lady le Straunge herself, as for instance such entries as " when you went a-hawking with my uncle, Roger Woodhous," or " to play at cards with my son Cressen^r." It is to be hoped that these singular Accounts, of which at present only selections, amounting to about one-third of the whole, have been published, may some day see the light in their entirety.

A few years ago Mr. Hamon le Strange, the late owner and representative of this ancient family, carefully indexed the four paper volumes containing these household notes, and, with this useful aid to work by, he has been able to look up many references to birds and fishes which are not in Daniel Gurney's abridgment in the "Archaeologia." The majority of the birds here named are not what we now call game, nor do they appear to have been regarded in that light, or to have been captured by the family and their friends for the sake of sport. They were looked on as a part of the produce of the country, to be netted, snared, or shot with the crossbow, either by le Straunge's paid keepers or by any other fowlers, and in the latter case they were paid for when brought to the buttery door in the same way as fish, pork and vegetables, and entered in the house-book by the housekeeper. In the remarks which follow, all these, with the dates which rightly belong to them, as fixed by Mr. le Strange, have been taken account of. The month and day are placed in square brackets, intended to indicate that they are not in the original manuscript books,

---

* Walter Rye, who gives many genealogical particulars of the Lestranges in his " Norfolk Families " (1913, p. 477), states that this knight was Esquire of the Body to Henry VIII. at the Field of the Cloth of Gold. The preparations for this great occasion appear in the Accounts for 1520.

† Vol. XXV., 1834.

where in most cases disbursements are entered under weeks calculated from the last festival. It will be seen that a great many records of birds additional to those in the printed Accounts can be cited, and three more species can be added, the Gull, the Godwit and the Scoter Duck. The entries of such an important species as the Great Bustard, hitherto supposed to be only two, are also shown by Mr. le Strange to be eight, while the number of Cranes, instead of being five, is at least twenty-eight.

It certainly cannot be said that justice has ever been done to the zoological aspect of these old Norfolk Accounts, although they are often quoted in the first two volumes of Stevenson's " Birds of Norfolk " and have formed the subject of a short but valuable article by the late Mr. T. Southwell in the ·"Transactions of the Norwich Naturalists' Society."*

Birds brought to Hunstanton Hall. — In the eyes of a naturalist, the birds are the great feature of these Accounts; forty-two species are enumerated, and all but two of them can be at once identified. Some species are repeated several times, and anything may be comprised in the general term of Wild-fowl. The Mallard would naturally be the most abundant, and accordingly it is brought in by the useful fowlers very many times, while the Swan—tame ones, it is to be presumed—the Pheasant and the Plover each come to the house repeatedly, and the Curlew, Redshank and Stint not much less often. Here it may be remarked that the word Plover is somewhat vague, not only in its use in these le Straunge Accounts, but wherever it occurs in bills of fare. What leads to some confusion is that in the succeeding century Sir Thomas Browne (*circa* 1662) applied the name Green Plover to what we now know as the Golden Plover as did Merrett in 1666 and Ray in 1676, a nomenclature which would have been copied by others.† When Thomas Pedder was sent to Walsingham to

* Vol. I., 1870.

† The Pewit (*Vanellus vulgaris*) is given by Ray under the appellation of Lapwing or Bastard Plover ("Ornithology," p. 307), the latter term denoting something inferior or worthless, yet neither of these names occurs in the le Straunge papers.

In Gage's "Antiquities of Hengrave in Suffolk," we meet with " bastard" among the household accounts. but only in one entry:— "October, 1572. To Damon the cater[er] for iij dosen bastard plovers vijs viijd—for ij dosen larks xijd.

buy Plovers and Rhine wine, and again when Barnaby Bryse
rode to the French Queen with Plovers, and had two shillings
for his trouble, it was, we may assume, Lapwings that are
meant.   Once only does Mr. le Strange find them specified :
" 1548 [November 15] It^m a gren plover j [penny]."   But
where the name Plover is associated with Stints and other
shore birds, as in the case of gifts from the Vicar of Thornham
(a parish adjacent to the sea), who was a somewhat frequent
contributor,* it is very possible that the Golden Plover is
intended.

Among so many items it is difficult to know which to
begin with.   The first one of a natural history character
which I come across is " C C & di. of Whyte heryng "
("Archaeol.," p. 417).   A white herring generally implies a
fresh herring, but so many as 250 must have been pickled,
and were probably in a barrel.

The herrings are followed by six Geese brought by a
woman from Yngaldesthorpe, doubtless tame Geese.   Then
come some chickens and a peck of oatmeal, and on the next
page " Itm pd. for Sethyng a Pykerell which my Mr. had to
ye Abbeye "—that is for boiling a pike.   Pykerell or Pickerel
was a common name for a small pike in various parts of
England.

The Geese fetched to the mansion seem to have been
generally tame Geese, sometimes spoken of as Green Geese,
that is to say grass-fed Geese, which have come off a pasture.
A Wild Goose might have been a tough morsel, and is only
specified occasionally.

The Brent Goose was no doubt a common bird in the
Wash then, as it is still, and would have been reckoned more
palatable.   Accordingly it is not surprising that Mr. le Strange
is able to give nine references to this species, which are here
subjoined, with the dates as supplied by him, most of which
come in mid-winter :—

1520 [January 15] ii dussen byrdys and a brant of store.

1523 [December 1] oon† wylde goose and oon brante.

1526 [January] Paid to a shepherd of Hecham for a wylde-
goos, iii brantes, a spowe and a redshanke xvi^d.

* " Archaeologia," Vol. XXV., p. 422.

† "One " is often spelled " oon " in the Accounts.

1527 [November 10] Paid to the blacksmith of Hecham for a brante.

1534 [February 1] a brant kyllyd with ye gonne.

1543 [December 1] oon wyldgoose, oon brant, store.

1544 [January] Brought into ye ketchyng the xvii of January a malard, and ii brannts of Cansellar's kylling.

1550 [November 25] a brantt & a mallard.

 [Nov. 26th] conys vi^d., a brannte store.

The Wild Swan is only specified once. " Sonday. lt^u", a swanne and ij malards kylled with ye crosbowe," but tame Swans and cygnets, somelimes spelled " synettes," are mentioned, and once or twice the taking of them at " broad-water," a sheet at Holme which is still undrained. No doubt they constantly appeared on the board with other viands.

There does not seem to be any passage referable to the Scaup, the Pintail, or the Pochard, although one would have expected them to have had separate designations, nor is the Sheld-Duck, which is a common species in the Wash, alluded to.

Mr. le Strange has drawn attention to two entries of "cockle ducks" in the unpublished Accounts, which it is to be presumed were Scoters, as these birds are common in the Wash and will eat small cockles, as well as mussels.

1537. [December] cocle dokes & sepys iii^s.

1538. [October 20] Item, paid to John Syff for a woodcock, a spowe and a cokell doke, iii^d.

The Wigeon has always had a good reputation for the table, but whether the following entries are strictly limited to what we now know as Wigeon may be doubted. According to the extracts kindly supplied by Mr. le Strange, the name occurs seven times in the unprinted Accounts and twice in the printed.

1522. [Dec. 21] a wydgyn, a tele & a redschanke, iii^d.

1527. [Dec. 29] vi sepys, a spowe, ii redshanckes & a wydgyn, x^d.

1533. [Jan. 25] a wydgyn kylled with the gonne.

1534. [Nov. 28] To John Syffe for a wygen.

 [Dec. 27] To Steven Percy for ix wigens & 1 curlewe xvi^d.

1536. [Dec. 4] Item paid for vii teles, iv wydgyns, ii malards, iiii spowes, & a dussen & di [18] smalle byrdes iii [shillings].

[Dec. 24] iv wyggyns.

1551. [Feb. 22] For a malard, iv wygges.

xxiiij of Febru. It^m a qrt of Mutton—ij wyggins.

Neither of these six Norfolk spellings is discoverable in " The Boke of Kervynge " (printed 1508), where we have the earliest mention of the species, as a " Wegyon." Forty years afterwards we find William Turner spelling it Wigene, which in 1570 had got back to Wigion, and at the present day to Wigeon. Saunders gives "Easterling " as an old Norfolk name for the Wigeon,* possibly quoting from Sheppard and Whitear's list (Linnean Soc., 1826), but I have never met with it, and it certainly is not taken from the le Straunge Accounts. The only other Ducks which are specified in the Accounts are the Mallard and Teal, which were doubtless more abundant than now, but " wyldfowle " is often heard of, which may have included other species. Once we meet with the expression '· wyld malards at 11d. the pece," so perhaps some of those elsewhere mentioned were tame ones. Teal were no doubt pretty common everywhere in Norfolk, a county so well suited to them. Teal is spelled in several ways—tealle, teille, tele, teel, teale : a significant entry in 1540 is " iii mallards & xiiii teelles for to entre yor hawkes withall." These must have been Peregrines about to be trained for hawking at the brook, but the Goshawk was also sometimes used for Wild Duck.

The Spowe or Spoe.—With regard to the shore-frequenting Waders there are a great many entries. One which at once bespeaks attention is variously called *spowe, spoe, spooe,* and *spow.* These names, which may all refer to the same species, come six times into the printed Accounts, and more than a dozen times, as I learn from Mr. le Strange, into the unprinted. November and December are the months when this unknown bird was oftenest obtained, but in 1538 six are brought in in September, and twelve in October, on one day. This name, which is evidently onomatopoeic, and almost identical with the Norwegian "spove," as remarked by Dr.

* Yarrell, " B.B.," 4th edition, IV., p. 400.

Ticehurst, as well as with the Swedish "spof" (a Curlew), was provisionally assigned to the Whimbrel by my father as long ago as 1846.* The fact that "spói" is the common name of the Whimbrel in Iceland, as pointed out by Prof. Newton in "Iceland, Its Scenes and Sagas"† further confirms his identification.

Another old English appellation for the Whimbrel, perhaps chiefly a book name, was Brue or Brewe, which was general in the seventeenth century.‡ This name does not come into the le Straunge or any other Norfolk accounts, and is certainly not used in Norfolk, where at the present day the Whimbrel is commonly termed a May-bird. Stone-Curlews are not mentioned, nor do we get the names Yarwhelp, Yelper or Barker, which might be looked for in an east coast list of birds. Neither is there any bird's name which can be assigned to the Glossy Ibis, a species supposed, though upon very slender foundation,§ to have been once abundant enough in the Wash to be called the Black Curlew.

There are two entries of Dotterel, which may be taken as referring to *Charadrius morinellus*: "1520 to Wat Dockyng for iij dotterells iij^d" (p. 443), and again "[April 28th, 1527] It^m to Blogge of Walsyngham for xxiv dotterelles ii^s." Walsingham is about four miles from the sea, and sixteen from Hunstanton, quite a likely place for these birds. Ten Dotterel, which were killed between April 29th and May 9th, 1548, were at that time of the year most likely to have been *C. morinellus*.

On the other hand, two more entries under the same name—in one of which forty-eight Dotterel with Godwits, and in the other six Dotterel with Stints, are brought in—probably mean the Ringed Plover, while the se- or sea-dotterel, which is occasionally distinguished in the Accounts, may very likely have been the Turnstone.

The Oystercatcher would naturally not be entered under that designation, which is as modern as it is inappropriate. Under its older and more sensible name of Sea-pie, or as

---

* "Zoologist," Vol. IV., p. 1323, and again, 3rd series, II., p. 289.
† Orn.: 15.
‡ *Ante*, p. 89.
§ *See* "British Birds," Mag., V., p. 307.

it is here written, "sepy," it comes three times into the Accounts, *e.g.*, when in December 1527 three Geese and six Sepys are charged at sixpence.   In the printed accounts it is mentioned once.*

Of the Knot or "knatte" there are a good many entries. As many as forty come in once (p. 107), and another time it is four Knots, three Redshanks, "& vi grete [great] byrds," whatever that may mean.

Woodcock and Snipe.—No bird is oftener alluded to than the Woodcock, whose merit for the spit was well known. This is one of the very few British birds which has not been provided with a string of provincial names.   It is *par excellence* the bird of the woods, and has been so looked upon ever since the Saxons named it wudecocc or wudu-coc—an appellation which, or its equivalent, is given it in many countries.† Especially numerous are the entries in 1548, in which year Mr. le Strange finds that sixty-eight were brought to the house, of which fifty-six were between October 20th and November 1st ;   probably most of them were caught with horsehair nooses.

The Snipe ‡ is mentioned eight times, as appears by the following entries, which have been extracted by Mr. le Strange :—

1520.	[18 November]	To Raff Ryches of Holme for ij Snypes	· i.^{d}
1523.	[18 January]	To Robert Barker for iiij teles, a Woodcoeke & viij. Snypes	vj.^{d}

---

* P. 470. Apparently it was not considered very eatable, yet we meet with it sometimes, as in the " Records of Lydd " (1541), in the " Household Account of The Princess Elizabeth " (1551-2), and in The Naworth Accounts (begun in 1612).

† Common as is the Woodcock at the present day, there must have been a time when it was far more abundant in England, where, though always looked upon as proper food, its money-value in the sixteenth century was small.   Taking the Northumberland household book as a fair standard, we find them only rated at a penny in 1512, and in the le Straunge papers twopence is the highest price.

‡ They appear in other Household Accounts.   Thorold Rogers, in his work on prices, before quoted, puts Snipe at fivepence or sixpence the dozen in 1555 (*l.c.*, IV., p. 344), at eightpence in 1591, and at no less than four shillings in 1594 (V., p. 369), but in this case there must have been something exceptional.

1523. [15 November] To Stephyn Percy for a Woodcocke, a grey Plou[r], and a Snype   iij.[d]

1534. [19 December] To Carston of Thornham, for iiij Curlewes & for Snype   iii. ix.[d]

    [20 January] Jhñ v. Snyppys.

    [21 „] Jhñ v. Snyppys of gist.*

1541. [9 January] To John Syff for Stynte and Snype   ij. o.[d]

1548. [11 November] For a Curlewe, a Tele, & a Snyppe   ix.[d]

The names of shore-birds generally occur in the Accounts together, as if there had been a catch received from the nets. To take an instance, " a curlewe, dosyn Knotts, a dosyn Redschanks & Stynts, ij Teals " : *i.e.*, twenty-seven birds are brought in, for which the fowler goes away with two shillings in his pocket.

Either Avocets were rare, or, what is more likely, were not considered very good to eat, for they do not come into the le Straunge Accounts, or into any other house-books of English fare, unless indeed they are meant by the occasional entry of a " White Plover." My father was more inclined to identify the White Plover with the Grey Plover,† a solution not altogether satisfactory, for in autumn there is little or nothing white about this species. The name spelled " whyte," or " whit," occurs four or five times, with those of other shore-birds.

Of the Grey Plover, Mr. le Strange finds one mention :—

1523. [November 15] " for a Woodcocke a grey plou[r] & a Snype . . . iij d."

The ffedowe or ffeddew.—The Godwit, presumably the Bar-tailed species, comes four times into the unpublished Accounts under its obsolete name of "ffeddowe " or "ffeddew," a name latinised by William Turner in 1544 (" De Avibus," p. 44), and by Gesner in 1555, as Fedoa. The Godwit is a bird which has had a good many designations, but this is the most curious of them, and unfortunately its meaning is lost.‡

* Gist, or gyste, was a payment in lieu of rent.
† *See* Stevenson's " Birds of Norfolk," II., p. 103.
‡ " Dictionary of Birds," p. 248.

There may be some connection between *Fedoa* and the name
Doe-bird, which, as pointed out by Mr. Harting, is in common
use for the Godwit in the United States.*

1520. [January 1]   Item paid to John Cawston for
a curlewe and a ffeddowe, vii d.

1537. [May 6]   Item paid to him [John Syff] for iiij
ffedours, viij[d].

1550. [December 17] Item paid for a ffeddew, iij[d].

1550. [Dec. 19] Item paid for iii ffeddewes, viii d.

This ends the shore-frequenting species, but there are
still sundry entries of " grete byrds " and " litell byrdes,"
which are not to be identified.   In one place we read of
" a spowe & iii grete byrdes," in another of " ii curlewes &
other small byrdes," in another of " v teles & x litill byrdes."

All these may have been from the shore, but in one
passage where " byrds " come between chickens and eggs,
and that in the month of June, something domestic would
seem to be intended.

The Great Bustard.   Nine brought to the Hall.—There is a
good deal to be learnt from these old paper books about the
Great Bustard, which held out in Norfolk after it had become
extinct in every other county.   It is true that it is only named
twice in the Accounts in the " Archaeologia," but these are
very incomplete.   In the unprinted Accounts there are six
other mentions of the Bustard, which—as extracted by
Mr. le Strange, with the dates—must be given in full :—

1520. [April 29] Item, a pygge, ij capons & a busterd
of gist.

1527. [April 23] Itm., a bustard & iij mallards kylled
with ye crosbowe.

[July 11] A crane & a busterd kylled with ye
crosbowe.

[November]   It. viij malards, a bustard & j
hernsewe kylled wt ye crosbowe.

1528. [January 1] viij malardes   a bustard & j
heronsewe kylled with ye crosbowe.

1537. Itm. in reward the xxv day of July to Baxter's
servant of Stannewyk for bryngging of ij yong busterds ij d.

* *See* Nuttall's " Manual of the Ornithology of the United States " (II.,
p. 174), and Samuels's " Birds of New England " (p. 464).

1540. Itm. in reward the viijth day of May to a ffelawe that brought a busterd from the parisshe prest of Burnham called Sir Raff, iiij d.

1543. [September 23] Itm. of Canseller's killyng oon busterd & iiij cranes whereof iij Cranes [were] given oon to Sir Roger Townshend another to Sir Ric[hard] South and the thred to my lady Hastinges.

1548. [September 16] Itm j bustarde.

Of these entries, the fifth has the most importance for the naturalist, which chronicles the bringing of two young Bustards. Most likely they were chicks caught by hand, and not too easily, we may be sure, for they learn to run very quickly. As the Bustard only lays two or three eggs, two would be a clutch.* These youngsters came from Stannewyk, also spelled Stanneugh, now known as Stanhoe, about eight miles from Hunstanton : it is the same parish referred to in Richards' " History of Lynn "† as a locality harbouring Bustards. It will be observed that one of the Bustards in the above list was killed in January, this was undoubtedly a migrant, which may have been driven from the continent by hard weather ; two more were killed in April, one in May (near the sea), one in July and two in September.

These dates are all plain, and quite coincide with what we have long known about the habits of the Bustard. It was evidently a species which, like the Norfolk Plover, summered in Norfolk and Suffolk, and went south with a host of other migrants about October. Any which in winter temporarily took the place of the breeding-race were not natives, but migrants from Europe. It is to be remarked that the first entry here quoted—that of April 1520—is really entitled to stand as the first record of this noble species in Britain, for the Northumberland Household Book, begun in 1512, which has generally had that credit, is merely a statement of what birds were suitable for principal feasts at Wresil Castle, and does not give the actual captures of the Bustard,

* Colonel Willoughby Verner tells me that in Spain Bustards will lay four eggs if undisturbed.

† Vol. I., p. 196.

or any other birds.* The truth is the sixteenth-century records
of the Bustard are very few in number, which point to its
having been confined to a limited number of localities.†

The Crane.—Another typical East Anglian species in
days of yore, the Crane, was a bird of the fens, not of the
plains like the Bustard and Norfolk Plover. We do not hear
of it as a Norfolk bird before about 1476, and then incidentally
from one of the Pastons, who acknowledges " a brawn and a
crane " from a friend at Reepham.‡ It is not likely that it
was rare in those days, but more will be said of its status in
East Anglia as a breeder in another chapter.§ It comes five
times into the Accounts printed in the " Archaeologia," but
Mr. le Strange has found twenty-three additional records in
those which are unprinted.

1519 [Jan.   2] To Thomas Bloye for a crane ij iiij^d.
     [,,   30] To Thomas Bloye for a crane, ij spowes
                   ij^s. ix^d.
     [Oct. 23] To Bloye for a crane & vi. plouers xx^d.
     [Nov. 21] A crane of gyste.
1525 [,,   12] To Clifton for a crane xx^d.
1527 [July 11] A crane and a bustard kylled wt. ye
                   crosbowe.
     [Dec. 15] A crane kylled wt. ye crossbowe.
1528 [Jan. 12]   ,,   Kyled with the crosbowe.
     [,,   14]   ,,   ,,   ,,   ,,
1533 [Sept. 25]   ,,   vi^d.
     [,,   28] A goos & a crane kylled with the gon.
     [Dec. 14] A crane kylled wt ye gunne.
1536 [Nov. 21] Three cranes from the fouler of
                   Tichewell [on the coast], v^s. & vi^d.
1537 [Jan. 14] One crane, xvi^d.
     [Dec. 23]   ,,   ,, & ii geese ii^s. viii^d.
1538 [Sept. 15]   ,,   ,,   xx^d.
     [Oct. 13] Two cranes, ii^s. ii^d.

* Mr. N. F. Ticehurst has supplied a still earlier record from the
Chamberlain's Books of the City of Canterbury, where, under date 1480-81,
there is found among other entries. ". . . . Item pro uno Bustardo
xvi^d." (9th Report Historical MSS. Commission, 1883, p. 136.)
† *See* p. 173.
‡ Historical Manuscripts Com., 12th Report, p. 11.
§ *See* p. 164.

1540   [Oct.   27]   One crane, ii^s.
1543   [Sept.   23]   Four cranes killed by Canseller [the
                          knight's keeper].
1548   [Oct.   22]   One crane.
1550   [Dec.   8]   One crane iii^s.
       [Dec.   15]   ,,
       [,,   28]   ,,

Of these Cranes, two are stated to have been killed with
the gun, and four in 1527 and 1528 with the crossbow, and
this is about the last occasion on which we hear of the crossbow, which was falling into disuse.   Between 1528 and 1533
the Crane is not recorded,* and then we read of one " killed
with the gun " on September 28th.   It is to be noted that
three were brought in on one day in November, and four
on a single day in September.   As regards the months, one
Crane was got in July, seven in September, five in October,
five in November, six in December, and five in January.
Its status in North Norfolk therefore was evidently that of a
winter bird, although possibly the July example was a breeder
and the five in September young birds.   For fourteen of them
no price is quoted, implying that they were procured on the
Knight's own manors, which doubtless included extensive
marshes at Hunstanton and Holme.

The Spoonbill.—That the Spoonbill comes into these
Accounts has not generally been recognised,† but as a matter of
fact it is there entered, seven times as " popelere " or " popelar,"
and three times as " shovelarde."   Popeler, like Shoulard or
Shovelard, was a mediæval name for the Spoonbill, but Shovelard is much the more frequent of the two in documents.
Yet Popeler must be the earlier designation, for it occurs
in connection with Norfolk in 1300, as poplo$_3$, a contraction
for poplorum (" Norwich Nat. Tr.," VI., p. 159).   Both
names refer to the spoonlike shape of the beak in this species.
The following passages, as supplied with the dates as calculated by Mr. le Strange, include twenty-three Spoonbills,
all of which were most likely " branchers " or young ones,

* But this does not necessarily imply that none were brought in, but
only that the accounts are imperfect, also between the same dates no Bustards,
Spoonbills, Snipe, Wigeon or Godwits are entered.

† Though alluded to in " The Birds of Norfolk " (Vol. III., p. 135, note).

in which state they were considered to be prime eating. They had to be secured by means of a hook on a pole, in the same way as young Herons, and the two species may have bred together. It will be observed that the entries run from April 30th to July 13th, and this is very suggestive of a breeding-place not far off, and probably it was on the estate, for in every case the Spoonbills are stated to have been of store.

1523.   [April 30] Item iij popeleres of store.
     [May   4] Item v herns and a popelere of store.
     [May   8] Item ii popeleres of store.
1533.   [June   1] Item iiij cople of rabbettes & a poplere of store.
     [June   2] Item ii popeleres & iiij cople of rabbettes of store.
     [June   8] Item ii popeleres & iii rabbettes of store.
     [July   9] Item iii hernes & iiij popeleres of store.
     [July   10] Item iii hernes & a popeler of store.
1543.   [May   20] Item spent iii shovelards that cam from thens [Hunstanton],—store.
1548.   [July   7] Item ij shovelardes.
     [July   13] Item ij shovelardes.

It may have been from a Hunstanton breeding settlement of Spoonbills that Cardinal Wolsey's table was once supplied, for Mr. E. M. Beloe has discovered an entry in the " Hall-Book " of King's Lynn,* setting forth that when Wolsey came there in August 1521, he and his retinue were presented with three " shovelardes " (*i.e.*, spoonbills), three Bitterns, ten cygnets, twelve capons, thirteen plovers, eight pike and three tench.

The Heron.—Herns and Hernshaws are continually put down ; the entries are too numerous to quote, but it may be observed that the latter name is not always restricted to young ones. Herons were reckoned to be of considerable account on a country property, as they are now, although for a different reason. Hawking them was, as Mr. Harting observes, thought to be "a marvellous and delectable pastime," and in some of the treatises upon falconry many pages are

* No. III., fol. 319. The passage is printed in Hillen's " The Borough of King's Lynn."

dedicated to this particular branch of sport. The strictness with which Herons had been for many years protected at their breeding-places is shown by the stringent statutes of James the First of Scotland in 1427, and James the Fourth in 1493, as well as by that of our Henry the Seventh in 1504. The first of these enactments lays down that there was to be no shooting with hail-shot or hand-gun within six hundred yards of a heronry, while Henry the Seventh's Act forbade all killing of Herons except by means of the hawk and the long bow, the more deadly crossbow which discharged bolts being excluded. It was in the interest of holders of manors on which herons bred to keep the laws in force, and not allow them to lapse, but whether this was really done is doubtful.

Ancient tenures of land sometimes particularise the yield of Herons, which the woods should annually afford, an asset of no small consideration (cf. " History of Fowling," p. 212). That they were held to be very good eating at Hunstanton Hall is clear, and evidently the majority of those brought in were the produce of the estate, although there is no Heronry there now.

On one page Herons and Rabbits " of store " occur five times running (p. 483), followed by a pig and a buck of store. This indicates pretty plainly that there was a Heronry not far off, especially as in another place four pence is given " to one that clymed the herons at Mr. Prattes."* Hooking down young Herons from the nest, or when " branchers," was the general way of taking them.†

The Bittern only comes once into the le Straunge Accounts, which is rather singular : " [April 22nd, 1527.] Item a buttour kylled with ye crosbowe "‡ somewhere on

---

* P. 556.

† In the " Account Book of Hurstmonceux Castle," 1643-49, communicated by Mr. T. B. Lennard to " The Sussex Archæological," there are several references to the practice of hooking Herons.
Paid for climing v dozon of herons.
 ,, ,, making a new heron rope.
 ,, ,, white leather for the herne climers use.
 ,, ,, a pole to his hearne hooke.
 ,, ,, the heron climer for climing viii dozon & a half of herons.
 ,, ,, climing xxx rooks for the hawks.

‡ P. 482.

the estate, where there may not have been enough suitable swamps for this species.

Partridges and Pheasants.—Partridges are mentioned a great many times, Pheasants not quite so often. No Pheasants are entered after 1549, but this can hardly be because none were procured. Partridges go on to 1548 and 1549, in which years Mr. le Strange finds repeated entries about them. None is stated to have been shot with the gun, and it is obvious that they were netted. But Partridges and Pheasants were also a favourite quarry for the Hawks, which accounted for a good many of them in the Hunstanton demesne. In some places there was an idea prevalent that they were more savoury when killed by a Hawk than if caught in snares (*see* Willughby's " Ornithology," p. 165).* At any rate the patrimonial estate of the le Straunges was well supplied with feathered game of this kind. In September 1527 the "sparhawke" accounts for twelve Partridges in four days, which would seem to imply that there was more than one hawking party. Again in 1530 a servant brings in twelve Partridges on September 17th† and here we seem to recognise a night's labour with the drag-net.

1536 may have been a good Partridge season, for in January 1537 Mr. le Strange finds Mathew bringing thirty-six Partridges on the 4th, quite a Christmas supply. No doubt Partridges were common, but that could hardly be said of Pheasants in the sixteenth century. Nevertheless Pheasants were to be had for the seeking, and one Towers, who was perhaps what we should call the gamekeeper, seems from time to time to have been sent in quest of them. This is the man who was repaid on the 12th of June for money which he had laid out at divers times, when he went to take Pheasants—whether with a hawk or with a net is not stated. Money again is paid in June to a servant for bringing three Pheasants—possibly live ones at that season of the year, or chicks to put in an aviary.

The Quail only comes twice into the Accounts, which is somewhat surprising, as one might have expected this little

---

* Because, observes Mr. Harting, the head was commonly pulled off.

† P. 497.

quarry, so good for the table, to have been more sought after:
1533 [September 14th] " ij ptryches & a quaylle kyllyd with
ye haukes."
1548 [April 29th] " Itm a quayle."

Pigeons and Fowls.—" Stockdowes," or as it is also
spelled, " Stockedoves," are brought in now and then, in one
place associated with two Cygnets and a " brid pye [bird-pie],"
in another with butter, eggs, and a venison pasty. These, it
is most likely, were either young Stockdoves or Woodpigeons
taken from the nest, domestic Pigeons being distinguished as
" pyggens." Certainly where Pigeons of store are named,
tame Pigeons bred upon the farm must be intended. In 1548
these latter become quite frequent, the number ordered for
the house being, as Mr. le Strange informed me, very considerable. In many parts of England these plunderers of grain,
as one indignant author terms the domestic Pigeons, were
getting so abundant that loud complaints began to arise*, but
it was not necessarily so at Hunstanton. Sixteenth-century
Pigeon houses were in some cases quite substantial brick
buildings, but whether there were any remains of one at
Hunstanton Hall in 1833 is not stated. Undoubtedly one
or more existed, and we also read of " ye olde douffehouse in
Fryng," another part of the estate about five miles away.

In another passage we are told of " a pound of comyng
[cummin seed] for the dowes,"† and again of two " salt stonys "
being bought for the " dowffhouse," presumably at Hunstanton (p. 448). Pigeons are fond of salt, and this may
have been done to keep them at home. In that case Mrs.
Margaret Ferefreye, whom the editor supposes to have been
housekeeper,‡ gave the order, as William Skyppon was clerk
of the kitchen at a later date,§ or the command may have
been from the farm.

* *See* William Harrison's " The Description of England " (1577)
and Hartlib's " Discourse on Husbandry " (1651). Harrison says:—
" . . . . Pigeons, now an hurtful foule by reason of their multitudes,
and number of houses daillie erected for their increase (which the bowres
of the countrie call in scorne almes houses, and dens of theeues, and such like)
whereof there is great plentie in euerie farmer's yard." Mr. Mullens observes
that bowres means " boors," or farmers.

† P. 513.

‡ P. 424.

§ P. 559.

In another place Mr. le Strange meets with a "dow skrapp"; by a skrap or scrap we understand a place for pigeons or fowls to scratch and busk in. Again he comes across a "cowl dow" or pigeon coop, and a "cowle for ye hens at Anmer," a manor about eight miles away, which formed a part of the demesne.

In domestic accounts of this kind, Barn-door Fowls naturally figure frequently, and in the Hunstanton ledgers they are generally accounted for as "checons." Once or twice only do we catch the name of cockerel or capon. Every farmstead or considerable house in East Anglia was no doubt supplied with Fowls, and especially Norfolk, which in the sixteenth century had come a good deal to the front.* Turkeys† and Guineafowls we could hardly look for in the Hunstanton farmyard, but the gaudy Peacock had long been a denizen of England, and must by this time have been well known in Norfolk.‡

Of this species the first notice is a payment in 1520 to the vicar of Thornham's servant for bringing a Peahen, and three young Peahens, and six Plovers (p. 447)—twopence. The gratuity seems a small one, but later on (p. 540) only threepence is paid for another and a Goose thrown in to the bargain.

Small Birds.—There is nothing about the Thrush, nor the "Fulfer," a characteristic Norfolk word, but Blackbirds often come in. In January 1520 four are brought, and then six more "of store," and after that come another six. In the thirty-ninth week of 1522 John Long and Stephen Percy bring four Blackbirds and eight Woodcocks. Judging from other household accounts, Blackbirds seem to have been rated a sort of delicacy. All this tribe of birds has greatly increased in England, and it is conceivable that four hundred

---

* Professor Thorold Rogers is of opinion that in 1503 Norfolk was the second most opulent county in England.

† The first mention of the Turkey as a denizen of Norfolk is discoverable in 1601, in "The Official Papers of Sir Nathaniel Bacon" (R. Historical Soc., p. 220): it soon became as common there as in other parts of England.

‡ *Supra*, p. 57, note.

years ago Blackbirds were nothing like as common as they are now ; perhaps if they had been of larger size our ancestors would have reckoned them as much worth catching as Woodcocks.

Entries of Larks come repeatedly, most often in summer, and generally for half a dozen or a dozen. Fifty-four are brought in on three consecutive days in June 1527, when the Abbot of Ramsey was on a visit at the Hall. Skylarks have always had a reputation for delicacy, so perhaps they were especially provided in this instance for the Abbot.

Again there is an entry of fourteen Larks killed with a Hobby in June 1533, and a fortnight afterwards twelve more killed with a Hobby, as well as five Coots and some Mallards taken with a Spaniel, probably when moulting (p. 528). In the fifteenth century, Mr. Harting observes, the Hobby was considered the hawk for a young man, and ladies also flew the Merlin ; but this latter is not mentioned in the Accounts.

The tenant must have been very poor who could render no higher rent than common Sparrows, but in July 1533, in default of anything better, twelve " sparouse " of gyste are accepted, and in the same week there also come " xij sparouse, iij herns," the latter probably nestlings, for which three halfpence is allowed. The Sparrows also, judging from the time of year, may have been young ones.

In July 1548, Mr. le Strange finds two dozen more Sparrows, and two dozen more in September, presumably for eating, as they could hardly have been bought for any other purpose, unless it was to feed the hawks.

Seamew.—Only one more species, the Gull, remains to be named. Under the name of Seamew, Mr. le Strange discovers six entries—

1536	[June 18]	xxxij	See mowes xi d.
1548	[July 11]	ij	semmywys.
,,	[,, 20]	x	semewes.
,,	[,, 22]		semewys.
,,	[,, ,,]	iiij	seebyrdes called See mewes.
,,	[,, 25]	iiij	semewes.

Probably these refer to the young of the Black-headed Gull, more commonly known as a " Puit," which may have had a breeding-place in the neighbourhood, but Gulls from the seashore were undoubtedly sometimes eaten.*

Hawking at Hunstanton.—That hawking was freely practised on the lands appertaining to Hunstanton Hall we have abundant evidence, nor does it look as if this was done for the entertainment of le Straunge and his frequent visitors, so much as for the more prosaic purpose of filling the larder. Be this as it may, in nearly every case it seems that the Goshawk was the species carried in the chase. It is specified by name at least sixteen times, and we shall not be wrong in concluding that it was generally the Goshawk which is intended by the entry " hawk " without a qualifying adjective. It goes without saying that much attention would have to be given to these valuable food providers, and accordingly it is not surprising to meet with such a payment as sawing for " ye dow house ende [pigeon cote] & board for ye hawk mewe." The mewe was generally some handy outhouse, in which the hawks could be kept clean and free from draughts. In 1519 there is an entry of ten shillings paid to John Maston for mewing & keeping of the Goshawks from Chrostyde [September 14th] unto the XVth day of November,† a liberal consideration for two months' care.

Without doubt the Goshawk (especially a large female) was the prime favourite in most country establishments of this date. Their value to the family at Hunstanton Hall is abundantly demonstrated, not only by the game which they killed, but by the price paid when a fresh hawk was required. Thus a new Goshawk, delivered in August 1533 (p. 550), cost le Straunge forty shillings, and another in 1541 nearly as much, and forty shillings, be it remembered, was a good round sum in the days when coins were few. Although said not to be always tractable in the training, yet to a country mansion such as Hunstanton Hall, the Goshawk, which acted as general provider, was more suited than the long-winged Peregrine, or the high-priced Gyr. Especially was the Goshawk, which has great

---

* Doctor Muffett (1595) says : " *White Guls, Grey Guls*, and *Black Guls* (commonly termed by the name of Plungers and Water Crows) are rejected of every man as a fishy meat : nevertheless being fed at home with new curds and good corn till they be fat, you shall seldom taste of a lighter or better meat. . . . ."

† P. 421.

speed for a short distance, adapted to rabbits, and even the hare could not escape so impetuous a pursuer. But the Goshawk was quite equal to taking winged game, viz., the Pheasant, and we are told no less than thirteen times of a Pheasant finding its way to the buttery which had been killed by a Goshawk. Goshawks were also flown at Partridges, which seem to have been abundant at Hunstanton. On one page (529) Partridges, or as they are written " ptryches," come into the Accounts four times, nine birds altogether, five of which at least were taken with a hawk of some kind.

On another page we have six rabbits, and two Partridges killed with " ye sper hawke " (p. 484). This was in 1527, in which year the trained Sparrow-hawks, if they really were Sparrow-hawks, were very active in the early autumn, accounting for two Partridges on August 25th, four on September 1st, one on the 2nd, two on the 4th, and five on the 5th, besides some rabbits.*

A female Sparrow-hawk might manage young Partridges in August or September, but that it should be capable of taking old ones strong on the wing and full-grown rabbits, though possible, would show a very high degree of training. It seems most likely that by the term " sper hawke " in these Accounts Goshawk is more often meant.†

Some of the disbursements in connection with hawking, in these well-kept Hunstanton books, are worth quoting. Hawks' food, always spoken of as Hawks' meat, is often set down, and occasionally there are expenses which have to do with hawking excursions, and the accompanying breakfast (p. 419). One significant entry is for expenses " when ye went on hawkyng to Woolferton wood for fyer & dryncke." Now we know that in after years a good Heronry flourished at Wolferton,‡ and accordingly it may have been Herons, which on that occasion were the quarry. If it were

---

* Dates as supplied by Mr. le Strange.

† This receives some confirmation from the " Survey of Cornwall " (1602) of Richard Carew. Alluding to the real Sparrow-hawk as employed in the sixteenth century for hawking, he remarks that she would serve to fly little above six weeks in the year " and that only at the Partridge, where the Faulkner and Spanels must also now and then spare her extraordinary assistance . . ." He evidently regarded Sparrow-hawks as too small for this flight.

‡ See Morris's " Naturalist," 1852, p. 204.

so, the Knight would hardly have flown anything at them but the Falcon, which he might have acquired locally, for Peregrine " eyesses " were to be obtained from Hunstanton cliff near by.* It may have been at Wolferton Wood also that the Spoonbills bred, but this is a mere conjecture, with nothing to verify it, unfortunately.

One item is twopence to Thomas Pedder—the same man who was sent for the Plovers—for a tame Mallard to lure back the hawks in Hunstanton Marsh (p. 441).† On the same page we read of " sekyng of ye haggard fawkon callyd Cheny " at Christmas time, possibly so named in compliment to my lady Chenys (p. 440), when as much as twenty pounds were laid out in costs. Elsewhere we hear of Hawks' bells, most important for the retrieving of a lost one, and of the wages paid to Saunder the falconer, and in one place of " fyer for the hawkys " (p. 9). Mr. Harting suggests that this should not read *fyer*, but *tyer*, *i.e.*, something to tire on or pull at, when sitting on the porch or block, to keep a hawk quiet. Nowhere is the Peregrine Falcon alluded to in the Accounts by name, yet the wild haggard " cheny " sounds as if she must have been one of this breed.

Any English falconer who had a Peregrine would have called it a Falcon or Lanner, or perhaps a Gentil Falcon in those days, the latter term being usually reserved for the female.

---

* Although Hunstanton Cliff, sometimes called St. Edmund's Point, was by no means lofty, and is now only sixty feet high, Peregrine Falcons persistently bred there for a great number of years, of which proof is given in the " Norwich Naturalists' Transactions " (Vol. V., p. 185). That they were known, and their value appreciated, as far back as 1604 is also certain, *see* " Norwich Nat. Tr." (IV., p. 658), for in the evidence room at Hunstanton Hall there exists a list of falcons taken from this cliff beginning with that year. This carefully kept falconer's list was drawn up by the Sir Hamon Lestrange of that date, who here records that between 1604 and 1653 he took on the estate no fewer than eighty-seven hawks, of which sixty-five were young ones from the nest. This eyrie is alluded to in Bishop Gibson's edition of Camden's " Britannia," 1772 (Vol. 1., p. 470). Mr. Harting has shown that according to Nicholas Stoleman of Snettisham, a parish a few miles away, it ceased to exist about 1818 (" Zoologist," 1890, p. 418).

† The luring of a lost hawk was a common practice. It is mentioned in the Middleton Accounts, where, under date 1524, we have " ij molerdes to hayse [*i.e.*, to lure or train] the hawkes " (*t.c.*, p. 368), and elsewhere allusions to it may be met with. Tame Ducks, which were good enough for this purpose, were to be distinguished from Wild Ducks. In the " Munimenta Gildhallæ Londonensis," a domestic duck is called a dunghill mallard for distinction's sake (Rolls Edn., I., lxxxiii.), and such a fowl would have answered the purpose of a lure.

To these falconers Peregrine was an appellation which really meant a hawk of foreign origin, in which sense the name *Helog Dramor* is applied to this species in the Welsh language. The truth is, the name Peregrine is a comparatively modern word, which was very little known to the falconers of the sixteenth century, although that great authority Turbervile does in one place in his " Booke of Faulconrie "* write about " the Haggart Falcon, and why she is called the Peregrine or Haggart "†

Other Means employed for Fowling at Hunstanton.—One thing which is somewhat inexplicable about these careful books is the constantly repeated formula, set down for some unknown reason, as to how the various birds were obtained, whether by crossbow, hawk or gun. Throughout the earlier part of the Accounts the crossbow was the weapon most commonly employed. The type of crossbow for fowling, of which a good example may be seen in Norwich Museum, was fitted with a wooden stock, and discharged metal bolts, being not much heavier than a modern gun. With such effect did the energetic fowlers handle their crossbows that the buttery was supplied with three Great Bustards, two Cranes, a wild Swan, a Bittern, a wild Goose and numerous wild Ducks. On one occasion a Bustard, eight Mallards and a Heron, all marked as killed with the crossbow, are brought in to the larder.

Water-dogs, here alluded to as " the spannyell," were trained to assist in taking wild-fowl. There is one entry of four Mallards, and another of six Mallards, and five Coots

---

* P. 33.

† A good deal of curious information about hawking in Norfolk and Suffolk, at about this period and also later, has been collected by Mr. J. E. Harting for the Norwich Naturalists' Society. *See* his articles entitled " Notes on Hawking as formerly practised in Norfolk " (" Trans. N. and N. N.," Vol. III., pp. 79–94) and " Further Notes on Hawking in Norfolk " (Vol. VI., pp. 248–254). Among the passages quoted by Mr. Harting in the latter paper, not the least singular is a communication accompanying the dispatch of a hawk, from one Jasper Meller to Sir Bassingbourn Gawdy of West Harling in 1598. Two days ago, the writer states, he caught with some labour this Tasslegentle [Tiercel], and afterwards found on him the Queen's varvaile [a ring bearing Elizabeth's mark] and one Mr. Throgmorton's name on the mayle [a small plate]. He desires Sir B. Gawdy to take the legal course, which was to inform the Sheriff of Norfolk. There are some other letters equally interesting, such as refer to the mewing of a " heroner," *i.e.*, a falcon trained to herons; to an old hawk " taken with the cramp and the quack "; to a " Jake-marlen [Merlin] "; to a lusty falcon, that is " ever raking out at crows "; and to " green geese " and ducks required for hawkes meat.

(p. 528) being captured with a dog of this breed. Most likely it was the spaniel's part to drive the Ducks into nets previously laid for them, and this may have been usually in July, when the old ones were moulting, and the young scarcely able to fly.

Nothing is said about a decoy, nor is it likely that the estate possessed anything which deserved the name of one; indeed, the method of decoying fowl on the Dutch principle by alluring them was not introduced into Norfolk until the seventeenth century (1610–1620).* The customary way of catching Ducks was to hustle them into a tunnel net, as shown in an old print reproduced in Payne-Gallwey's "Book of Duck Decoys."†

The first bird shot with a gun was in 1533, nothing more considerable than a Waterhen which might have been got any day in the moat; but very quickly the new weapon is put to better account, and kills a Crane, two Mallards, and a Wigeon. However, perhaps powder was scarce, for we do not hear much more of it, nothing being shot after a Brant Goose in 1534.

The smaller waders. such as Dunlin and Knot, would not have been deemed worth powder and shot, or even bolts from a crossbow; they were evidently captured in upright nets set near the sea, which on dark nights are a fatal trap.‡ Nets of this kind have been in use in the Wash for a very long time; I can remember seeing them erected in lines as far back as 1862, and they were no novelty then.§ Although they are

---

* The oldest East Anglian decoy of which we have any precise particulars, situated at Steeple, in Essex, near the mouth of the Blackwater, was constructed in 1713, and curious details of its working have been given by Mr. Cordeaux and Mr. Harting. ("Field," April 6th, 1878, and July 5th, 1879.)

† P. 5.

‡ Sir Thomas Browne, writing a century later, alludes to this method of taking Knots on the Norfolk coast. We learn from the Gawdy Papers that in 1563 Knots cost five shillings a dozen and that they were commonly caught at Terrington near Lynn ("Norwich Naturalists' Trans.," VI., p. 253).

§ The catch on December 18th, 1862, was: Dunlin 34, Knot 15, Curlew 3, Golden Plover 3, Grey Plover 3, Oystercatcher 2, Woodcock 1, Bar-tailed Godwit 1, Redshank 1, Great Black-backed Gull 1, Black-headed Gull 2. These nets were for many years the property of Mr. Frank Cresswell of Lynn, who generally placed them at high-water mark. In eleven consecutive years, beginning with 1859, Mr. Cresswell took 3,693 birds, but of late years from various causes the nets have not been so much used. The above is given as an example of a good night's work. Illustrations of these nets are given in Dawson Rowley's "Ornithological Miscellany" (Vol. II., p. 373).

not alluded to in the " Archaeologia," Mr. le Strange has given
me four or five entries from the unpublished Accounts which
refer to the making of shore bird-nets.

1543 [November 8th] To a woman of Thornham for a
li [*i.e.* a pound] of stryng for the stynt nette.

1543 [November 14th] To a woman for twyn for ye
stynt nett vii^d.

1543 [November 26th] To a woman of Thornham for a
li of twyne for the stynt nette.

1543 [December 19th] For a stynt nette for Jekes, &
the brayding thereof viii^d.

But Stint nets were not the only ones used by the fowlers,
for another entry is tenpence for twine for the Partridge net,
most likely in this instance a draw net. With this a covey
of Partridges could be encompassed at night by two men,
each holding one end of the net : the spaniel, which was
their indispensable companion, having first scented out the
whereabouts of the game. A second plan was to use them
by day with a trained Falcon aloft, which, no matter at what
height she hung, would be seen by the Partridges, which then
squatted close in terror of their natural enemy. Another
entry communicated by Mr. le Strange runs :—

" 1540 [June 6]. It^m p^d the same day to Gyburn for
suche things as he haue bought vz.,* iij ffesaunt nettes & a
Cloth ij^s viij^d, for ij ptrich nettes v:x^d, iij^s hoby nettes xj^d,
for a sawe ij^d." . . . On the same page of the Accounts
Mr. le Strange finds : " It^m p^d the viijth day of May to
Gybson for his costs when he went a ffyssyng & a Taking
of the Hobye . . . vj^d." The "hoby" nets were perhaps
intended to catch Skylarks while the Hobby waited overhead. The employment of a small Falcon for this kind of
sport was called "daring," and is described by Turbervile
in his "Booke of Faulconrie" (1575). A well-known
poet alludes to it when he writes, "As larks lie dar'd
to shun the hobby's flight" (Dryden). In the second
entry, perhaps, the allusion may be to a Hobye-horse, and
not to a bird.

* Namely.

As Woodcocks were only visitants, we should scarcely expect to find, as in some Cumberland Accounts,* entries of hankes of yarn, *i.e.*, spun wool, for the cockshut net, a device used in the west, but apparently not in Norfolk, for taking Woodcocks in their evening flight, so le Straunge does not seem to have had any at Hunstanton. We have entries of " packethrede for ye haye," and " a haye of 1 fadam long " (p. 423), which was a net for catching hares, also of " twyn for yo' foxe netts "† which looks as if reynard had been troublesome in the poultry yard.

With the spread of cereal crops, both hares and rabbits we may presume were increasing, at all events 1,514 rabbits were consumed in the house in less than a year. In one place there is an entry which points to another form of sport, viz., 2 lb. of twine " for the hunt[er] to make up his nett & to Mason for [fish-] castyng nettes." But possibly these were only to be used at the stew-ponds, of which some remains are still to be seen in the park. Among the many entries which Mr. le Strange has marked are three which refer to Bat-fowling (or -folding), of which one runs :—

" 1543. [29 December.] Itm Spent in Wildfoule vz., v dosen Styntes, iij mallardes, ij ffesauntes, viii ptriches, v spowes, j curlewe, iij Redshankes, oon Tele, ij dosen Batt ffowling Bryddes."

Mr. le Strange did not come across any mention of a crow-net, yet such a necessary item could hardly have been lacking, nor are crow-boys named among the papers. Mr. Harting has found a figure of a sixteenth century Crow-net, which shows the type commonly used in Leonard Mascall's " Booke of Fishing with Hooke and Line " (1590).‡ Every parish had to provide itself with one, and could be fined under the statute of 24 Henry VIII. (1533) if it were not forthcoming.

* The following is from the larderer's book of Naworth Castle in Cumberland. " October 23 [1624]. To Robert Stapleton for hempe yarn in March for making a drawing net [doubtless for Partridges] v s. : and for iij hankes of yarn for a cockshott nett at Brampton parke iij s."
The earliest reference to a cockeshot is in Wynkyn de Worde's " Treatyse of Fysshynge with an Angle."
† P. 550.
‡ *See* article on " Choughs, Crows and Rooks " (" Zoologist," 1894, p. 47).

The fact of such a law being necessary indicates that Rooks were very numerous. Sir Thomas Browne (1665) speaks of the great plenty of Rooks and Rook-groves in Norfolk, while another writer of the next century observes that England has bred more Crows than any country in Europe, no doubt meaning to include Rooks.

Of items which bear indirectly on Natural History there are not a few. The careful diarists put down the price of apples and medlars, of the pasty of a stag, and the quarter of a porpoise, of a hundred eggs, etc. The King's falconer has his reward, and we are duly told what was paid to the bringers of a couple of whelps, or a " yolle of fresh salmon."*

On page 420 there is an allusion to the shoeing of a " stawkyng horse." The stalking horse appears to have been in great favour for approaching fowl, and even a stalking ox, behind which the fowler could screen himself, and so get within short range.

As a sample of the many good things which passed through the buttery door into the hands of the housekeeper at Hunstanton Hall, here is the well-kept inventory of one week :—†

Sunday, [November 1519.] One Goose, a Pig, 6 Conies. 6 Plovers, 2 Mallards, 12 Birds [not named].

Monday. Two Geese, 2 Pigs, 1 Crane, 7 Conies, 1 Curlew, 3 " Spowes " [*i.e.*, whimbrel], 3 Mallards.

Tuesday. One Goose, 3 Mallards, 2 Teal, 3 Conies.

Wednesday. One Pig, 1 Woodcock, 2 Conies, 2 Mallards.

Thursday. One Goose, 3 Conies, 2 Mallards.

Friday. One Codling, 10 Plaice.

Saturday. One Cod, 2 Codling, 10 Plaice, a Salmon-Trout and half a Ling, besides Butter, Eggs, Beef, Mutton, and Ale.

This was rather a special week, but there were many others nearly as productive. It will be observed that four

---

* Mr. Walter Rye observes that " yolle " is a variorum reading of jowl, a jaw or head. In that sense the word is used in the Duke of Buckingham's Household Book, and in Russell's " Boke of Nurture " (L. 622).

† P. 426.

sorts of fish are here mentioned ; fish were largely consumed and continually come in throughout the Accounts.*

But Hunstanton Hall, with all its many advantages, was not free from one defect, and that was the presence of rats, which must have been Black Rats, for *Epimys norvegicus* did not come until the eighteenth century.   These undesirable visitors had found their way into the house, and in 1520 were such a nuisance that ·· Peter Ratonar "--who took his name from his profession—had to be paid twenty pence for laying of the chambers with poison (p. 478).   Again the same man,

---

* For the following list of the fish, etc., enumerated, I am indebted to Mr. le Strange :—

Fish Eaten at Hunstanton.

Basse.

Bretteor Bretcocke (Brill). My father could remember when this name, which was possibly applied to the Turbot as well, was in use at Wells. In the Kenninghall Accounts it is spelled *bryt* in 1525 (" Norfolk Arch.," 1904, p. 54).

Butte (Plaice).

Butt sprag (*Sprag* was used for a young cod-fish or salmon, and according to " The English Dialect Dictionary," *butt* was a basket for catching fish.

Cockyll.

Cod.

Cod Waxen (large Cod).

Codlyng.

Congre.

Crabbe.

Cravose (Lobster).

Eell.

Fawke (? Flounder).

Flathe (Skate).

Gurnard.

Haburdyn (Salted Cod from Aberdeen, a town famous for curing fish).

Haddock.

Herryng, fresh.
,,   full.
,,   red.
,,   shotten.
,,   white.

Lampre.

Lyng.

Mackerell.

Mullett.

Muschelle.

Oyster.

Perch.

Purpose (Porpoise, often mentioned, and reckoned as quite eatable. Six shillings and eightpence was paid for a whole one).

Purwynckle.

Pyke.

Playce.

Roche.

Samon.
,,   salted.
,,   Trowght.

(During the early part of 1548 Mr. le Strange finds that over thirty Salmon were brought to the house, about half of which were salted Salmon, while the remainder were fresh.)

Skull slyce (also spelled sculleslyes and skulk Slyce. Probably the Plaice, *skolla* and *Sand-skädda* are stated to be Swedish names for this species, and *skulder* Danish. Mr. Norgate suggests that Slyce may be equivalent to Low German *slick* = mud.)

Shrymp.

Smelt.

Sole.

Spratt.
,,   red.

Sturgyn.

Spyrlyng (Smelt).

Stockfysshe.

Tenche.

Thornbacke.

Turbutte.

Whytynge.

Wylkes.

and John Audeley, are a second time each remunerated with twenty pence for killing rats with "ratton bayn."* It is to be hoped that they succeeded in clearing the mansion effectually of such undesirable marauders.

Few departments of English history have been less cultivated than that relating to the household accounts of the upper classes in the sixteenth century, which tell us about their meals and manners, and considered zoologically often present an aspect of very great interest. Not a few of them were kept in eventful and troubled times—a period which in the case of le Straunge and his family takes us through the greater part of three reigns, ending in 1578, the year which witnessed Queen Elizabeth's stately entry into Norwich.

The House and Farm Accounts of the Shuttleworths.†— There are not many existing household accounts of the sixteenth century on the lines of le Straunge : the most appropriate with which to compare them are the Middleton Accounts (Hist. MSS. Com.), and those of Shuttleworth of Lancashire, which latter contain also some references to falconry. About twenty-five species of Lancashire birds are here enumerated, some of them under rather peculiar names, viz. : the skergrys or scargrasse, which, according to Mitchell's "Birds of Lancashire" (p. 166), was the Water Rail, the tullette‡ (Ringed Plover, *idem*, p. 177), the curlue hilpp (Whimbrel, *idem*, p. 200), the snipe knave (*qu.* Jack Snipe), the pire or piere (Dunlin), ooselles, youlwringes (Yellow Hammers), dige brides or digge birdies (young ducks),§ etc. Ducks received in lieu of rent are entered as boon-ducks.|| Dunes were not Pochards, as the editor supposes, but Knots (Mitchell, *t.c.*, p. 192). Twelve scriltes, or scrittes, brought home in June with Lapwings and a Grey Plover, were most likely

---

* P. 524.

† "The Shuttleworths of Gawthorpe Hall in the county of Lancaster, from September 1582 to October 1621," edited for the Cheetham Society by John Harland (1856-58).

‡ Probably from its cry, as Borlase tells us, for the same reason Sanderlings were called in Cornwall *Towillees* (" Natural History of Cornwall," p. 247).

§ *Cf.* "English Dialect Dictionary," art. *digg*.

|| "Boons," *i.e.*, gifts.

Mistle Thrushes as suggested, but it is not very probable that " thrie whekeres " for which sixteen pence was paid in December 1591 were Wheatears. Neither *scrittes* nor *whekeres* are included in a list of Lancashire bird names printed in Hardwicke's " Science Gossip,"* but *scaragrice* is given for the Water Rail, literally, the timid bird of the grass. Prices in Lancashire did not differ sufficiently from those at Hunstanton to call for remark : Woodcocks varied from twopence to fourpence.

Hawking items are scattered through the Accounts. Thus we find that 9s. 6d. was spent in bringing hawks from London, another time 1s. 4d. for hawks' hoods, again 6d. for hawks' bells, and 4d. for beef for them to eat, while some necessary repairs to " the haucke mue," *i.e.*, the shed where they were kept, cost 2s.†

Henry VIII. and Queen Elizabeth fond of Falconry.— The sport of falconry, to which our ancestors were enthusiastically devoted, has been shown to have been pursued by the le Straunges, as well as by the Lancashire family of Shuttleworth. The popularity which it had attained may be judged from Shakespeare's plays if by nothing else, for they are full of allusions to it. Perhaps it was the example of the Sovereign which did a good deal to augment a taste for this form of the chase, for Queen Elizabeth was fond both of hunting and hawking, and in Mr. Harting's opinion the latter diversion had hardly obtained its full development before her reign. An observation by the German traveller, Paul Hentzner, may be said to confirm this view, in a passage where he remarks, when visiting England in 1598, on the circumstance of Falconry being then the general sport of the English gentry. In that rare and fine old work, George Turbervile's " The Booke of Faulconrie or Hauking," printed in 1575, there is a picture of good Queen Bess mounted on horseback, and gallantly taking her part in the chase. Two herons have been roused, and three falcons are circling in the sky overhead, preparatory to making a stoop, while another has just been cast off at the

* Vol. XVIII., (1882), p. 164.

† Little inferior in importance to the le Straunge and Shuttleworth accounts is the household book of Naworth Castle in Cumberland, made public by the Surtees Society, which commences in 1612 and therefore refers to a later period but is quite as full of items of zoological interest.

quarry by one of the falconers. Elizabeth, active by nature and a good horsewoman, had inherited a taste for hunting and hawking from her father, Henry VIII. Like him, she was at home in the saddle, and when bent on pleasure was often to be seen at the head of a brave retinue in the field.

On some occasions her royal parent appears to have been over-bold in his adventures. It is related that once when leaping a dyke with his hawking pole, the staff broke with his weight, and the King would have been in no small danger of being smothered in the mud had not one of the royal falconers been there to drag him out. Another time the house in which he was lodging caught fire, which, says the chronicler of events, put the King in great fear, but fortunately in no jeopardy.* On a third occasion Henry shot a tame buck by mistake, at least we may presume it was not done on purpose, for which seven and sixpence had to be paid by way of compensation.

Modern enthusiasts for the sport of falconry think themselves fortunate to possess one at least of Henry VIII.'s Household books, which has escaped destruction ; although it only runs from 1529 to 1532,† there are quite a number of allusions to the King's hawks in it. The best falconers were Flemings, a reputation long maintained, and Sir N. Nicolas considers that the king employed ten at least, each of whom had a livery costing twenty-two shillings and sixpence.‡ One Nicholas Clamp received ten pounds a year,§ while others had a groat (fourpence) a day, and a penny for the food of each hawk.

Brought up with falconers, and probably himself no mean judge of the points of a good hawk, Henry VIII. was partial to one species in particular. This was the Goshawk, if we may so argue from the circumstance of its being brought into these curious old accounts by name nine times. On one occasion the King, when he had sallied forth for an

* " Hall's Chronicle," edn. 1809, pp. 50, 697.
† " The Privy Purse Expenses of King Henry VIII.," edited by Sir Nicholas H. Nicolas (1827).
‡ *T.c.*, pp. 142, 198.
§ Preface, xxxix.

expedition, met with a Goshawk upon the cage, or " cadge,"*
a sort of wooden frame on which hawks were commonly carried
hooded.   Taking a fancy to the bird, the King purchases it
for three pounds, which is duly paid by one, Master Walche,
who was perhaps the steward.   There are many other entries
in the King's accounts about hawks and hawking.

* Cadger, as applied to an itinerant hawker, is said to be derived from
this word, of which also the epithet cad, used in an opprobrious sense, is
considered to be an abbreviation.

CHAPTER X.

SIXTEENTH CENTURY (3RD PART).

The Sixteenth Century (3rd part) : 1544. William Turner. 1555. Conrad Gesner. The Solan Goose.

William Turner, afterwards Dean of Wells.—No annals of ornithology would be complete without proper reference to the labours of William Turner, who has been called the Father of British Ornithology, for with the aid of this enquiring and industrious man we may make some tolerable attempt to sketch the status of British birds in the sixteenth century. Whether Turner's ornithological tastes continued in later life we are not told, but he was to the last a botanist. His reputation as a lover of birds rests on a small but very learned work, the " Avium Praecipuarum, quarum apud Plinium et Aristotelem mentio est, brevis & succincta historia," which is an attempt at identifying the birds given by these old writers. This volume was printed at Cologne, in Germany, in the year 1544, and contains most valuable information about British and German birds, which, but for Turner, would not have come down to us. The great rarity of the original edition, and of Dr. Thackeray's later one printed in 1823, have prevented the work from being generally known. Accordingly a new edition in 1903, with an excellent translation by Mr. A. H. Evans, was exceedingly acceptable to all ornithologists.*

Dean Turner furnishes a contribution to the history of the Solan Goose, which, although well known, will bear quoting again from Mr. Evans's translation. The Solan Goose, he tells us, evidently deriving his information from some original source, " . . . looks to its young with so much loving care that it will fight most gallantly with lads that are let down in baskets by a rope to carry them away, not without danger of

---

* " Turner on Birds : A short and succinct History of the Principal Birds noticed by Pliny and Aristotle, first published by Dr. William Turner, 1544." Edited by A. H. Evans, 1903.

life. Nor must we fail to mention that a salve, most valuable for many a disease, is made by Scots from the fat of this Goose, for it is wonderfully full of fat. . . ."

Mr. W. H. Mullens, the author of a very good memoir of Turner, to be consulted with advantage,* is of opinion that he owed something to Bartholomæus Anglicus. The "De Proprietatibus Rerum" of this writer is stated by Mr. Mullens, in his "Bibliography of British Ornithology," to have been probably written between 1248 and 1267,† but in any case it does not detract from the merits of the scholarly Northumbrian, if he did use it.

The Rev. H. A. Macpherson, who has written with justifiable enthusiasm about Turner, conjectures that he was thirty-seven when the "Avium Praecipuarum . . . historia" was printed ;‡ but as Mr. Mullens finds that he graduated in 1529-30, he possibly was not so old as that. It may have been, as both Mullens and Macpherson suggest, the proximity of the Cambridgeshire fens which directed Turner's attention to birds, during his ten years' residence at the university, where he had already brought out a book on botany.§ Be that as it may, the result was the invaluable "Avium Praecipuarum," which predates the "Histoire de la Nature des Oyseaux" of Pierre Belon and the great work of Conrad Gesner. With Gesner, Turner was in close friendship, and much mutual assistance these two men rendered to one another; indeed, Gesner quotes nearly every observation which Turner has made.

From our point of view, by far the most important part of the "Avium Praecipuarum" is not that which comments on Aristotle and Pliny, though Turner meant it to be so, but his own personal observations on birds. Many of these may have been made on preaching tours in the east of England, as for example where he notes that Cormorants breed in Heronries in Norfolk. It is difficult to say how

* "British Birds," Mag., II., p. 5. The series communicated by Mr. Mullens, comprises lives of Turner, Carew, Merrett, Martin, Plot, Pennant, Ray, Willughby, Bewick, Montagu, Macgillivray, Yarrell, Tradescant, Charleton, Muffett and Sibbald. It is to be hoped that these valuable articles will be continued.

† "Bib. B.O.," p. 45.

‡ "Zoologist," 1898, p. 337.

§ The "Libellus de re herbaria novus," of which an excellent reprint was issued by Mr. B. D. Jackson in 1877.

many birds Turner meant to enumerate as British, but evidently the ninety-five to which he gives English names are to be so accounted. Not the least singular of the many facts, with which his pages abound, is the curious reference to white Herons in England, from which we can only conclude that Turner had come across an albinistic race of them somewhere, which is all the more remarkable because Herons are little subject to variation. As regards the status of the birds of prey, other than those used in falconry, we know but little. The Peregrine falcon, and the Gyr falcon prized for their high qualities do not seem to have been very easy to procure, while of the smaller hawks, such as the Kestrel, the Hobby and the Merlin, there is little or nothing which can be said with certainty, either as to their abundance or their distribution. Turner, with his usual discrimination, distinguished the Hobby, of which he says: "It catches for the most part Larks and Finches, nests on lofty trees, and is not seen in winter anywhere." All, or nearly all, Turner's remarks may be taken as applying to England, unless the contrary is stated, yet it has to be remembered that he resided for four years in Switzerland and Germany, before the publication of his book.

What Turner took to be the Sparrow-hawk of the English and the Sperwer of the Germans, was the bird which we now call a Goshawk, which there is every reason for believing was a not uncommon breeder in the British Isles (*supra*, p. 82), while the real Sparrow-hawk (*Accipiter nisus*) was possibly less abundant than at the present day. The bird which Turner had in his mind was large enough to prey upon Doves, Pigeons, Partridges, and the bigger sorts of birds, and this description fits the Goshawk. The Marsh Harrier, he tells us, a bird nearly brown in colour (*fusco proximo*), "lives by hunting ducks, and the black fowls which Englishmen call couts," its fierce attacks on which he had himself often seen. To the Hen Harrier, another plunderer, Turner can give no praise, it "gets this name among our countrymen from butchering their fowls," which condemns it. The Buzzard was probably very generally distributed, both as breeder and migrant, in the British Isles, and being looked upon as a rather useful scavenger which did not molest chickens, was tolerated, as it still is in some parts of the continent.

In one of his letters to the Swiss naturalist Gesner, a translation of which is given by Macpherson in the " Zoologist,"* Turner, writing of the Kite, says :—" We have Kites in England, the like of which I have seen nowhere else. Our birds are much larger than the German birds, more clamorous, tending more to whiteness, and much greedier. For such is the audacity of our Kites, that they dare to snatch bread from children, fish from women, and handkerchiefs from off hedges, and out of men's hands. They are accustomed to carry off caps from off men's heads when they are building their nests."† This recalls the description by the Venetian Ambassador before quoted,‡ and to go much further back, the testimony of Ælian, who speaks of the daring of Kites in the second century, and accuses them of snatching hair from men's heads, when engaged in nesting.§ In spite of such delinquencies, they have ever been given special protection, nor was this withheld from them in England, where there was a fine for killing one.|| At the present day the Red Kite, *Milvus ictinus*, would be considered commoner than *M. migrans* in Western Germany.

The (? Golden) Eagle, the Erne, and the Osprey are all distinguished by Turner and named as inhabitants of England, but the Peregrine Falcon appears to have escaped him. Of Owls he recognised three, of which one was the Long-eared Owl and one the Eagle Owl.

Turner died in 1568, his age is not known, but he did not live to be seventy. A monument was put up to his

---

* 1898, p. 340.

† " Historiæ Animalium," lib. II., p. 586. Reference supplied by Mr. Mullens.

‡ *Supra*, p. 82.

§ Ælian, " De Animalium Natura," lib. II.

|| That the Kite did not cease to be common in the British Isles until long after this is certain. Francis Willughby and John Ray must have been familiar with their gliding flight, the former (who died in 1672), describes them as " very noisome " to chickens, ducklings and goslings, probably referring to Warwickshire, where most of his short life was spent.

In churchwardens' books we not infrequently find entries of moneys paid for their destruction ; the church accounts of Tenterden in Kent show payments for three hundred and eighty in fourteen years, commencing 1677 (N. F. Ticehurst, " Brit. Birds," Mag., XIV., p. 34).

memory in St. Olave's Church, Crutched Friars, and on it we
may read, says Macpherson, that the great naturalist was
"ac tandem corpus senio, ac laboribus confectum " when he
answered the last roll call. By the kindness of the Rev.
T. Wellard, the rector of St. Olave's, a photograph of
this tablet, which was erected by the affectionate care of
Turner's widow, is here reproduced.

Pierre Belon.—Peter Belon, a French naturalist, was born
about 1519, and was the author of an illustrated work on
ornithology, bearing the title of " Histoire de la Nature des

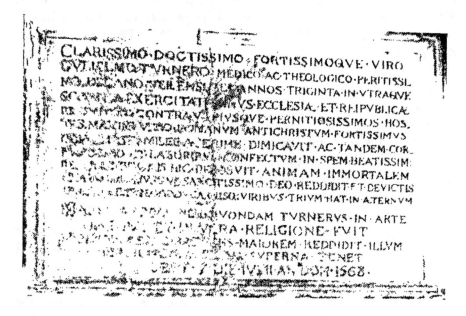

TURNER'S TABLET.

Oyseaux " (1555), which contains a good deal that is original
—as, for example, passages referring to the Barn Owls at
Metz (p. 144), the Pelicans at Rama (p. 155), the Mergansers
on the Loire (p. 164), the Gulls at Havre and Dieppe (p. 170),
the white Herons which Turner saw in England (p. 191), and
the Storks on the Hellespont (p. 202). When visiting England
Belon met with the Stone Curlew (p. 239), while he notes the
protection given to Ravens (p. 279), and to Kites (p. 131),
but not much else apparently. However, in his own country
he had more opportunities, and here he does not fail to tell
us about the breeding of the Spoonbill. In his day, the

" Pale Poche " nested on tall trees in Brittany and Poitou (p. 194), perhaps near the home of his youth.

Treating of the Sparrow-hawk (Esperuier), of which he gives a fairly good figure and description (pp. 121–3), Belon mentions its partiality for Chaffinches which descend into the plains in winter, and then continues :—[" When] we were at the mouth of the Euxine Sea, where the Straight of the Propontis [Marmora] commences, having climbed the highest hill which is there, we found a fowler taking Sparrow-hawks [Esperuiers] in a clever way. And as it was near the end of April, when all birds are nesting, it seemed strange to us to see so many Kites [Milans] and Sparrow-hawks coming from the right-hand coast of the great sea. The fowler caught them with great industry, and did not miss one. He took more than a dozen every hour. . . . No man could easily imagine from whence such a multitude of Sparrow-hawks should come. For in the two hours' time that we were spectators of that sport, we saw more than thirty taken, whence one may conjecture that one fowler in the space of a day might take more than a hundred." (*Translation.*) Under the heading of " Milan noir " (p. 131) Belon alludes again to the same bird-catcher, expressing his surprise at the Kites which came to the net in such great companies. Since Belon's time, other naturalists, particularly Alléon and Vian, have described the Bosphorus, and remarked on the biannual passage of birds of prey which is to be seen there. " Au printemps," write these authors, " et à l'automne, le Bosphore présente, pour les naturalistes un spectacle vraiment merveilleux par les migrations des oiseaux de proie ; leur nombre dépasse tout ce que l'imagination peut supposer."*

John Maplet, 1567.—This was an author who wrote " A Greene Forest, or a naturall histoire," almost the earliest treatise of its kind, but admittedly a compilation ; Maplet describes twenty-eight birds, besides three which are fabulous ; an account of him is given in the " Bibliography of British Ornithology." Mr. Harting observes that errors are to be detected in the descriptions of the Falcon and Goshawk.†

---

* " Rev. et Mag. de Zoologie," 1869, p. 258. In another place (p. 260) the same authors speak of " l'agglomeration de ces bandes fabuleuses d'oiseaux de proie."

† " Bibliotheca Accipitraria," p. 10.

Dr. John Kay or Caius.—To the " Avium Praecipuarum
. . . historia " of Turner, that portion of a kindred work, the
" De Rariorum Animalium atque stirpium Historia," which
relates to ornithology, is a useful sequel. This was published
in 1570—twenty-six years after Turner's book—by Dr. John
Kay, or Caius as he is commonly called,* a native of Norwich,
although he does not seem to have lived there long. Mr.
Evans gives the whole of the bird part of it with a translation,
as an appendix to his edition of Turner. Kay only describes
thirteen birds in his " De Rariorum," but at some length ;
of these eight are British species, and what he has to say
about them is quite to the point. Noteworthy are his remarks
on the Gannet and the Puffin—one of the latter he actually kept
alive for eight months in his house, which nowadays would
be looked upon by aviculturists as a good performance. It
bit with right good will, but was satisfied with little food,
yet when there was none, begged with the cry of " pupin,
pupin." Our author has a good deal to say about the Solan
Goose, but his dissertation on that species is entirely from the
writings of others, except where he compares them to Puffins
for flavour and fatness. Of the Meleagris or Guineafowl he
furnishes quite a lengthy description, penned with great
accuracy, which is repeated, but not without acknowledg-
ment, in Gesner's " Historia Animalium," where there is an
admirable figure of this bird under the name of *Gallus
numidicus aut moritanus.*† The species to which Kay,
for some unknown reason, limited himself, are :—

Sea Eagle (Osprey).
Brent Goose (Barnacle Goose).
Bass Goose (Solan Goose).
Indian Duck (Muscovy Duck).
The Turkish or Second Indian Duck (doubtful).
Sea Pie (Oystercatcher).
The Domestic Getulian Hen (a breed said to come from
Africa).
The Meleagris (Guineafowl).

* Mr. Evans, to whose assistance I am much indebted, points out that
other spellings are Keys and Kees, *see* Venn's " History of Gonville and
Caius College," p. 30.
† Liber III., p. 772.

The Morinellus (Dotterel).

Puphin or Pufin (Puffin) and Cormorant.

The Spermologus or Frugilega (Rook).

The Sacropsittacus (Parrot).

White Ravens (two in Cumberland, August, 1548).

It has been thought that this tract, which can hardly be all that Kay wrote about birds, was part of a longer treatise intended as a contribution to Gesner's " Historia Animalium," but that, in consequence of Gesner's early death, it was never communicated.

Conrad Gesner and the Solan Goose.—In passing under review some of the early classics of ornithology, we take note that the Solan Goose is not described by Eber and Peucer (1549), nor by Pierre Belon (1555), nor is it given a place by that great authority on gastronomy, Dr. Muffett, or Moffett (? 1595). Accordingly we must turn, as in many other instances, to Conrad Gesner (1555). Gesner was a Swiss physician, a man of the highest erudition, a great seeker after knowledge, and the friend of William Turner. There must have been much in common between Gesner and Turner, both of whom died in middle age, the former being no more than forty-eight and the latter only fifty-six. So highly was Turner's knowledge esteemed by Gesner that, as Mr. Evans shows, he was continually quoting some of his observations, *e.g.*, his notes about the Brent and Barnacle Geese, the Nightjar, the Night Heron, and the Pelican. In the famous " Historia Animalium "—the ornithological part of which* came out in 1555, only a year before its author died—Gesner includes the Solan Goose, but, adhering for the most part to an inconvenient alphabetical arrangement, he puts it after the true Geese, and before the Bustard, which here bears the name " Gustarda," also used by Boece. After quoting William Turner, Gesner continues :—(*Translation.*) " I lately received from a learned Scot those Geese called Solendgens which are longer than tame ones, but not so broad : they lay their eggs on rocks : and with one foot placed upon them (whence perchance the name from *solea*, that is, the sole of the foot, and the Germans also so name them) at length hatch them. Plenty of them are taken at

* Liber III., " De Avium Natura."

the Bass island, near the river Forth, which flows by Edinburgh in Scotland ; nor are they found anywhere else. They go far, even six miles, from the shore. It is their nature that when they see a fresh fish they throw up a former one, and this

SOLAN GOOSE ("HISTORIA ANIMALIUM").

they do very often, and carry the last to their young. Moreover, so many fishes do they throw up that those who form the garrison of the fortress collect the ejected fishes for food. They are easily taken, nor do they drive away their captors."

It is not clear to whom Gesner alludes as Germans, but it is presumably to some author or authors. Apart from the letterpress, one cannot, with all desire to praise, say much for Gesner's artist, for his figure,* which is the earliest attempt at delineating a Solan Goose, is poor, and not without reason did Mathurin Brisson ironically designate it as " icon pessima." On the other hand, some of Gesner's pictures are excellent, considering the date and the circumstances under which they were done, as, for example, that of the Cormorant,† which is one of the best in the book.

Another good one is the Bittern, of which our author gives a very full history, quoting Turner, but there is not much that is original in the rest of his narrative, a few paragraphs of which may be worth translating.

" In Italian it [the Bittern] is called *Trumbono*, from its having the voice of a trumpet, as I think : and it is called the trumpet bird (whether this or another) among the Greeks ; by others *Tarabusso* [bull-roarer], or *Terrabusa* [earth-roarer], especially by those of Ferraria, as if it blows through the earth, for with its beak plunged in the marshy soil it gives forth a terrible noise. I think it is the same as, with diminished voice, they call *aigeron*, that is *ardeola*, for they say that it is rufous. . . . its voice when strained being as great as that of a bull, which may be heard at the distance of half a German mile, that is half an hour's journey : and it is said to be a sign of rain. The inhabitants of our lake Tigur [in Zurich] rejoice when this noise is heard, and promise themselves a fruitful year. . . . The *Ardea stellaris* which I myself have seen was smaller and shorter than the other, whose description we shall subjoin together with its shape : with the same colours all over its body, variegated and choice, after the fashion of the country partridge, or woodcock, russet or somewhat yellow, sprinkled with black spots and all shiny, especially on its back, with legs of a greenish-yellow, with black head, and neck the length of three spans and three fingers : the remainder of its body only three spans long. Its big claw was toothed on one side, the middle toe exceeded the human middle toe by a nail and a half's breadth. Its

* *T.c.*, p. 158.
† P. 132.

body almost as thin as that of a young cock : and its wings
also almost like those of fowls.   It flies away with difficulty
unless it has previously sprung up [*lit.* jumped].   It lays
eggs to the number of eleven or twelve, or fewer.   I saw its
nest interwoven with reeds in a certain lake, with twelve
eggs.*   In colour indeed it is so near that of the reeds, that it
can scarcely be observed when lying among them."

William Harrison.   1577.—William Harrison was a canon
of Windsor, who, among other things, wrote an account of
the birds of England, which is prefixed to "Holinshed's
Chronicles," and which, though short, is from its early
date, very important.   He has a good deal to tell us about
birds generally, particularly about the birds of prey, under
the head of "Hawkes and Rauenous Foules."   After
first describing the Golden Eagle's nest at Castle Dinas
Bran in Denbighshire, originally recorded by John Leland,
the antiquary, he continues :—" I have seen the carren crowes
so cunning also by their own industry of late, that they used
to soar over great rivers (as the Thames, for example), and
suddenly coming down have caught a small fish in their feet
and gone away withall without wetting of their wings.   And
even at this present the aforesaid river is not without some of
them, a thing in my opinion not a little to be wondered at.
We have also ospraies, which breed with us in parks and woods,
whereby the keepers of the same do reap in breeding time no
small commodity : for so soon almost as the young are hatched,
they tie them to the butt ends or ground ends of sundry trees,
where the old ones finding them, do never cease to bring
fish unto them, which the keepers take and eat from them,
and commonly is such as is well fed, or not of the worst sort."†

It would seem that in the Middle Ages the Osprey was
very much commoner in the British Isles than it is at the
present day.   That it was plentiful in England in the sixteenth century is certainly implied by William Turner, to
whom it was probably no unfamiliar sight, although he does
not actually say that he had met with it, contenting himself
with the comment that the Osprey was " a bird much better
known to-day to Englishmen than many who keep fish in

* A nest containing twelve eggs cannot have belonged to a Bittern.
† Edition 1807, Vol. I., p. 582.

M

stews would wish ; for within a short time it bears off every fish."*

In the seventeenth century it was becoming rarer, the introduction of firearms having begun to lessen its numbers. The poet Drayton, whose description of Lincolnshire was published in 1622, speaks of " the Osprey, oft here seen, though seldom here it breeds,"† which does not imply great abundance.

It has been supposed that the Osprey was sometimes tried by falconers, but probably with no success. An Act in the reign of William and Mary prohibiting the taking of salmon by Hauks, Racks, Gins, etc.,‡ has given colour to this idea, but the " Hauk " here alluded to was a kind of fish-trap, and not the bird.§ Mr. Harting, however, has shown that Ospreys were certainly kept by James I. with Cormorants and tame Otters on the Thames at Westminster.||

Various other birds are enumerated by William Harrison, among which are the dotterel or wind, so named from the windy or foolish character which it bore, the pauper [Spoonbill], crane, bitter, bustard, snite, pewet [Black-headed Gull], notte [Knot], oliet or olife [Oystercatcher], dunbird, kite, woodspike and woodnawe [Woodpeckers], ruddock [Robin], washtaile [Wagtail], cheriecracker [?], tiuit ? [Tit], and several more.

Aldrovandus.—There is not a great amount which is original in Aldrovandus's sixteen portly volumes—the " Historia Naturalium " (1599–1603)—a work of compilation stated by Newton to have been mostly printed after the author's death in 1605,¶ and altogether very inferior to that of Gesner, from whom the whole of Aldrovandus's account of the Solan Goose (Tom. ter., liber XIX., ch. xx.) has been appropriated. Aldrovandus gives as many as seven illustrations of the Ruff and Reeve, and of these, one has been discovered by Mr. W. H. Mullens to have been copied from

---

* Evan's translation, p. 37.
† "Poly-Olbion," S. XXV.
‡ This Act is given in Nelson's " Laws Concerning Game," 1751, p. 88.
§ The " New English Dictionary " (Vol. V., p. 131) cites as the earliest use of the word " hawk " in this sense a passage in John Worlidge's " System of Agriculture " (1669), where it is described as a fish trap.
|| " Essays on Sport and Natural History," p. 429.
¶ Three volumes completed by 1603 ("Dict. of Birds," p. 6).

an anonymous pamphlet, printed in England soon after 1586.* The cut, which is quite meritorious, represents in very characteristic fashion, one of a flock of Ruffs, which were "intangled and caught" at Crowley in Lincolnshire. Mr. Mullens is of opinion that in this pamphlet, which was evidently written as a protest against the extravagant fashions of the day, we have the earliest mention of the Ruff as a British bird, together with the first published figure and description of it. The pious John Ray and his pupil Willughby went to see Aldrovandus's collection on their Italian travels and it may be assumed jotted down many memoranda for future use.† This was on February 22nd, 1664, when the former writes of it in his journal : " Among many natural and artificial rarities therein preserved, we took more especial notice of ten volumes of the pictures of plants, and six of birds, beasts and fishes, drawn exactly in colours by the hand."‡ All these volumes may have been laid under contribution for Ray's subsequent works on plants, birds and fishes, for which they would have furnished useful material. Sir Thomas Browne's son was another naturalist, who wrote to his father that he went to see Aldrovandus's collection in 1665.§ Whether these books are still in existence, I have had no means of ascertaining.

It may not be amiss to give the following table of dates, which help to the better understanding of these authors and their writings, while it will be seen from it that Turner was the first of the five to publish.

1510	Caius born.	1564	Gesner died.
1512	Turner ,,	1568	Turner ,,
1516	Gesner ,,	1570	Caius published.
1544	Turner published.	1573	,, died.
1555	Gesner ,,	1595	Muffett wrote.
1555	Belon ,,	1599	Aldrovandus published.

* *See* " British Birds," Mag. XIII., p. 13.

† Aldrovandus probably had a fine collection, which passed to Cospi of Bologna (" Ann. Rept. Museums Association," 1891, p. 34). Gesner also had a museum, which must have contained treasures among its birds, and another collection of mark was that belonging to Kentmann of Dresden *t.c.*, p. 29).

‡ " Travels through the Low Countries," by John Ray, F.R.S., p. 200.

§ Browne's " Works," (Wilkin's edn., Vol. I., p. 89).

CHAPTER XI.

THE CRANE, BUSTARD, SPOONBILL AND BITTERN.

The Status of the Crane* in the British Isles.—We have
now carried these Annals through sixteen centuries, not without
some profit, I hope, and before proceeding any further it is
proposed to make a digression, · there being two or three
species which it may not be amiss to treat separately, even
though it may involve a little repetition, and conspicuously
among them stands the Crane, so intimately associated with
the pleasures of sport in the Middle Ages.   We have already
quoted such allusions to the Crane in the thirteenth and
fourteenth centuries as came to hand, and to some extent the
same ground has been gone over by Mr. J. E. Harting,† so
on that head no more need be said.   Nor need we again
refer to the finding of its bones : the fact of their having
been dug up in a semi-fossilised state in sundry parts of
the kingdom, which were doubtless once fenland, proves
that the Crane must have been a tolerably common bird.   As
regards the fifteenth century, the Crane was still pretty
plentiful, but probably more so as a winter visitor than as a
breeder.   It will be remembered that it was in the month of
September that two hundred and four Cranes were commanded
in 1465 for the great Neville banquet (*supra*, p. 87).   Cranes
were a festival dish in high favour,‡ and from their large size
even more so than Herons, so long as they were procurable,
but it is hardly likely that 204 were actually brought to table.
Such an order, with many other birds besides, would have

---

* *Grus communis*, Bech.

† The " Field," Dec. 23rd, 1882. There is an entry of fourpence in
the Countess of Leicester's Roll (*antea*, p. 50), 1265, paid to a boy for
seeking a Crane, *gruem in puteo*, but Mr. A. H. Evans tells me that this does
not mean in a well, as has been supposed, but in a spring, or marsh.
In the ancient Account Rolls of the Abbey of Durham, printed for the
Surtees Society (1898), entries of Cranes occur in 1312, 1358, 1375 and 1390.

‡ One of the earliest articles in " Archaeologia " is " A Dissertation
on the Crane as a Dish " (" Arch.," 1773, p. 171).

been very difficult of execution, and more than the fowlers of England could supply. For the sixteenth century it is to William Turner's writings that we chiefly look for information concerning the Crane, and the same may be said of many other species, regarding which this talented man has left invaluable notes behind him. Turner has been often quoted on the subject of the Crane, and perhaps too much stress has been laid on his remarks. What he says is : " Cranes, moreover, breed in England in marshy places. I myself have very often seen their pipers [young ones], though some people born away from England urge that this is false." * He appears to have written to Gesner to the same effect,† and the passage is copied by Aldrovandus ‡

Turner's expression " very often seen " in the " Avium Praecipuarum . . . historia" is explicit, and admits of no denial. Young Cranes, which soon learn to use their legs, may have been caught by countrymen and brought into Cambridge. That they were sometimes kept as pets is indicated, as Mr. Harting points out in his valuable essay, by an inventory of the chattels of Thomas Kebeel § in 1500, where three live Cranes are valued at five shillings,‖ perchance some which had been taken when young in the fens. In the same way Turner, in some of his botanical rambles, when he was a student, may have come across them. Although no one doubts Turner's word, there is only one witness who is able to support it, for Dr. Kay, who could have given some confirmation, says nothing. This witness is Dr. Thomas Muffett, or Moffet, a learned physician who wrote about 1595. In his " Health's Improvement "¶ Muffett states that " Cranes breed, as old Dr. Turner wrote to Gesner, not only in the northern countries, but also in our English fens."

It remains doubtful whether Muffett had any independent knowledge on the subject, or whether he was merely quoting Turner, whose work he had doubtless seen.

* Evans's edn., p. 97.
† See " Historia Animalium."
‡ Liber III., p. 511.
§ or Kebel.
‖ " Gentleman's Magazine," 1768, p. 259.
¶ For the loan of which I am indebted to Mr. H. S. Gladstone: for a life of Muffett see " British Birds," Mag., V., p. 262.

When Cranes were thus breeding in the fens of Cambridgeshire, there can be little doubt that some also mated in the
marshes surrounding what are now known as the Broads
of Norfolk, as well as in the tract near Lynn which was called
Marshland, and in the fens of South Lincolnshire. Proof
of the first supposition regarding the Broads has been
discovered by Mr. J. C. Tingey in the Chamberlain's accounts
of Norwich, where he has found an entry of a payment in
June, 1542, to one Notyngham of Hickling of five shillings
for a young Crane, and fourpence for the carriage of it to
Norwich.* As to what parts of England were inhabited by
Cranes besides Cambridgeshire, Norfolk and Lincolnshire, we
have unfortunately little information, but from the habits of
the bird it must have been strictly dependent on fen country.
As regards Wales, there is the evidence of George Owen of
Henlys † that the Crane was a breeder in Pembrokeshire
in the sixteenth century, and that it was also common there
long before that time is made tolerably certain by old laws in
the possession of the Welsh school.‡

As early as the time of K'ng John the Crane was a
favourite quarry for the Falcons of royalty, and there seems
to have been no difficulty in coming across them. When the
King had no inclination to go sporting, safe-conducts were
granted at Westminster to fowlers to proceed to divers parts
of the kingdom for the purpose of catching Cranes and other
birds,§ and in this way the palace was supplied with what
was then considered to be game of prime quality. Very
likely Herons were sometimes made to do duty for Cranes,
yet it cannot be doubted that Cranes were still tolerably

* *See* T. Southwell " On the Breeding of the Crane in East Anglia "
(" Norwich Naturalists' Trans.," VII., p. 168).

† *See* Owen's " Description of Pembrokeshire " in the " Cymmrodorion
Record Series " (1892, No. 1, p. 131), edited by Mr. Henry Owen of Poyston,
from which considerable extracts were given in the " Zoologist " (1895, p. 245).
There is at least one modern occurrence of the Crane in Wales, and that
was also in Pembrokeshire, April 28th, 1893, but the notification of two
in Carliganshire in May, 1696 (" The Philosophical Transactions," V., p. 33),
must be dismissed as doubtful.

‡ The Master of the Hawks was to be honoured with three presents the
day his Hawk kills one of these three birds : a Bittern, a Crane, or a Heron.
" The Ancient Laws of Cambria," translated by William Probert, 1823
(p. 100).

§ " Calendar of Patent Rolls, 33, Edward I." (pt. I., p. 321).

abundant in districts suited to their habits, and these districts would be known to the falconers.

Protection for Crane's Eggs.—But a change was soon to come, and of this we get a decided hint in the Act of 1534, passed under Henry VIII., who was a keen falconer, and had an eye for any birds which afforded good sport.

Act of 1534.

25 Henry VIII., Cap. XI.

An Act to avoid destruction of Wild-fowl.

Section 4 prohibits the taking of the eggs of any kind of Wild-fowl from the 1st of March [1533], and the last day of June, and so on yearly, under pain of imprisonment, besides having to forfeit for every egg of any Crane or Bustard twenty pence, of a Bittour (Bittern), Heronne, or Shouelard (Spoonbill) eightpence, and for every egg of Mallard, Teal or any other wild-fowl, except Crows, Ravens, Bosardes (Buzzards) and other fowl not used to be eaten, a penny.*

Unfortunately this Act protected the eggs only, and not the birds which laid them, an oversight which, as Professor Newton is at pains to point out,† was fatal, yet that its intention was good cannot be doubted.

Gradually, as guns and gunpowder came into use, the days of the Crane were numbered. It was natural for men to wish to try the new weapon on the largest bird in the land, especially as in this case it would fetch a good price for eating ; accordingly what the crossbow and its metal bolts failed to do, the gun soon accomplished. The Crane from its great size was readily discovered : it had no means of concealment, it was commoner than the Bustard, and less difficult of approach. Moreover, the fact that, like the Bustard, it was a ground breeder would go against it, and in the end be certainly fatal to its continuance. Its eggs were only two in number, and the nest rather easy to discover,‡ while the young ones, although

---

* A part of this Act, which was found to be too oppressive, was, it is stated, repealed in 1550, but not that portion which prohibited the taking of eggs.

† " Dictionary of Birds," p. 226.

‡ In Spain the old Cranes form tracks to their nests like a cattle path (" Ornithology of the Straits of Gibraltar," p. 179).

they quickly learnt to use their legs, could be sometimes caught. Such as did not fall victims in one way or another, before long found themselves too much harried to remain in England, and accordingly when the migratory season came round, experience taught the survivors not to return.   Quickly, then, the Crane's loud trumpet, which was to the peasants of that wide marshland tract, which included the " Great Bedford Level," one of the heralds of spring, ceased to be heard.   But the remembrance of the stately Crane, as the poet Drayton aptly terms it, could not fade away from their minds.   Its memory remained, and it is significant of this that there were, long afterwards, taverns to be seen which exposed a signboard bearing as an emblem—The Three Cranes.*   The actual date at which the Crane left off breeding in the British Isles can never be fixed, but that it had entirely ceased to do so before 1700 there is every reason to believe ; yet it is true there are some Lincolnshire Fen laws, which Pishey Thompson cites in his " Boston and The Hundred of Skirbeck " (p. 368), which protected the eggs of Swans and Cranes as recently as 1780.

The Crane as a Winter and Spring Visitant.—Putting the question of breeding aside for the present, we come next to the second phase of the Crane's history, viz., its status in Britain as a winter and spring visitant, but apparently less common in autumn : this phase of its career may be judged to have exceeded a century, roughly from 1650 to 1750.   After that the Crane seems to have bequeathed its name to the Heron, which was the bird that it most resembled,† and to have become, what it is at the present

---

* Larwood and Hotten particularly allude to a house of that name in Thames Street, London, which was known and frequented in the sixteenth century (" History of Signboards," p. 204).   *See* also Harben's " Dictionary of London " (pp. 495, 577) ; at the present time there are, according to Harben, four Crane courts in the Metropolis, including the court in Fleet Street, which was burnt in the great conflagration of 1666.

† Mr. Swann is of opinion that " The numerous place-names derived from Crane refer obviously in most cases to the Heron " (" Dictionary of English and Folk-names," p. 62).   Thus Cranshaws Castle in Berwickshire may have earned its name from the young Herons which were to be had there, then perhaps known to the country people as Craneseughs or Craneshaws, but " shaw " also sometimes means a wood.   In Norfolk we have Cranwick parish and Cranworth, the prefix in both cases being Anglo-Saxon (*see* Munford's " Derivation of the Names of Towns and Villages," p. 90), so in this case, the names are more likely to have reference to Cranes than to Herons.

day, merely a rare and occasional migrant driven to the British Isles by accidental circumstances. This is the only character which Thomas Pennant is able to give it in his " British Zoology," in 1768.* Here the Crane is included in the appendix, with the comment that the inhabitants of Lincolnshire and Cambridgeshire appeared to be scarcely acquainted with it. " We therefore conclude," adds Pennant, " that these birds have forsaken our island."

Albin, perhaps less well informed than Pennant, considered it more common,† but in 1787 John Latham, while referring to its ancient abundance, had only three modern occurrences to give his readers, all evidently migrants.‡

Going back to the sixteenth century there are a good many scattered records to be dealt with, forming enough materials to build up quite a tolerable history of this bird. The first mention to hand is in 1502, when twelve pence was paid on October 6th, as appears from the " Privy Purse Expenses of Elizabeth of York " (p. 51), to a servant for bringing the Queen a Crane. Presumably it was for eating; other items are for " an hert," " woodcokkes," " a present of byrdes," and some " quayles," all of which were for the table.

The next allusion to be cited is one in 1512, contained in the Regulations of the Household of the Earl of Northumberland, where, as was to be expected, the Crane is set down as being a proper and obtainable viand, but by implication a winter one :—

> " Cranys must be hadde at Cristymas ande outher Principall Feists. . . ."

Attention has already been drawn to the references to Cranes in the Norfolk Accounts of le Straunge, where we have no less than twenty-eight entries, all of them with one exception in the autumn and winter (*supra*, p. 130). The Crane is named three times in the Middleton (Notts.) Accounts. Here two of the entries are particularly noteworthy, because they have reference to captures in the spring, the first time being in April, 1522, and the second in June, 1523,

---

* 8vo ed., Vol. II., p. 629.

† " Natural History of Birds," II., p. 60.

‡ " General Synopsis of Birds," Suppl., p. 298.

a date when Cranes would be nesting.* On the first occasion as many as eight Cranes are brought in (p. 340), which sounds as if the fowlers had caught a party on migration : on the second the number is not stated, but may have been considerable, as it was " a gaynste Maystrys Alyse weddyng " in the beginning of June (p. 357).

In 1525 the Duke of Norfolk built himself a palace at Kenninghall in Norfolk, and from the " Expencys of howshould " Mr. R. Houlett has drawn up a tolerable list of fish, birds and minor provisions which were consumed there.† The Crane, however, is only twice mentioned, and in neither case is the month given.

In 1526, at a banquet given by Sir John Nevile in Yorkshire, nine Cranes were provided at a cost of thirty shillings, and at another banquet in 1530 twelve more were had at three shillings and fourpence each,‡ but the month of the year is not recorded. There is no reason for supposing that these were not real Cranes ; Heron-sewes and " bytters " are mentioned as well.

When the French Ambassadors came to England in 1528, the citizens of London presented them *inter alia* with twelve Cranes, twelve Pheasants and thirty-six Partridges.§ The time of the year was, it appears, October, and that the birds were real Cranes, and not Herons, which would have been a gift of less consequence, is most probable. In 1531 the first entry of a Crane which Mr. Tingey has traced occurs in the Norwich City Accounts, and is followed by other records of these large birds being brought for festival occasions.|| In 1530 and 1532 Eltham Palace in Kent was supplied with two Cranes in October, and four Cranes and two Bustards in January.¶ Between 1537 and 1554 the Registers of Lincoln record the presentation to the Duke of

---

* " Report on the Manuscripts of Lord Middleton " (Historical Man. Comn., 1911, pp. 340, 357). What adds considerably to these accounts is the statement in the introduction that they were partly arranged in bundles, some of which I have had the privilege of seeing, by Francis Willughby and John Ray.

† " Norfolk Archæology," XV., pp. 57, 58.

‡ " The Forme of Cury," by Samuel Pegge [the elder], 1780, pp. 165, 183.

§ " Hall's Chronicle," edition 1809, p. 733.

|| " Privy Purse Expenses of Henry the Eighth," pp. 85, 187, 188.

¶ *Cf.* " Norwich Naturalists' Trans.," Vol. VII., p. 163.

Norfolk and others of twelve Cranes,* to be eaten on special occasions, but no exact dates are given.

In 1555 Sir William Dugdale tells us seven Cranes were received as contributions from different people† at the dinners which took place in October at the elaborate festivities of the Serjeants of the Inner Temple, in London. Thirty-six Herons and Bitterns were also brought to table.

In 1567 no less than nine Cranes, all killed in November, with five Herons and sixteen Bitterns, were sent from Norfolk for a wedding-feast.‡ The bride was Elizabeth More of Loseley, near Guildford, and the ceremony and subsequent feasting took place in the Blackfriars, London. Also at the same time there were forwarded by the donor, who was a Mr. Balam, twenty-two Godwits—probably Black-tailed Godwits—fifty-two Knots and ninety Stints; all these birds came out of Marshland, the flat tract between Wisbech and Lynn, and are as likely to have been killed in Cambridgeshire as in Norfolk.

On the occasion of Queen Elizabeth's visit to Kirtlinge in Cambridgeshire, on the 1st of September, 1577, only one Crane was provided for her entertainment, as against seventy Bitterns, twenty-eight young Herons, and twelve Spoonbills. The time of year—September—was not favourable for procuring Cranes, we may assume, or there would have been more. This may end the list of Cranes so far as England is concerned, although it is likely enough that research could add a few more records. But the eleven passages which have been called in evidence imply that the Crane was no rare bird.

Cranes in Scotland and Ireland.—In Scotland there are but few sixteenth and seventeenth century records of the Crane. In 1503 some live Cranes were brought to James IV., when in Dumfriesshire, but possibly, as Mr. H. Gladstone suggests, they were only Herons, which were often called Cranes.§ In the Household Accounts of James V., " Excerpta E Libris Domicilii Domini Jacobi Quinti, MDXXV.—MDXXXIII., ‖ we find about six and twenty

* " Hist. MSS. Com." XIV. Report. app. : VIII., pp. 35, 41, 46, 48.
† " Origines Judiciales," pp. 132-135.
‡ " Archaeologia," XXXVI., p. 36.
§ " Birds of Dumfriesshire," p. 359.
‖ Contained in " The Proceedings of the Bannatyne Club," Vol. LIV.

references to the Crane, the correctness of all of which may
be accepted, as the Heron is always separately named. The
months in which the entries come may be specified : two are
in January, two in February, as many as seven in April and
four in May, while for the autumn there are four in October,
five in November and two in December. Although four
Cranes were taken in May and one as late as May 30th, it
cannot be said that there is anything here which proves
breeding. Hector Boece (1526) does not name the Crane,
which is perhaps surprising, but in 1529 the great bird appears
among the good things at the Earl of Atholl's feast. In
the Rental of Cupar Abbey, a Cistercian monastery in Angus,
printed for the Grampian Club—an antiquarian society
which no longer survives—there are (as I am informed by
Mr. R. K. Hannay) agreements, dated 1541 and 1547, with
a fowler, that he shall have five shillings for each Crane and
Swan,* a price which in 1550 and 1554 was raised to six
shillings and eightpence.†

The former figure agrees very well with a Scotch Act
of 1551, fixing the prices of wild-fowl, in which the Crane
is rated at five shillings.‡

The above are not quite all the allusions to the Crane
in Scotland, for in 1578 John Leslie, Bishop of Ross, who wrote
a history of Scotland, speaks of " Grues plurimi, sicut et

* Vol. II., pp. 13, 56.
† Vol. II., pp. 241, 254.
‡ In this Act the Heron is not mentioned, but five shillings seems too
high for a Common Heron. As the Act is little known, a copy of it, from
" The Laws and Acts of Parliament of Scotland," 1682 (Part 1, p. 276), with
which Mr. Quinton has obliged me, may be here inserted. It is entitled,
" Of the prices of wild and tame meates."
    " Item it is statute and ordained . . . That is to say, in The first, the
Cran five shillings : The Swan five shillings : The Wild Guse of the great
kind twa shillinges : The claik [Barnacle Goose], quink [Golden-eye Duck]
& rute [Brent Goose], the price of the peece, auchteene pennies. Item the
Plover & small mure fowle, price of the peece, foure pennies : The Black
Cock and gray-Hen, price of the peece sex pennies : the dousane of Powtes
[young Moorfowl] twelve pennies. Item the Quhaip [Curlew] sex pennies.
Item the Cunning [Rabbit] ij shillings unto the feast of Fastens-evin nixt
to cum, and fra Thine fourth XII pennies. Item the Lapron [young Rabbit]
twa pennies. Item, the Woodde Cocke, foure pennies. Item, the dousane
of Lavorockes [Sky Larks] and uthers small birdes, the price of the dousane,
foure pennies. Item, the Snipe and quailzie [Quail], price of the peece
twa pennies. Item, the tame-guse xvj pennies. Item, the capone, twelve
pennies. Item, the Hen and pultrie, aucht pennies. Item, the chicken,
foure pennies. Item, the gryse, auchteene pennies."

ardeæ " as if he supposed them to be equally common.
There is nothing to show that Cranes have ever bred in
Scotland, but this may be because written records of North
Britain are so few.

In Ireland the Crane is supposed to have been formerly
common, but Mr. Ussher is unable to cite any documents
to prove it, between the time of Giraldus (*supra*, p. 46), whose
testimony is not very conclusive, and 1739.* The country
is suitable for Cranes, which still visit Ireland from time to
time as migrants, and no more than that can be said.†

The Status of the Great Bustard ‡ in the British Isles.—
The early status of the Great Bustard as an inhabitant
of England is somewhat clouded and, much as we should
like to fathom the obscurity of the past, it cannot be
done. In one respect its history differs from that of the
Crane, for the Crane was known from the earliest times,
and is often cited by name in historical documents ; but not
so the Bustard, which had no Saxon appellation and does not
come into early British history. Some there are who have
thought, with the late Mr. Howard Saunders, that it inhabited
all the undulating plains and wolds from the British Channel
to the Firth of Forth,§ but is there really enough evidence
to warrant such a conclusion ? To begin with, we find an
echo of its former existence in Yorkshire in the family name

* *Cf.* " Birds of Ireland," p. 246.

† Although it does not pertain to the sixteenth century, one is tempted
to recall a remark of Sir Thomas Browne, made by him about 1662, viz.,
that Cranes were often to be seen in Norfolk in hard winters. What
Willughby and Ray have to tell on the matter fourteen years later is also
rather important. In the first or Latin edition of their " Ornithologia " (1676),
p. 201), these authors say :—
" Sæpissime ad nos commeant, suntque in palustribus agri Lincolniensis
& Cantabrigiensis æstivo tempore magni eorum greges."
But in the English edition, issued two years after the " Ornithologia,"
Ray omits the important words " æstivo tempore," and says : " whether or
no they breed in England I cannot certainly determine either of my own
knowledge or from the relation of any credible person."
In the " Synopsis Methodica Avium," which was published in 1713,
five years after Ray's death, the words " hyberno tempore " are substituted
for " æstivo tempore."

‡ *Otis tarda*, Lin.

§ *See* Yarrell's " British Birds," Vol. III., p. 195.

of Bustard, and that so long ago as 1391.* Perhaps this does not go for a great deal, but it is not improbable that the name came from the bird, but, even if it did, this neither proves nor disproves its abundance. Again, we have Sir William Dugdale giving Busterdesdole (*i.e.*, Bustard's boundary) and Bustard's lode (*i.e.*, watercourse), in his " History of Imbanking," as ancient names near King's Lynn in Norfolk.†

The Bustard is one of the thirty birds enumerated in 1413 in the " Boke of Keruynge," and it is named among the cooking recipes in John Russell's rhyming " Boke of Nurture " (*circa* 1450) :—

" Pecok, Stork, Bustarde and Shovellewre,
Ye must unlace them in the plite [manner] of the crane
    prest and pure . . . "

These allusions, which may be taken as applying to the British bird, show that it was appreciated for eating in spite of its somewhat rank smell, which gave it a bad name with some. We have already enumerated the partially unpublished records of Bustards in the le Straunge Accounts, one of them being as early as 1520, and on that head no more need be said, although they are of great value, going back, as they do, nearly four hundred years.‡ Tantalising in his brevity, Dr. Kay does not allude to the Bustard at all, and William Harrison merely sets down its name without remark, while we may conclude that Turner had not personally met with it in England, although possibly he had seen it in Germany. Turner calls it a Bustard or Bistard,§ the latter spelling, which is obsolete, being the same used by Christopher Merrett.‖

It can hardly be said that before 1555 the Great Bustard had its place as a British species recognised. About that time appeared Conrad Gesner's well-prepared folios, from which the study of ornithology received a great impulse,

---

* *See* " Testamenta Eboracensis," Part I., p. 153. Also in Fines Roll, 16 Edward II. (1323).

† Pp. 244, 286.

‡ As pointed out by Dr. Ticehurst (p. 130), there is a record for Kent of a Bustard in 1480.

§ Evans's edn., p. 167

‖ A century later. *See* " Pinax," p. 173.

and in the third book of the " Historia Animalium "—*qui est de Auium natura*—the Bustard is described twice over. First in the character of a Scotch bird (p. 159), but Gesner's discrimination was too acute not to realise that the bird known to Hector Boece as "a Gustard" was the same as the " Trapp " of the Germans. Of this he gives a very good figure (of a female, p. 468), accompanied by a rather lengthy description, in the course of which, referring to England, Gesner observes :—" Trappos permultos in Anglia esse audio, & locis gaudere aquosis [errore]. Sylvaticus tardam avem in aqua degere scribit. In segetibus [corn-fields] sæpe inveniuntur . . . . . ." (p. 470).

The statement here quoted, that there were very many Bustards—" Trappos permultos "—in England, is somewhat remarkable. Mr. W. H. Mullens has pointed out that the same is repeated by Aldrovandus in his Liber XII., but it must be remembered that the " Historia Naturalium " is little more than a compilation. Mr. Mullens thinks it hardly likely that this information was communicated by William Turner, although Turner is the only Englishman known to have been in regular correspondence with Gesner. Aldrovandus's words translated are : " I hear that there is an abundance of Bustards [copiam Otidum] in England from those who have travelled through that island."

This is not exactly what Gesner says, yet it is probably borrowed from him. Gesner goes on to say, on the authority of one Sylvaticus, that Bustards were taken with dogs and falcons, and that their feathers were in request with fishermen for dressing flies. In Sylvaticus, Mr. Mullens recognises Matthæus Silvaticus of Salerno in Italy,* so we may presume that this latter passage is not to apply to British Bustards.

Dr. Thomas Muffett, whose " Health's Improvement " is supposed to have been written in 1595, gives, under the heading of Tardæ, quite a long space to the merits of the " Bistards or Bustards."†

" In the summer towards the ripening of the corn," he says, possibly referring to Salisbury Plain at the time when he lived at Wilton in Wiltshire, " I have seen half a dozen

* The author of a medical work in 1474.
† Edition 1655, p. 91.

of them lie in a wheat field, fatting themselves (as a Deer will doe) with ease and eating; whereupon they grow sometimes to such bigness, that one of them weigheth almost fourteen pounds.* Now as they are of an extraordinary bulk, so likewise are they of rare nourishment. . . ."

In spite of Gesner's unknown correspondent, we must judge the Great Bustard never to have been a very common species in the British Isles. It required wide extents of open country, not timbered, and there cannot have been a great many such districts available apart from the plains in Cambridgeshire, Suffolk, and Wiltshire. On Salisbury Plain, and also on the wolds of Lincolnshire, and the still more extensive high grounds of Yorkshire, and on the downs of Sussex, small droves of Bustards, in companies of ten or a dozen, lived and flourished for a long time. But although they maintained their existence it was far from being in unmolested retirement, even at the period of which we are writing.†

There is no indication of the Bustard having ever been a native of either Wales or Ireland, while in Scotland only one locality was known, and that in the extreme south, the Mers (or border district) of Lothian, and here Boece says they were few in number. Boece spells the name with a G —Gustard, and Muffett Gusetard—but that was merely the Scotch way of pronouncing it. The only other Scotch authority for the Great Bustard is the " Prodromus Historiæ Naturalis " (1684) of Sir Robert Sibbald, where we read :

" Otis, the slow bird of Aldrovandus. This seems to be that which is called Gustard by our writers. In size it is fully equal to a turkey. It is said to frequent Merse, and I was recently informed that one had been seen in East Lothian not long since." (*Translation.*)‡

---

* Old males weigh much more than this.

† The last of the native race—or very nearly the last—was shot at Lexham in Norfolk, in May, 1838, and was, I believe, seen in the flesh by my father, who, in a note made at the time, remarks that the plumage was much worn on the back as if the bird had missed its moult (" Zoologist," S.S., p. 4724). As it was not likely to have found a mate there could have been small chance of its breeding, even if it had been spared. In 1876 I saw a migrant in February at Hockwold in the same county.

‡ As given by Mr. Mullens in " British Birds," Mag., VI., p. 41, and compared with a MS. translation in the possession of Mr. H. S. Gladstone.

The Status of the Spoonbill.*—The former status of the Spoonbill in England presents a problem which, however considered, must cause some regret for the loss of such a fine resident. There is besides the reflection that if the Spoonbill be lost, other good species, as for instance the Night-Heron, may have gone, of which we have now no knowledge. It is now well known that Spoonbills, or Shovellers (shouelard) as they were called, must have bred in heronries, or by themselves, in some of the more southern English counties, a fact to which Mr. J. E. Harting was the first to draw public attention. In addition to breeding in Sussex and Middlesex, as shown by Mr. Harting, and probably also in Kent, Spoonbills nested in the thirteenth and fourteenth centuries, and doubtless much later, in at least three spots in Norfolk (*supra*, p. 58), to which may be added Feltwell, where a fen on the Little Ouse was known as Poppylot.† Also we know that in the sixteenth century they bred somewhere near Hunstanton, as shown in the ninth chapter (*supra*, p. 131), as well as at Claxton and Reedham on the Yare. In the seventeenth century we have it on the authority of Sir Thomas Browne that there were Spoonbills at the mouth of the Orwell at Trimley in Suffolk. The position of all these places can be best explained by marking them on a map of Norfolk and Suffolk (p. 178).

Again there is the best of reasons for believing, on the trustworthy evidence of George Owen, who lived in the Elizabethan age, that Spoonbills bred in at least one place in Wales, viz., in Pembrokeshire.‡ Turning to the legislation of the sixteenth century, there is a good deal to be elicited about Spoonbills, implying breeding in the provinces. First we have the Act of 1534 (*supra*, p. 167) in which a fine of eightpence an egg is imposed on robbers of the nests of the Bittour, Heronne and Shouelard. As " Shouelard " here

---

* *Platalea leucorodia*, Lin.

† Professor Newton (Norwich Nat. Trans., Vol. VI., p. 159). The word " Popeler " occurs at least three times as a surname in Yorkshire poll-tax returns of the fourteenth century (" Dictionary of English and Welsh Surnames " by C. Bardsley), which is not surprising, for not many names of birds have escaped usage among people at one time or another.

‡ " Cymmrodorion Record Series," p. 131. I am indebted to the Editor for Part I.

clearly means the Spoonbill, this law would almost prove, if
no other evidence were forthcoming, that it was looked
upon as a regular breeder in England.   Although in this Act
the Spoonbill is called a " Shouelard," in a later Act (1564,

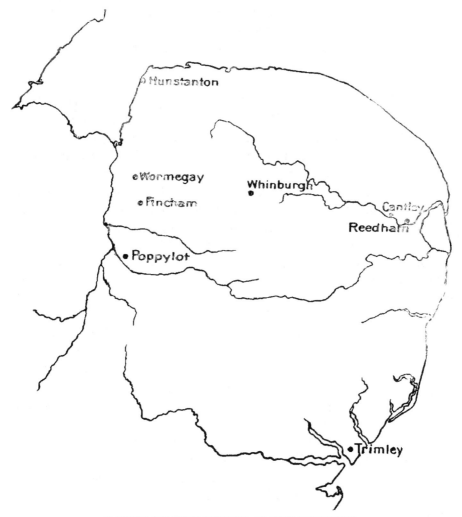

FORMER NESTING HAUNTS OF THE SPOONBILL.

8 Elizabeth, c. 15), intended for the compulsory destruction
of Rooks, a second name seems to be used.   Here a saving
clause is inserted protecting " Herons, Egrytes, Paupers,
Swannes or Shovelers " from disturbance.   Probably Pauper
is a variant of Popeler, the intention being to make the working
of the Act more certain by giving both the mediæval names

of the Spoonbill, whereby no loophole was left for an offender to escape his fine.

In William Harrison's list of birds in 1577 (*supra*, p. 162) we get a slightly different spelling—Pawper. Harrison says: " As for egrets, pawpers, and such like, they are dailie brought unto us from beyond the sea, as if all the foule of our countrie could not suffice to satisfie our delicate appetites."* Two other spellings in old MSS., both of the fifteenth century, have been discovered by Mr. John Hodgkin, as I learn from Mr. Mullens. From a list of carvers' terms he quotes the expression " Papyr ys lowryde [lurid]," while in the menu of a feast at the wedding of the Earl of Devonshire, he finds the word " Poper," which comes next to " Mawlard de la Ryner." Mr. Hodgkin suggests that the Goose is the bird here alluded to, in support of which he refers to the Italian name of " Papero," for a green goose, or a gosling. (" Notes and Queries," March 18th, 1911, p. 216. Reference supplied by Mr. Mullens.) In the passage quoted, it hardly seems from the context as if the Goose could have been intended. A third variation of the name spelled " Popard " (1413) is cited in " The New English Dictionary," but the editors refrain from attributing it to any particular species.

To see how various the spellings of birds' names were, one has only to turn to the " Promptorium Parvulorum," an English-Latin Dictionary of the fifteenth century.† Here we have the spellings popler, popelere and poplerd, as well as schovelerd, sehoveler, scholarde and schoues bec, while in the nearly contemporary " Boke of Nurture " (1452) the latter name is written shovellewre and shovelere, which half a century later the poet Drayton (1613)‡ abbreviates to shouler. In the " Fantasticks " of Nicholas Breton (1626) there is the further alteration to shoulard.

As regards the derivation of the name Popelar or Popler, Professor Newton pronounces it to be a corruption of Lopeler, —*i.e.*, Lepelar Dutch, Lepler German, with which Mr. Harting agrees.§ The word means a spoon or a shovel, and bears

---

* " Holinshed's Chronicles," Bk. III., ch. II.
† Said to have been composed about 1440 by a friar of King's Lynn.
‡ In Song XXV., line 353, of the "Poly-Olbion."
§ *See* Stevenson's " Birds of Norfolk," Vol. III., p. 135, and " Handbook of British Birds," 2nd ed., p. 210.

reference to the peculiar shape of the Spoonbill's beak, having in fact the same signification as shouelard, and other cognate names in use in Europe.

Dean Turner was apparently not aware of Spoonbills breeding in England, but there really is nothing remarkable in his reticence on this point. At the same time his incidental reference to the Spoonbill in identifying the Albardcola of Aristotle,* is not suggestive of its being very rare in this country. But it certainly is very strange that the circumstance of Spoonbills breeding, or having once bred, in England was unknown at a much later date to two such careful collectors of facts as Francis Willughby and John Ray (to say nothing of Merrett), both of whom were in correspondence with Sir Thomas Browne, who was quite aware of the fact.

Considering its known range, the Spoonbill is not very likely ever to have bred in Scotland, where Sibbald, writing in 1684, merely says of it : " Huc advolat quandoque," nor is there the slightest evidence of its having nested in Ireland.

Spoonbills and Young Herons considered a Delicacy.— Throughout the records of the sixteenth and seventeenth centuries we get many hints that fish-eating birds, both those frequenting fresh water and those from the shore, were thought worthy of the best tables. Young Solan Geese, which, as Ray said of them, " both smell and taste of herrings," were in high favour, and other birds which we should now think very rank. That Spoonbills were considered not only quite fit for the board, but when young, an equal delicacy with Herons is certain, of which there is plenty of evidence, apart from their protection by legislation. At the same time the Spoon-bill was only a summer visitor, not to be looked for at winter festivities, when the Crane and the Bittern were in season. One passage furnished by Master Robert Laneham deserves to be quoted.† He is treating of the sumptuous entertainment provided for Queen Elizabeth at Kenilworth in Warwickshire in July 1575. Describing the preparations, Laneham

---

* Evans's translation of Turner, p. 39. Turner's remarks are, as usual, repeated by Gesner, from whose pages we judge the Albardeola to have been one of the Egrets.

† " The Progresses and Public Processions of Queen Elizabeth," by J. Nichols, Vol. I., p. 432.

says : " Upon the first payr of posts " of a fair bridge, twenty feet wide and seventy feet long, over which the Queen was to pass " were set too cumly square wyre cages, each a three feet long, too foot wide ; and by in them live bitters, curluz, shoovclarz, hearsheawz, godwitz, and such like dainty byrds, of the presents of *Sylvanus* the god of Food." These birds, together with the fruit with which the second pair of posts were garnished, were no doubt served to the royal party after the pageant, but this, Laneham, who was doorkeeper of the council-chamber, does not tell us.

Although it was the young Spoonbills which were generally eaten, in England at all events, there is a passage in Gesner's " Historia Animalium "—possibly on the authority of Albertus or Turner—which shows that a custom existed of catching older birds on the shore, presumably by netting them. Gesner, who gives a very good plate of the Spoonbill, which he remarks the English call " a schofler vel shouelard," says : " Platea nostra . . . *(translation)* " is taken on the sea-shore in England, and fed in confinement on fish, and the insides of fowls, and other offal from the kitchen."* In another place, relating his experience, he says: " In England I hear that Spoonbills are tamed; at Ferrara in Italy I have seen tame ones, which were fed on kitchen refuse."†

The following recipe for dressing Spoonbills, written by that very learned doctor, Thomas Muffett, about 1595, seems to apply to adult birds, rather than to young ones : " Plateæ Shovelars feed most commonly upon the Sea-coast upon cockles and shell-fish ; being taken home and dieted with new garbage and good meat, they are nothing inferior to fatted gulls." This was high praise. young Black-headed Gulls, well fed on bullock's liver, being in great favour for the table. The native race of Spoonbills has passed away from England, but the regularity with which migrants return in the spring to Breydon Broad in Norfolk, and to one or two spots on the coast of Kent, indicates an inclination to breed with us again. That they would do so in some of our Heronries if they were as well protected here as they have been in Holland, there can be little doubt.

* *Op. cit.*, Liber III , p. 641.
† *Op. cit.*, p. 642.

The Status of the Bittern.*—That in the fifteenth and
sixteenth centuries the Bittern was diffused throughout the
marshes of England, in its double capacity of a breeder
and a winter visitant, admits of no doubt. And, moreover,
that it continued to be common in the seventeenth and
eighteenth centuries, we have abundant evidence in the
literature of the period. The factor which has banished it
from Britain was partly drainage, but still more fatal than
drainage has been the use of the gun. We should like to
know rather more both of its English and Irish distribution,
yet must not complain, seeing that there exists a history of it
in the sixteenth century by a good ornithologist of that day,
William Turner, who has left quite a considerable account
as appears from Mr. A. H. Evans's excellent translation of
the "Avium Praecipuarum . . . historia," from which the
following extracts are quoted.†

"Stellaris," says Turner, taking the name from Aristotle,
"is that kind which Englishmen denominate buttour or
bittour, and the Germans call pittour or rosdom. Now it is
a bird like other Herons in its state of body generally, living
by hunting fishes on the banks of swamps and rivers, very
sluggish and most stupid, so that it can very easily be driven
into nets by the use of a stalking horse." This, however,
was not by any means the employment to which a stalking
horse was usually put in England. That Aristotle was aware
of the Bittern's sluggishness is indicated when he says :
"stellaris piger cognominata . . . . atque, ut cognomen
sonat. iners ociosaque est."   "So far as I remember," continues
Turner," it is nearly of the colour of a Pheasant and the beak
is smeared with mud : it utters brayings like those of an ass.
Of all birds it aims at men's eyes most readily." That it is a
dangerous bird when wounded is well known, but that its beak
should have been smeared with mud must have been an accidental circumstance in the examples which Turner examined.

In another place in this valuable bird-book, when
discussing the identity of Aristotle's *Onocrotalus,* Turner
returns again to the subject of "the loud-sounding lacustrine

* *Botaurus stellaris* (Lin.).

† "Turner on Birds," edited by A. H. Evans, M.A., 1903, pp. xv. and
41, 125, 127.

bird called Buttor by the English, and Pittour or Rosdomm
by the Germans." Some of his experiences, and that of sundry
German friends, whose veracity he is careful to vouch for,
including " a physician much renowned among the men of
Cullen " are then given regarding its habits. " It sits about
the sides of lakes and marshes, where putting its beak into
the water it gives utterance to such a booming as may easily
be heard an Italian mile away. It gorges fishes, and especially
eels most greedily—nor is there any bird, except the Mergus
[Cormorant], that devours more." As is now well known,
this time-honoured legend of the Bittern immersing its beak
—a fable by no means confined to Germany—or inserting it
into a hollow reed, is entirely without foundation.*

Assisted by a professor and the before-mentioned learned
doctor, Turner went to some trouble in dissecting a Bittern,
his chief object being to examine the æsophagus, which is wide
and expansible. He found "the gullet most capacious, and it
uses it in the place of a crop. It has a belly not like that of other
birds, but like that of a dog†; it also is large and capacious."

He further goes on to describe the Bittern's brown
speckled plumage, so imitative of the reeds it lives in, from
which is taken its name of *stellaris*, also the shape of the
bird, and its neck " marvellously thick with plumes," and
finally its " very long claws, for that which serves in birds
the purpose of a heel exceeds an inch and a half in length,
on which account our countrymen use it to pick their teeth and
mount it in silver. The middle toe of either foot, which is
longer than the rest, has a prodigious claw, that is to say,
toothed and serrated, ..."

Among the various names bestowed locally on the Bittern,
most of them onomatopoeic, the first in point of date seems
to be myre dromble or mirdrommel. We find Bartholomæus
Anglicus giving the name rather vaguely, while Turner also
employed it.‡ Literally it means the sluggish bird of the
marshes, but corrupted as it soon became into the shorter
name of miredrum, it signifies the bird which drums or booms.

* One of the first to ridicule it was Sir Thomas Browne, in " Pseudodoxia
Epidemica," ch. XXVII.

† Evans's edn., p. 125. Belon makes the same comparison.

‡ Evans's edn., p. 38.

CHAPTER XII.

SEVENTEENTH CENTURY (1st PART).

The Status of the Black-headed Gull.*—Very different from that of the birds which we have been describing, was the status of our familiar favourite, the Black-headed Gull, which one may suppose to have been always common, although probably never so abundant in Great Britain as now. As it has been clearly shown to be of considerable use to agriculturists by feeding upon their enemies, the wireworm and the larvæ of the crane-fly,† it is to be hoped that it will continue to multiply, and to receive the protection which it deserves. What is known about the distribution of this inland breeding Gull in former times is not much. As in the case of many other birds, we must begin with Turner, for there is nothing earlier, but he fortunately has left us rather a good account of it,‡ though he does not say that he had ever seen a breeding-place. To him, as he watched its graceful flight, this bird was known as the grey gull " a se cob or a see-gull," which came up rivers, the bird " always querulous and full of noise," as it flew round his ship when at anchor. Very descriptive is his sketch, where he likens it to a Daw in size, but goes on to note that its wings are sharper and longer. It may have been on the same great River Thames that John Ray, an Essex man, made its acquaintance, for he remarks especially on the number of them which there were at Gravesend.§ Ray also gives a good description both in his " Ornithology " and in one of his Itineraries.

1. One ancient settlement of Black-headed Gulls, which has had its ups and downs, but which is still fairly well populated, is situated at Scoulton in Norfolk, where there is a mere

---

* *Larus ridibundus* Lin.

† *See* Reports issued in 1907 by the Cumberland County Council, and in 1913 by the Suffolk and Essex Fishery Board (" Zoologist," XVIII., p. 181).

‡ " Turner on Birds," edited by A. H. Evans, pp. 77-79.

§ " The Ornithology," p. 347.

of about seventy acres. How far this historic Gullery goes back is not known, but it may well date to the thirteenth or fourteenth century. At that period the manor of Burdeloss-cum-Scoulton was held by its occupier for the service of being a chief "lardiner" (or larderer) to the King, and Stevenson plausibly suggests that the "service" in this instance may have been the rendering of young Gulls in their season.* Some may think this far-fetched, but we know that from early times young Gulls were considered a delicacy, and further we learn from Sir Thomas Browne that in the seventeenth century they were sent to London from Scoulton mere, a practice which may have been going on a long time. The name of the parish, Scoulton, however, is in no way connected with the Gulls, being from the old Norse *Skule*, which means a shelter, or place of refuge.† Scoulton Mere as far as is known has never dried up, and there is no record of the Gulls having forsaken it, even for a year.

2. Sir Thomas Browne also mentions another Gullery on Horsey Broad, which is much nearer the sea. Writing about 1662, he tells his unknown correspondent‡ that there were at that time "puets in such plentie about Horsey that they [*i.e.*, the country folk] sometimes bring them in carts to Norwich, and sell them at small rates." These two Gulleries, Scoulton and Horsey, are among the oldest of which naturalists have any record in England, but that at Horsey is deserted, the Gulls having shifted to another Broad.§

3. Yet of equal antiquity were the two important Gulleries in Essex and Staffordshire, the former near Harwich, the latter—one of the most inland known—at Norbury. Of the one in Essex there is an excellent description in that curious old volume, Thomas Fuller's "Worthies of England,"‖ which has been often quoted, and it is from this source that the references by Merrett and Charleton to the settlement are borrowed. Samuel Dale, when writing his History of Harwich,

* " Norwich Naturalists' Trans.," Vol. I., 1871-2, p. 25.
† Munford's " Derivation of the Names of Towns and Villages," p. 182.
‡ Possibly Sir Nicholas Bacon.
§ They were breeding there as recently as 1816. (Norwich Nat. Trans., III., 243.)
‖ 1662, p. 317.

must have had this same Gullery in his mind, and had probably visited it, for he comments on the young " Pewits " as being " esteemed proper for the table."[*]   Another witness, hitherto overlooked, who had seen these Gulls at their nests, was the amusing diarist Henry Teonge, a chaplain on board the " Assistance."   Teonge records his visit on July 8th, 1678, to the Gullery : " This day I went with our captaine on shoare to Puett Iland, where wee tooke above 10 douzen of young puetts."[†]   It would, however, seem highly probable that this was not the only settlement of Black-heads at that period in Essex, for Mr. Miller Christy points out that no fewer than three islands on the coast bear the name of Pewit Island.[‡]

4.   Of the Staffordshire Gullery Fuller makes no mention, but we have two excellent accounts, one by John Ray in 1662,[§] and another, which is still more complete, by Robert Plot in 1686.   It was already an ancient settlement when they went to view it, having flourished on the same estate " *ultra hominum memoriam.*"   Plot gives a clever picture of the lake where he saw them breeding, with eight men engaged in driving the young Gulls towards a net, within which are two pens to put them into when caught.[||]   This quaint illustration has been given by Mr. W. H. Mullens in " British Birds," Mag. (Vol. II., p. 220) with a good biography of Plot, and with Mr Witherby's permission is again reproduced.   Unlike the Norfolk Puets, which were sold at small rates, and their eggs used for puddings, the Gulls at Norbury were reckoned of no little consequence, the young ones, after a course of feeding, being worth five shillings a dozen, so that in some years the mere had produced a profit of sixty pounds.

It is difficult to point to the whereabouts of more than these four Black-headed Gulleries in the seventeenth century in England, but what may be called secondary evidence is to be had of at least sixteen others, and these shall be briefly enumerated.

---

[*] " Antiquities of Harwich," 1732, p. 402.
[†] " The Diary of Henry Teonge," 1675-1679, p. 245.
[‡] " The Birds of Essex," p. 267.
[§] P. 218.
[||] " Natural History of Staffordshire," chap. VII

5.   In Gage's "History and Antiquities of Hengrave" in Suffolk, we read under date of July 1574, among a great variety of disbursements, " For iij livers for the puets and the other mewed fowls, vjd.,"* which is suggestive of a Gullery not far off.

6.   The existence of a Gullery near Hunstanton has been already hinted at (*supra*, p. 138).   Mr. R. Gurney tells me there is still a place known as Mow Creek at Brancaster.

7.   While that another was known to Thomas Pennant in south Lincolnshire seems probable.†

8.   That a Gullery flourished at Hornsea Mere in Yorkshire in 1693 is to be inferred from the " Diary of Abraham de la Pryme," as quoted in " The Birds of Yorkshire,"‡ unless the birds were Black Terns.

9.   There was also a Gullery in 1702 between Barnard Castle and Bedale, according to the following entry in Bishop Nicholson's diary :   "Thornton Bridge, thousands of the Blackcap Mews breeding in a moss."§

10.   In a description of Delamere Forest in Cheshire in 1617,‖ we read of " great store of Fish and Fowl in the Mears, Puits or Sea Mawes in the flashes " which conveys the impression of a Gullery.

11.   Time out of mind there has been a settlement of Black-headed Gulls at Pallinsburn in Northumberland, which Mr. Harting believes is traceable as far back as about 1750,¶ but they are not mentioned by Wallis.**

12.   It is pretty evident that Ravenglass in Cumberland held an ancient settlement of Gulls, at least nine allusions to Gulls are met with in the Household Book of Naworth Castle †† which commences in 1612.   Macpherson supposes that there was also a second Gullery which furnished the castle as well.‡‡

* P. 202.
† " British Zoology," II., p. 541.
‡ Vol. II., p. 657.   From the Publications of the Surtees Society (LIV., p. 272).
§ As quoted in " The Birds of Yorkshire," Vol. II., p. 670.
‖ Quoted in Coward's " Fauna of Cheshire," Vol. I., p. 426.
¶ " Field," Feb. 16th, 1884.   Bewick alludes to them in 1804.
** "The Natural History and Antiquities of Northumberland," 1769.
†† Naworth is near Carlisle, and was the seat of Lord William Howard, whose household books have been printed for the Surtees Society.   (Trans., Vol LVIII., p. 90, *et seq.*)
‡‡ " Fauna of Lakeland," by H. A. Macpherson, p. 427.

13. Besides, judging from a passage in the " Antiquities of Westmoreland,"* there must have been a settlement at Helflack Moss, also in Cumberland.

14. According to a quotation in Pennant's " British Zoology "† there was a Gullery near Portsmouth, which produced to its owner forty pounds a year by the sale of " Pewits," and it is suggested by Kelsall and Munn that the site may have been on Pewit (locally Pewty) Island.‡

15. From the Household Book of Hurstmonceux Castle in Sussex (1643 to 1649) we learn that the fare included puets, sea gulls and sea mewes, but§ whether this can be accepted as proof of a Gullery on the manor seems doubtful.

16. Mr. Harting brings forward evidence of an ancient Gullery near Eastbourne in Sussex, but it is not quite clear that the Gulls nesting there were of the present species.||

17. A remark of John Aubrey's points to the presence of a seventeenth century Gullery in Wiltshire : " Sea-mewes. Plentie of them at Colerne-downe ; . . ."—an inland parish.¶

18. In 1602 Richard Carew, a Cornish historian, enumerates Gulls and " Pewets," (by which he does not mean Lapwings), among the birds of Cornwall, and says they breed upon little islands, laying their eggs on the grass.**

Here the list ends, but it is possible that there were Black-headed Gulleries in the north and east of England, and certainly there must have been more in the west than the four here mentioned. One indication of it is that " puets " are repeatedly named among the table provisions for Judges on the Western Circuit, and this, be it noticed, was always in July, just the time at which the young Gulls would have been ripe. Unfortunately these Assize accounts only run from

---

* By J. Nicolson and R. Burn, 1777. (Vol. I., p. 225.)

† " B.Z.," II., p. 543.

‡ " Birds of Hampshire," p. 335.

§ Communicated to the Sussex Archæological Society (Vol. XLVIII.), by T. Barrett Lennard.

|| " Zoologist," 1891. p. 194.

¶ " The Natural History of Wiltshire," edited by J. Britton, p. 65.

** " The Survey of Cornwall," 1811 edn., p. 109.

1596 to 1601,* but in that short time Puets are entered ten
times in the lists of eatables served up to the representatives
of the law.

There is no information to hand for Ireland and Scotland,
but as regards Wales we have John Ray's journal, in which he
notes of Caldey, one of the Pembrokeshire islands, which he and
Willughby visited on June 10th, 1662 : " In one part of this
island the puits and gulls, and sea-swallows' nests lie so thick
that a man can scarce walk but he must needs set his foot
upon them."† Further than this, from Thomas Pennant's
" Tour in Wales," we are able to say that about 1781 and no
doubt earlier, Gulleries of this species flourished at two lakes
in Carnarvonshire, Llyn Llydan and Llyn Conwy.‡ §

The Young Gulls commonly Fatted and Eaten.—Nowadays
people eat the eggs of the Black-headed Gull, although
they are very inferior to those of the real Peewit, but
formerly the young were thought preferable. The mode of
catching them, by driving them into nets before they could
fly has been already alluded to. After that, placed in pens,
and well supplied with bullock's liver, they soon fattened,
and were served at table as wanted, but others elected to
have them fed with corn or curds from the dairy, which may
have imparted a pleasanter flavour. The excellent Thomas
Fuller, who had a high opinion of " puetts " as a table dish, in
giving his experience says : " Being young they consist only
of bones, feathers, and lean flesh, which hath a raw gust of
the sea. But poulterers take them then, and feed them with

* Printed in " The Camden Miscellany," 1858-9 : the accounts enumerate
many birds besides " puets."   Gulls are named thirteen times in the
month of July, probably young Herring Gulls from the rocks, the Great
Bustard comes in once (when the Assizes were held at Salisbury, June 23rd,
1600), Turkeys, under the name of Gannyes twice (pp. 19, 27), Oxen and
Kyne—supposed to be Dunlins—once (p. 26), Partridges and Quails very
often. Black Grouse four times, the Woodcock only twice. Puffins are
associated with fish, while young Herons, esteemed a festival dish, are brought
to the judges under the appellation of Heronshaws, on no less than fourteen
occasions.

† " Memorials of John Ray," p. 175.

‡ "Tour," Vol. II., pp. 140, 180. These places have probably been long
deserted, *see* Forrest's " Fauna of North Wales," p. 380.

§ For a full and excellent account of existing British Gulleries, up to
1884, by Mr. J. E. Harting, *see* the " Field " for that year, pp 165, 204.   The
list has been well carried on by Mr. Robert Gurney in The N. and Norwich
Naturalists' Trans. up to 1919 (Vol. X., p. 416).

gravel and curds, the one to scour, the other to fat them in a fortnight, and their flesh thus recruited is most delicious."*

To the Norwich philosopher, Sir Thomas Browne, ever on the look-out for paradoxes, it seemed inconsistent to eat such birds, and at the same time to refuse other animals whose food was no more impure,† but we have seen that the plan was to diet them, by which means this objection was partly overcome. In the " Health's Improvement " of Dr. Thomas Muffett, the dictum of a physician in the reign of Elizabeth— which refers apparently to this species—inclines to the views of Sir Thomas Browne, declaring that " Sea-mews and Sea-cobs feed upon garbage and fish [and are] thought therefore an unclean and bad meat ; but being fatted (as Gulls used to be) they alter their ill nature, and become good."

Perhaps in no Household accounts are there more refer- ences to Black-headed Gulls than in the entertaining papers of Naworth Castle, before alluded to. Here, as Macpherson shows,‡ we come across allusions to the number of young Gulls brought to the larderer, the dates at which they come in, a carpenter's charges for making a pen, and such entries as " a knife to cut the gull's meat," and again " a crook for the gull house "—this latter for the cook to hook them by the neck when wanted. Two or three times they are brought to the castle with " sampier," i.e., samphire for pickle, or with young " hernsues," likewise a dainty. Puets always made good money, but the highest price paid for them is that given by Thorold Rogers, who says they were retailed to certain Oxford colleges in 1569–70 at 2s. 3d. and 3s. 4d. apiece.§

Names formerly employed for the Black-headed Gull.— It is natural that, bearing the name of *Pewet* or *Puet*, these small Gulls should be commonly supposed by editors of sixteenth and seventeenth century accounts to be Lapwings. By some inadvertency this mistake has even got into the fourth edition of Yarrell's " British Birds,"‖ but it must be

* " The Worthies of England," p. 318.
† " Pseudodoxia Epidemica," chap. XXV.
‡ " Fauna of Lakeland," p. 427.
§ " A History of Agriculture and Prices," Vol. III., pp. 198, 696 and pref.
‖ Vol. III., p. 286.

admitted that the similarity of the names—both of which are derived from the cry of the birds—is very misleading. Although *puit* or *puet*, a name distinctly expressive of their note, was the almost universal appellation in former days for these Gulls, in Kent they were known as *crocards* or *crockers*, literally birds which croaked. We meet with the *crocard* among the good things to be served to Henry VIII. and his court. Thus at Eltham Palace, a favourite resort of the Plantagenet and Tudor monarchs, the table viands in 1531 included *crocards*, as well as *winders* (Wigeon), *runners* (Rails), *grows* (Black Grouse) and *peions* (Pigeons).* Dr. Ticehurst tells us that the name is by no means obsolete† in Kent.

1603. GEORGE OWEN.

We are now in the seventeenth century, and with it a wide field is opened to the enquirer, for ornithology at length begins to find itself upon a firmer footing. Its devotees are still few and far between, but the study of birds is no longer looked upon as beneath the notice of learned men ; in fact, a few of the best brains in England occupied themselves with it more or less, in conjunction with botany. Not the least of this little band were John Ray, Francis Willughby, Ralph Johnson, Jessop of Sheffield, Sir Thomas Browne, and a Welshman named Owen.

George Owen, lord of Kemes, a native of Pembrokeshire, who died in 1613, has left behind him a very singular account of the birds of that county,‡ in which he mentions, among other things, the breeding of the Spoonbill and Crane. Part of his narrative, referring to the abundance of the Woodcock, and the modes of taking them, appears to be worth quoting, and is as follows : " If any easterly wind be aloft," says Owen, in his quaint English, " we shall be sure to have him [*i.e.*, the Woodcock], a fortnight, and sometimes three weeks before Michaelmas, and for plenty it is almost incredible. For when the chief time of haunt is [*i.e.*, the autumn migration], we have more plenty of that kind of fowl than all other sorts laid

* " Archaeologia," 1786, p. 154.
† " Birds of Kent," p. 511.
‡ *Supra*, p. 177. The whole of Owen's relation is given in the " Zoologist " for 1895 (p. 241).

together, the chiefest plenty between Michaelmas and Christmas, and in these three months he visitest most houses [dead
ones, that is, are brought in for eating].   Their chief taking
is in cockeroades in woods, with nets erected up between two
trees, where in cocke shoote time (as it is termed) which is the
twilight, a little after the breaking of the day, and before the
closing of the night, they are taken, sometimes two, three or
four at a fall [of the net].   I have myself oftentimes taken
six at one fall, and in one roade at an evening taken eighteen ;
and it is no strange thing to take a hundred, or six score, in one
wood in twenty-four hours if the haunt be good, and much
more hath been taken ; though not usually. . . .   The plenty
of this, and other kind of fowl hath been such in a hard winter,
as I have heard a gentleman of good sort and credit report that
he had bought in St. David's two Woodcocks, two Snipe, and
certain Teal and Blackbirds for a penny."

If the Woodcocks arrived in Pembrokeshire, as Owen
tells us, a fortnight before Michaelmas, that is about the 15th
of September, their habits must have changed somewhat, as
Welsh sportsmen do not expect them so early as that now, nor
do they any longer come in the same plenty as formerly.

The cocke shoote or cockshot referred to by Owen was a
well-known device, consisting of one or more nets suspended
in some convenient ride, while the cockeroades were the
aforesaid rides or glades, up and down which the Woodcocks
were expected to fly about twilight.   The practice of netting
Woodcocks was so general as to suggest the employment of
the phrase " cock-shut time " as a synonym for twilight as
in the play of " Richard III."

1605.   CAROLUS CLUSIUS.

We next come to consider the labour of a great Flemish
botanist, de l'Escluse, a physician of Arras, whose name is
usually latinised into Clusius.   To criticise Clusius's figure
of the Solan Goose to be found in the " Exoticorum Libri
decem,"* a quaint, but on the whole creditable representation,
would hardly be just.   The block drawn and engraved from
a sketch by Clusius's correspondent, James Plateau, which by
the good offices of Dr. B. D. Jackson I am able to reproduce,

* 1605, Bk. V., Ch. VII., p. 103.

is good for when it was done, though it would be easy to discover faults in its composition. Clusius, who is less known to fame as an ornithologist than as one of the early fathers of botany, gives figures of about fourteen other birds in this volume, including the Dodo and the Great Auk, but they are somewhat rudely done. The Great Auk is wrongly represented in the attitude of a Goose, but the Penguin from Magellan is correctly given an upright attitude, with the remark, " illas autem a pinguedine qui erant præditæ,

SOLAN GOOSE (AFTER CLUSIUS).

Pinguins appelarunt. . . ." This derivation of its name, however, is questionable.*

1613. MICHAEL DRAYTON.

The famous " Poly-Olbion " of Drayton professes to include the animal products of the various counties which it versifies, yet Norfolk and Suffolk are dismissed in scanty fashion, but to the birds of Lincolnshire the poet devotes eighty-eight lines naming thirty-seven species of birds, with which however, he had evidently had no personal acquaintance. With these we have not here to do, but in the first edition of

* *See* Newton's " Dictionary of Birds," p. 703.

the "Poly-Olbion" (1613-22) there is something which calls for remark in connection with the Solan Goose. This is a map of Devonshire, quaintly embellished with symbolical figures, of which one is the Nymph of Lundy standing between Neptune and Amphitrite, with a Gannet on her head and two

Conies at her feet. The accompanying poem to these appropriate symbols runs as follows :—

    " This Lundy is a nymph to idle toys inclin'd,
       And all on pleasure set, doth wholly give her mind
       To see upon her. shore her fowl and conies feed,
       And wantonly to hatch the birds of Ganymede."

    The idea, which is rather fanciful, is supposed to have been derived by the poet from the translator of De la More's

Life of Edward II. A photograph of the figures by Mr. Donald Payler, giving their exact size as in the map, which accompanies the poem, is reproduced.

1633. LORD WILLIAM HOWARD.

Here it may be convenient to refer to certain passages in The Household Books of Lord William Howard of Naworth, a border castle in Cumberland.* On August 25th, 1612, the larderer writes : "My Lord Crainston's man bringing solom-geese, Vs." On August 14th, 1623, he enters : "To the Lord Crainston's man bringing iiij Solamosse geese iij, iiij," and on August 23rd, 1633—ten years later—"To 2 boyes bringing 10 sollemgeese from my Lord Cranston X.s." It is possible that in the second entry, not Gannets, but domestic geese from "the moss," or grasslands of the Solway, are intended. Mr. H. S. Gladstone finds these lands marked as Solanmoss or Sollan Mosse in an old map of 1654, see the "Scottish Naturalist," 1912, p. 90.

1654. ROBERT GORDON.

Sir William Brereton's account of the Bass Rock in 1635, and William Harvey's in 1641, entertaining as they are, having been given at length in another work,† need hardly be repeated, but the story of the Bass by Robert Gordon of Stralloch seems too important to be omitted. It is here quoted from an excellent translation supplied by Mr. H. S. Gladstone, from Blaeu's great Dutch "Geography," to which Gordon contributed.‡

"On the very top [of the Bass Rock in Scotland] is a little chapel, and a remarkably clear spring ; there is barely enough pasture for twenty sheep. The inhabitants have no coals in the winter, but burn for the most part the nests of birds. This island has (besides other birds which the [adjacent] island of May also produces), a quite wonderful bird usually called the Bass Goose, somewhat smaller than a Common Goose, but much fatter, for they live on the Herrings, and have the same taste when eaten. They surpass in fatness

---

* Printed for the Surtees Soc. (Trans. LVIII.).

† "The Gannet : a Bird with a History," pp. 197-201.

‡ "Geographia Blavianae, Volumen Sextum," 1654 (Lib. XII., XIII.).

all other birds, of whatever kind they be. These Geese come
in the month of April and May to this island, and then every-
body must be quiet, but when they have begun to make their
nests they are not frightened at any noise. The people of
Edinburgh sell their feathers (which are nice for making
beds) dearly enough to their neighbours, who pay twenty-
five shillings [Scotch, worth a penny] for one Goose. Each
of these Geese lays one egg, and that at least once in the year.
They place their eggs so cleverly that if anyone takes one out
of the nest, he cannot put it back in the same place. They
do not sit on their eggs like other birds, but set the sole of
their foot on the egg, and thus hatch the young one. While
they are chicks they have ashen-grey feathers, which become
white when they are full grown. They have a long neck,
like the Crane's, and a very sharp beak, as long as our longest
finger, and yellow [? white] in colour. The bone which we
commonly call " the bril " [the furculum] in other birds can
be separated from the breast-bone, but in these Geese it
cannot ; indeed, so firm is it that no force can divide
it, and it is attached in this manner to the breast-bone in
order that when they chase the Herrings, and plunge
into the sea, they should not break their necks by their
extreme violence. In the month of August [most of] the
young ones are taken and are sold to the neighbours at a
high price, and the others fly away until the following year.
Many of them, nevertheless, are killed in the following
manner. The sailors prepare a smooth board, and make
it white, and fasten herrings on it ; which board they make
fast to the stern of a fishing-boat. The Geese, seeing the
Herrings, try to seize them with their beak, and drive it so
deep into the board that they cannot pull it out again, and
thus are taken, or rather take themselves. Moreover, if
these Geese alight so far from the sea that they cannot see
it, they can neither raise their bodies from the ground nor
fly away."

The notion that the egg of a Solan Goose when once taken
up cannot be replaced, which the people of the place seem to
have also told William Harvey in 1641, is a fiction, but a very
persistent one, for we get it again from Morer in 1702 and
from Defoe in 1722.

1653. LEONHARD BALDNER.

Leonhard Baldner was a fowler and river fisherman at Strasburg, whose paintings of the birds of his native Rhine, together with a written account of them, were bought by Francis Willughby, when passing with John Ray and Philip Skippon through that city in 1663, *see* " The Ornithology " (Preface *et seq.*). At Nuremberg Willughby also bought a volume of bird pictures, still in existence at Wollaton Hall, Notts, the residence of Lord Middleton, where his collection of medals is also preserved. Baldner's paintings, fresh as when the colour was laid on, are still in the British Museum, bound in a book, only twelve inches by eight, together with a translation of his notes, made from the German for Willughby after his return to England.* Full justice has been done to the Strasburg fisherman by Robert Lauterborn, by whom his work was printed and edited in 1903.† Lauterborn enumerates other copies of the Baldner MS., with paintings, of which one in Cassel, containing a hundred and fifty coloured drawings, is stated to be the most perfect, but the English copy in the British Museum is the earliest known, the preface to it being dated Dec. 31st, 1653. The following is a list of Baldner's plates numbered according to the London copy, with some (translated) extracts from his remarks.

1. Mute Swan.
2. Black-throated Diver.
   " This great *See-flutter* I shot the 12th of December 1649 " (MS.).
3. Pink-footed Goose. The description better applies to a Bean Goose.
4. Brent Goose. " I had two the 27th February, 1649, they are altogether unknown in our country " (MS.). *See* Ray's comment in " The Ornithology," p. 360.
5. Cormorant.
6. Red-breasted Merganser.
7. Goosander.

---

* Addl. MS. 6485 and MS. 6486.

† " Das Vogel- Fisch- und Thierbuch des Strassburger Fischers. Leonhard Baldner, aus dem Jahre 1666." Edited with an introduction by Robert Lauterborn, 1903. This volume is the subject of an excellent article by Dr. Hans Gadow in the " Field " of Oct. 26th, 1907.

✓ 8. Golden-eye Duck.
✓ 9. Mallard. "They have a very quick scent, in so much that they smell out a man, though they do not see him, if they have but the wind from him" (MS.).
10. Pintail.
11. Pochard.
12. Gadwall. Baldner's description of the *Brog Vogel* does not fit this species.
13. Wigeon.
14. Shoveller.
15. Great Crested Grebe. "This Fowl 1 shot, and some more I got, which were taken in a net. There are but few of them" (MS.).
16. Ferruginous Duck.
17. Tufted Duck.
18. Garganey Teal.
19. Smew.
20. Little Grebe. "Come to us about St. Michael Feast, and tarry till Easter" (MS.).
21. Teal.
✓ 22. Osprey. "June 15th, 1654, I got an Osprey . . . . I found a stone of carp in his throat" (MS.).
23. Great White Egret. The description applies to the Common Heron.
24. Heron.
25. Purple Heron. Bittern. A part of Baldner's description applies to the Bittern, and a part to the Purple Heron, while it is evidently the latter in immature plumage that is represented in his drawing. "One may hear their cry," he says, "half a mile off, which they lift up on high through their long nostrils, and the bill, and this the female does more than the male, as much as I know of them.* They abide with us a twelve month, and hatch two or three young ones." One which Baldner dissected contained an entire mole.

* This is disputed, some naturalists even doubting if the female booms at all. Miss Turner's experience is that it sometimes utters a soft booming sound ("British Birds," Mag., XIII., p. 8).

26. Night Heron. " Sent me the 24th of April 1649 from a fisher at Pothsenhausen, who had found him dead " (MS.).

27. Avocet. " This *Uberschnabel* was catched in 1647 " (MS.).

28. Squacco Heron. " The 4th of July 1646 I shot this Fowl just as he is drawn, none could give him a fit name, ... the 24th of May 1651 I shot again such a Fowl " (MS.).

29. Spotted Redshank. Represented in the painting in its summer plumage.

30. Green Sandpiper ?

49. Do. do.

31. Black Tern, adult. " They arrive in our country in the month of May . . . . . the 2nd of May 1651 I killed four of them with one shot " (MS.).

34. Black Tern, young.

32. Caspian Tern. " This great Sea-mew I shot the 23rd of May 1649, such like has not been seen in our country . . . ." (MS.).

33. Common Tern.

35. Black-headed Gull.

36. Lesser Tern.

37. Gull ? Here it is difficult to decide from its very dark colour for what Gull the painting is intended.

38. Coot.

39. Spotted Crake.

40. Water-Rail.

41. Redshank.

42. Golden Plover.

43. Lapwing.

44. Ruff. *See* note by Ray in " The Ornithology," p. 304.

45. Ringed Plover. " They come into our country in the month of June, and tarry here till October" (MS.).

46. Snipe. The description applies to the Snipe " an extraordinary good fowl, very savoury and always fat " (MS.), but the picture represents a Grey Phalarope.

47.   Common Sandpiper.

48.   Kentish Plover.   The description is probably intended for a Jack Snipe, but the picture represents a Kentish Plover.

50.   Dunlin.   " The young ones come to us in the month of September, many of which I shot " (MS.).

51.   Water Pipit, or Meadow Pipit.

52.   Kingfisher.

53.   Pied Wagtail.

54.   Grey Wagtail.

Dipper.   No description in the London MS.

Eider Duck.   Do.   do.

Curlew.   Do.   do.

With this the Birds end, and are followed, at all events in the London copy, by descriptions of forty species of fresh-water fish, with illustrations, as well as by about fifty-two mammals, insects and molluscs.

1662.   SIR THOMAS BROWNE.

In 1902 an excellent edition of Browne's treatises on Birds and Fish was published, with notes by Thomas Southwell, assisted by Professor Newton,[*] but the complete edition of his works is that by Simon Wilkin.[†]   Among other topics on which Browne touches is the migration of birds, and here he is the first English writer to offer us anything definite. In the seventeenth century not very much was known about the movements of birds, indeed the majority of scientific men were still reluctant to abandon the theory of hibernation, one of the chief exponents of which had been Olaus Magnus, the Swede.   Absurd as it now seems to us, it was not more so than a much later theory, viz., that birds migrated to the moon, an idea promulgated in all good faith in 1703 by F. Roberts, and subsequently by Charles Morton.[‡]   Browne knew very well that it was from oversea countries, and not from the moon, that birds came.   Forced on his notice every autumn, far more in Norfolk than if he had lived in one of

---

[*] " Notes and Letters on the Natural History of Norfolk from the MSS. of Sir Thomas Browne."   Edited by Thomas Southwell, 1902.

[†] Issued in 1835 in four volumes.

[‡] " Harleian Miscellany," Vol. II., p. 578.

SIR THOMAS BROWNE TO DR. MERRETT.
(Southwell's edn. of Browne's "Natural History.")

the central counties, his was much too inquiring a mind not to attempt an investigation of migration, accordingly we find him writing as follows :—

"Beside the ordinary birds which keep constantly in the country, many are discoverable both in winter and summer which are of a migrant nature and exchange their seats according to the season. Those which come in the spring coming for the most part from the southward, those which come in the autumn or winter from the northward. So that they are observed to come in great flocks with a north-east wind [in the autumn] and to depart [southwards] with a south-west [at that season]." I have added in brackets what Browne apparently intends to be understood in the last sentence.

In another passage, evidently not quite certain in his own mind about the direction of the wind preferred by birds in the autumn, he says they come with a north-west—not a north-east—wind. This correction occurs in his tract on Hawking,* where, after alluding to the speed of trained Falcons, Browne says :—

"How far the hawks, merlins, and wild-fowl which come unto us with a north-west wind in the autumn, fly in a day, there is no clear account : but coming over sea their flight hath been long or very speedy. For I have known them to light so weary on the coast, that many have been taken with dogs, and some knocked down with staves and stones."

The question of birds and wind has been much debated by ornithologists, and very opposite opinions have been held, and still are held, as to the effect of wind—both in its direction and force—on migratory birds, especially on the east coast of England.†

---

* Wilkin's edition of "Works," Vol. IV., tract 5.

† At the present day, a north-east or east wind, not so strong as to be a gale, is considered by the majority of observers on the Norfolk coast to be the most favourable for bringing over autumnal migrants to Norfolk and Suffolk, and the same rule probably applies to all the eastern counties. Any birds which arrive on the coast so weary that they can, as Browne says, be knocked down with stones, are delayed birds, and probably the survivors of many others which perished in the sea. Any also which are to be seen arriving in the morning, against a west wind, or during the day, whether tired or not, are to be looked upon as delayed birds.

By that term is meant birds which, with a moderate wind at their backs, would have made the passage across the North Sea in one night, and been on English soil before daybreak, if not impeded.

It is to Browne that we owe, among many other things, the first intimation of the Solan Goose in Norfolk, of which he says :—

" A white, large and strong bill'd fowle called a Ganet which seemes to bee the greater sort of Larus, whereof I met with one kild by a greyhound neere swaffam, another in marshland while it fought and would not bee forced to take wing, another intangled in an herring net wch taken aliue was fed with herrings for a while . . . . "

Browne alludes to the very great store of Partridges, a species which, as already shown by the le Straunge accounts, was abundant in Norfolk in the sixteenth century, but goes on to say that the Red-legged Partridge (*Caccabis rufa*) was not found. The date of its introduction to England has been commonly placed at towards the end of the eighteenth century, but it would seem that a few French Partridges were brought to England before that. In November 1682 a brace of " curious outlandish partridges," which may have been of this species, were sent to Belvoir Castle.* There is doubt about these, but none about some which were bred at Wimbledon in Surrey, prior to 1751,† and before that they were known to have been turned out at Windsor.‡

Browne is almost the only author who vouchsafes anything definite about the Quail, which was by no means such a common bird in England as some have supposed, though probably more abundant in Ireland.§

Alluding to the Sheld-Duck, Browne informs his correspondent that Barganders, *i.e.*, burrow-ganders, bred about Norrold, which Stevenson identifies as Northwold near Stoke-Ferry, adding that they are " not so rare as Turner makes them."

Concerning other Norfolk wild-fowl, about which Browne has a good deal which is valuable, some might consider the identity of Arts, Ankers and Noblets, all local names, to be

* 12th Report of The Historical MSS. Commission, II., p. 78.

† " Natural History of Birds " by George Edwards, IV., p. 223.

‡ Daniels, " Rural Sports," III., p. 95.

§ Robert Payne, writing in 1589, says it was plentiful, and that a dozen could be bought for threepence ("Irish Archæological Soc." 1841), of which later records are confirmatory.

lost. But the first named can be identified, for according to the " Ornithologia Svecica " of Nilsson, *Arta* is Swedish for a Garganey Teal, and was probably used in Norfolk for any Teal. In 1824 C. S. Girdlestone states that Arps, evidently a variant of the same word, was a name used in some parts of Norfolk for Tufted Ducks,* and it is mentioned again by Bewick in 1826.† Noblet was probably some species of duck with a knob on its head, which may mean a tubercle, such as the Sheld-Duck and Scoter possess, or it may mean a crest. Forby gives Knobble-tree as a provincial name for head.‡ With regard to Anker, this would be the same as ancre, that is, a nun, an old name sometimes given to the white male Smew.

Professor Newton was always in hope that a fair copy of Browne's two " Accounts " would some day turn up, being of opinion that the papers in the British Museum were but a rough copy. If that be so, it may account for the omission of the Owl, Pheasant, Snipe, and Wood-Pigeon ; that some pages of the original are missing seems almost certain. At the same time it was evidently not Browne's intention on this occasion to give his correspondent an enumeration of all the small birds, which would have considerably extended the list. As it now stands, it embraces eighty-nine species, to which are subsequently added in his letters to Ch. Merrett a few others, viz., the Hobby, Merlin, Waxwing, " Beebird " (Spotted Flycatcher), Tufted Duck, Garganey Teal, Golden-eye and Guillemot. Browne's enumeration commences with the birds of prey, but it can hardly be said to possess any order, and much pertinent matter is omitted, some of which had found a place in his " Enquiries into vulgar and common errors," as for example what he has to say on the Bittern.§

Who Browne's correspondent was must be a matter of conjecture. It is clear that these notes on Birds and Fishes— so carefully penned and original—were not intended for Dr. Ch. Merrett, nor were they meant for the use of Ray, who in

* " Norwich Naturalists' Trans.," Vol. II., p. 396.

† " History of British Birds." Vol. II., p. 328, note. On the authority of a Norfolk correspondent.

‡ " Vocabulary of East Anglia," 1830, Vol. II., p. 187.

§ Wilkin's edition of Works (1835), Vol. II., pp. 521-3

1662-68 was not occupying himself with birds, although much engaged in botany. It is possible that Browne drew them up for Sir Philip Skippon of Wrentham, with whom he was acquainted, but more likely still is the hint thrown out by Evelyn that they were intended for Sir Nicholas Bacon, who it would seem at one time resided in Norfolk.

The words with which they commence : " I willingly obey your commands in setting down," etc., clearly show that they were written for some one who took an interest in natural history, and the tract on " Plants mentioned in Scripture " was addressed to Bacon.*

---

* *See* Wilkin's edition (Vol. III., p. 381, and IV., p. 191), also " Norfolk Families," by Walter Rye (pp. 16, 17).

CHAPTER XIII.

SEVENTEENTH CENTURY (2ND PART).

1665. JOHN EVELYN.

John Evelyn, though not an ornithologist, was a virtuoso
of great talents, and has some claim to be considered the
founder of the Royal Society, while his visit to Norwich, where
he made the acquaintance of a kindred spirit in Sir Thomas
Browne, is almost historical. Evelyn kept a careful journal,
and in October 1671 he puts down as follows : " Next morning
[October 17th] I went to see Sir Thomas Browne, with whom
I had some time corresponded by letter, though I had never
seen him before ; his whole house and garden being a paradise
and cabinet of rarities, and that of the best collection, especially
medals, books, plants and natural things. Amongst other
curiosities, Sir Thomas had a collection of the eggs of all the
fowl and birds he could procure, that country (especially the
promontory of Norfolk) being frequented, as he said, by several
kinds which seldom or never go farther into the land, as Cranes,
Storks, Eagles, and variety of water-fowl. He led me to see all
the remarkable places of this ancient city. . ." Sir T.
Browne's collection of eggs and the dried " cases " of the
Stork and other birds in his cabinet of rarities have long since
perished, and a hundred and twenty years ago his house was
also demolished, but some carving from it is still preserved.
From Evelyn's description it appears to have had a garden
behind, but it must have been a small one.*

Recording a visit to Charles the Second's London mena-
gerie or rather collection of waterfowl, Evelyn says :—

" February 9th [1665]. Dined at my Lord Treasurer's.
. . . I went to St. James' Park, where I saw various animals,

* Browne's library of books, which doubtless embraced many treasures,
and his MSS. were kept together until 1830, and then sold ; his copy of
Justus Lipsius, presented in 1666 to the City of Norwich, is still preserved in
the Free Library.

and examined the throat of the *Onocrotylus*, or pelican, a fowl between a stork and a swan ; a melancholy water-fowl, brought from Astracan by the Russian Ambassador ; it was diverting to see how he would toss up and turn a flat fish, plaice or flounder, to get it right into his gullet at its lower beak which, being filmy, stretches to a prodigious wideness, when it devours a great fish." This was perhaps the same Pelican described by Ray and Willughby.* " Here was also a small water-fowl, not bigger than a moorhen, that went almost quite erect, like the penguin of America [Great Auk] ; it would eat as much fish as its whole body weighed ; I never saw so unsatiable a devourer, yet the body did not appear to swell the bigger." It was probably a Guillemot or Razorbill. Evelyn next goes on to say something of the Scotch Solan Goose or Gannet : " The Solan Geese here are also great devourers, and are said soon to exhaust all the fish in a pond. . . . ." Dr. Edward Browne, who must have known his father's friend, has something to tell us about St. James's Park, in February, 1664, one year earlier than Evelyn's visit. " I saw many strange creatures, as divers sorts of outlandish deer, Guiny sheep, a white raven, a great parrot, a storke, which having broke its own leg, had a wooden leg set on, ..."† He does not allude to the Solan Geese mentioned by Evelyn. The collection was evidently quite considerable, judging from the preceding extracts, and also from some allusions to it in Charleton's " Exercitationes de Differentiis et Nominibus Animalium " (1677). We have a reminiscence of it in the name Bird-Cage Walk.

1666. CHRISTOPHER MERRETT.

In the " Pinax Rerum Naturalium Britannicarum," of Dr. C. Merrett, we are in possession of the earliest printed catalogue of English birds, although it only extends to fifteen pages, and the information afforded is rather poor, neither has much attempt been made at classification, which, joined to one or two avoidable mistakes in the text, probably induced Ray to condemn the production as Merrett's bungling Pinax. The life and labours of Christopher Merrett have been

---

* " The Ornithology," p. 327.

† Browne's " Works," edited by Wilkin, Vol. I., p. 50.

made the subject of very good biographical articles by Mr. J. E. Harting and Mr. W. H. Mullens.*

1668. FRANCIS WILLUGHBY.

Francis Willughby, whose name has been held in such high honour, was born in 1635 and died in 1672 at Middleton Hall, near Tanworth, in Warwickshire.   The house still stands, and is the property of his descendants, but has been altered and added to since Willughby's day.   Lord Middleton, its

MIDDLETON HALL, 1918.

present owner, to whom the reader is indebted for the view of it, possesses good oil paintings of the naturalist,† and of his mother, Lady Cassandra Willughby, the former has long combed hair, and both of them are in costumes suggestive of Cromwellians of a Puritan type.

* The "Field," Oct. 10th, 1903, and "British Birds," Mag. (Vol. II., pp. 109, 151).   Mr. Mullens possesses Thomas Pennant's copy of the "Pinax," with his book-plate, but it only contains one or two brief memoranda.

† Reproduced by Sir William Jardine, in "The Naturalists' Library" (Orn., Vol. V.), and the original of the bust at Cambridge, as well as of the tablet in Southwell Cathedral.

Willughby's first contribution to ornithology, and indeed the only one of which he can be considered as sole author, was a

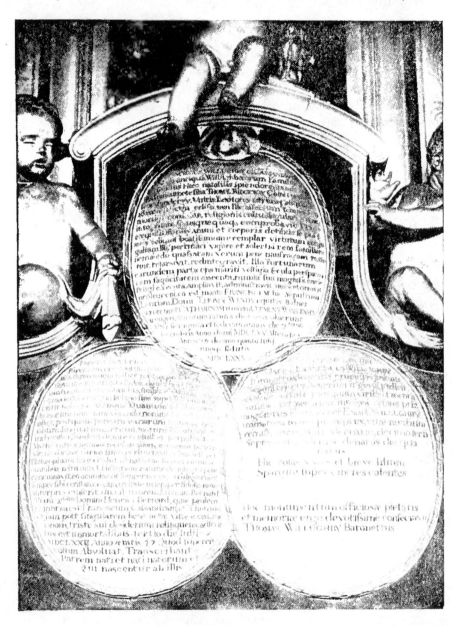

TABLET TO FRANCIS WILLUGHBY.

Table of Birds drawn up for Dean Wilkins, afterwards Bishop of Chester; Professor Boulger, however, is of opinion that here

he received Ray's assistance, which is very possible, as they
worked so much in common. This elaborate "Table" appeared
in Wilkins's "Real Character And a Philosophical Language,"
which was printed in 1668, and in it eight pages are devoted
to a scientific arrangement of birds by Willughby. The
system on which it is based divides all known genera into
nine groups, viz., six for the reception of land species, commencing with the carnivorous birds (with which he associates
the Cuckoo, Raven, Parrot and Woodpecker) ; and three for
aquatic species, that is such as live " near wet places," or are
" much in the water." At the conclusion of the List,
Willughby adds a few remarks which as coming from his pen
are interesting, but they treat of only six or seven species,
namely, the Wild Swan, of which he remarks, " Hooper, having
the wind-pipe going down to the bottom of the breastbone "
—wild geese " whereof one [kind] is black from the breast to
the middle of the belly, called Brant-Goose "—" the Widgeon-
kind," and " the Teal-kind," to which " should be reduced that
other fowl . . . called Gargane." He concludes with one
observation, to which naturalists would hardly now assent, viz.,
that " to the Gull-kind doth belong that other Bird, of a long
slender bill bending upwards, called *Avosetta recurvirostra.*"

I am indebted to Lord Middleton for permitting me the
use of what must certainly have been Willughby's own copy
of Wilkins's " Real Character." It is interleaved, and ten or
eleven pages, commencing with p. 122, are translated into
Latin in Ray's hand, but there are no notes by Willughby, and
this is disappointing ; also the owner's name, written on the
first page, is not his, but that of his son, Sir Thomas Willughby.
This volume is preserved with other treasures, at Wollaton
Hall in Nottinghamshire, a stately edifice built by one of the
Willughbys in the reign of Elizabeth, and here are also many
other works on Natural History which belonged to Sir Thomas
Willughby, the son of the naturalist, for they bear his name
on the fly-leaf. One of these, the " Libri de Piscibus Marinis "
of Rondeletius (1554) is furnished with a manuscript index,
incomplete and roughly written on the back of a letter, which
has been identified by Mr. W. H. Stevenson* as being in the

---

* Inspector to The Historical MSS. Commission, and Editor of The
Middleton Papers. (Report on MSS. 1911.)

handwriting— oblique and very scratchy—of Francis Willughby.
Besides this, there are a few other volumes, such as the works
of Gesner, Aldrovandus and Piso, and the "Dell' Historia
Naturale" of Ferranti (1590), which probably belonged to
Francis Willughby, but there are no marginal notes, nor
anything to indicate ownership, and the bulk of the books
appear to have been purchased by his son. When on the
continent in 1663—(a full account of which journey will be
given later)—Willughby is recorded to have bought a
volume of coloured pictures of birds at Nuremberg, and this
relic is still in Lord Middleton's safe keeping at Wollaton,
although in a somewhat tattered condition. Willughby, in
his zeal for information, may have got together a good
many pictures of birds and fish at one place and another,
and either he or Ray, or possibly Sir Thomas Willughby, evidently pasted some of them into the same volume with the
Nuremberg collection, adding sundry engravings at the end.
These engravings are taken from Pietro Olina's "Vccelliera"
(1622), a book of which Ray subsequently made great use, and
from Adrian Collaert's "Avium vivae Icones" (*circa* 1580),
which is not so often quoted. No manuscript, beyond a few
names in German, accompanies the Nuremberg plates, which
represent about eighty species of birds, some well painted,
some badly. A few of them bear brief memoranda in Ray's
hand, but of little importance, *e.g.*, where he remarks satirically
on the picture of the Sand Grouse (*Pterocles alchata*) that the
colours have been "corrupted" by the painter, which perhaps
partly accounts for his subsequently omitting the species
altogether from the "Ornithologia." Another painting represents a hybrid duck, but although in this case the colour
has been artistically laid on, it is difficult to put a name to
the anomalous bird.

Willughby's bird skins, if he ever possessed a collection,
have passed to the mite and the moth, except a few tough
beaks of the Toucan and Albatross, and the foot and head of
an Ostrich, but the remnant of his egg collection still exists in a
cabinet at Wollaton Hall. Most of the eggs have been written
upon, and the writing is still legible, although the eggs themselves are very faded and mostly cracked. Some Heron's eggs
remain intact, and these and an inscribed Shoveler Duck's egg

may have been procured by Willughby or Ray in Warwickshire, but we are tempted to associate a Night Heron's egg (?), marked " Quacke Belge," with their visit to Sevenhuys in Holland.

1676. WILLUGHBY AND RAY.

It was Francis Willughby who collected the materials for —and John Ray, who, after his friend's early death at thirty-seven, completed, in retirement in Warwickshire—the famous " Ornithologia."* This great work, which won the praise of Linnæus and Cuvier, intended for a history of the birds of the whole world as they were then known, will ever stand as a monument to the industry of these two naturalists. Nevertheless, however industrious and talented Willughby was, considering his youth when he died, it is difficult to give him credit for very much of it, yet but for the liberality of his widow the world might never have had the book.

To apportion this joint production would not be easy, but the story as told by the Rev. William Derham, who spent the latter part of his life at Upminster, some twenty-five miles from the home of Ray, is sufficient, since he had it from Ray's own lips, a few months before the great naturalist died.

In connection with Ray's labours, it is curious to peruse the correspondence which went on at this time, which the Ray Society have so judiciously printed.† There are many very remarkable letters from Martin Lister, the author of " Historiæ Animalium tres Tractatus," Sir Philip Skippon, Jessop of Sheffield, Johnson of Brignal, and Sir Tancred Robinson, author *inter alia* of a paper " On the French Macreuse and Scotch Barnacle." Also from the antiquary Aubrey, Sir Hans Sloane and others, all of whom were desirous of lending a helping hand with the " Ornithologia," on which Ray was known to be engaged.

* " Francisci Willughbeii De Middleton in agro Warwicensi, Armigeri, E Regia Societate, Ornithologia Libri Tres." 1676. This work, which must have entailed immense labour, was probably written at Middleton Hall, near Tanworth, where Ray took up his residence after Willughby's death in 1672, and where he, in 1673, married Margaret Oakeley.

† " The Correspondence of John Ray " (Ray Society, 1848, p. 33). *See* also " Philosophical Letters " (1718) and " Original Letters of Eminent Literary Men " (Camden Society, 1843, pp. 194–210), as well as " Unpublished Material relating to John Ray," by G. S. Boulger (The " Essex Review," 1917, pp. 57–129).

THE HOME OF JOHN RAY, WHERE HE DIED IN 1705.

No letter from Sir Thomas Browne is among the collection, but in his preface Ray acknowledges the assistance of the celebrated "Professor of Physick in the City of Norwich," who had communicated drawings of the Manx Shearwater, Little Auk, Stork, Turnstone, Scoter Duck, etc. Some of these drawings, which are life-sized, and really very creditable, are preserved in the British Museum (Bibl. Sloane, 5266). They are obviously the same which were made use of by Ray for "The Ornithology" (Tables LII., LVIII., LIX., LXXVIII.), and which were also communicated to Christopher Merrett. They have Sir T. Browne's name on them, as well as the name of the bird, in Merrett's handwriting, in nearly every case. There is one drawing among them which represents a dead Ringed Plover, on which Merrett has written : "a ringlestone or stone runner which breeds on the shingle on by Yarmouth. S. T. B." Neither he nor Ray refer to this name, here given on Browne's authority, which is in allusion to the ring, or circle of stones, within which the Dotterel lays its eggs. It is probably quite obsolete now, but "ringle" is still in provincial use. Another drawing, which came from Sir T. Browne or his artist, is of a Great Crested Grebe's leg bone, showing its peculiar formation and the "sharpe processe extending above the thigh bone," to which Browne alludes in his catalogue. This sketch would almost have done duty for the Diver's leg bone which Ray figured (Tabl. LXII.). A third draught is "the morinellus or sea doterell," that is the Turnstone, which is mentioned in Browne's fifth letter to Merrett, where he remarks "these sea-dotterells are often shot near the sea [in Norfolk]." Browne adds, what is very true, that his artist should have painted "a greater eye [or shade] of dark red in the feathers of wing and back," but with this exception the painting is passable. In the same letter to Merrett, Browne speaks of sending a picture of his "whin-bird." This, which is rather rough, is also in the Sloane Collection, but it is quite good enough to prove that the "whin-bird" was a Goldcrest, not a species which frequents furze.

Other pictures of birds were communicated to Ray by Sir Philip Skippon, whose residence was at Blythburgh in the north of Suffolk, but it is not likely that they were so important as Browne's. Among these letters there is not any communication, as might have been expected, from Christopher Merrett, of whom, it seems, Ray had not a very high opinion.

1658–1664. JOHN RAY.

The Early Itineraries of John Ray. First Itinerary, August and September, 1658.—Perhaps nothing better shows the enquiring spirit with which Ray and a few friends of like tastes set to work, than the diaries of certain " simpling journeys," as he called them, undertaken in quest of herbs, when he and Willughby were young men, but Ray was seven years the senior. The first of these simpling expeditions was in 1658, at which time Ray (or as he then spelled his name, Wray) was only thirty years of age. Yet, young as he was, he had already made his mark at Cambridge, where he had been elected Greek and Mathematical Lecturer to Trinity College. Full of enthusiasm for botany, but at present taking not much thought of birds, and solitary, for on this occasion he had no companion with him, the scholar starts from Cambridge on August 9th, 1658, on horseback, riding thirty-one miles the first day. Among enquiring minds of the stamp of Ray's, it is plain that Botany claimed far more attention than Ornithology in the seventeenth century; by physicians and laymen alike the medicinal value of herbs was held in high repute, and it was still thought that in many a familiar shrub some undiscovered secret might lie. This summer expedition took Ray to Northampton, Warwick, Coventry, Ashby and Buxton, as far north as Lancashire, after which he visited Wales, and returned home by Gloucester. The Itinerary contains nothing about birds, and on his return he devoted his time to the " Catalogus Plantarum circa Cantabrigiam," which proved to be his first step to fame.

Ray's Second Itinerary. July and August, 1661.—The journal of Ray's second Itinerary, commencing on July 26th, is longer, and has a good deal in it which appeals to lovers of birds. " We began our journey northwards from Cambridge, and that day passing through Huntingdon and Stilton, we rode as far as Peterborough, twenty-five miles. . . . August the 8th, we arrived at Scarborough, distant from Malton sixteen miles. This town hath a great trade of fish taken thereabout. We saw ling, cod fish, skate, thornback, turbot, whiting and herring. They take also conger, bret [brill] and mackrell. . . . August the 9th, from Scarborough we journeyed to Whitby, twelve miles. . . . The country people hereabout told us the story related by Camden, that wild geese, if once they light in Whitby strand, cannot rise again or fly away. . ." This venerable legend, which claims such high antiquity, runs in the Cottonian MSS. thus: " Not farre from Whitby is a peice of grounde called Whitby stronde, over which the inhabitants affyrme that noe wildgoose can flye, . . ." William Camden, the historian, does not mention a strand, but locates the dangerous spot " over certain neighbouring fields hereabouts." Very likely, as in the case of other legends, it had a foundation in incidents now long since forgotten.

After passing within sight of Holy Island, " but the tide served us not to pass over," and the Farne islands, the travellers lodged at Berwick, that is John Ray and Philip Skippon, for Scott's statement * that Willughby was one of the company must be erroneous.†

About birds there is nothing more until they crossed the Scottish border and came to the Bass Rock, of the celebrity of which Ray was doubtless well aware. He thus refers to what has always been the most eastern station of the Soland-Goose.‡ " August 17th [1661], we travelled to Dunbar. . . . August the 19th we went to Leith, keeping all along on the side of the Fryth. By the way we viewed Tontallon Castle, and passed over to the Basse Island, where we saw, on the rocks, innumerable of the soland geese. The old ones are all over white, excepting the pinion or hard feathers of their wings which are black. The upper part of the head and neck, in those that are old is of a yellowish dun colour ; they lay but one egg apiece, which is white and not very large. They are very bold, and sit in great multi-

* ";Select Remains of The Learned John Ray," p. 132, by George Scott (1760).

† As pointed out by Professor G. S. Boulger. *See* " Correspondence of John Ray," p. 3 (published by The Ray Society).

‡ " Select Remains," p. 191.

tudes till one comes close up to them, because they are not
wont to be scared or disturbed. The young ones are esteemed
a choice dish in Scotland, and sold very dear (1s. 8d. plucked).
We eat of them at Dunbar. They are in bigness little inferior
to an ordinary goose. The young one is upon the back black,
and speckled with little white spots, under the breast and
the belly gray. The beak is sharp-pointed, the mouth very
wide and large, the tongue very small, the eyes great, the
foot hath four toes webbed together. It feeds upon mackerel
and herring, and the flesh of the young one smells and tastes
strong of these fish. . . ." Besides this narrative, of which
the whole is not here quoted, we have a very excellent account
of the Solan Goose in " The Ornithology," to be found in
the Latin edition at pages 247, 265, and in the English edition
at pp. 328 and 348. Here, as well as in Ray's earlier " Catalogue of English Birds " in 1674,* it is spelled Soland Goose,
which is the Lowland Scotch way of writing it.†

This journey ended on September 7th, on which day
they returned to Cambridge, and the week after Ray writes
to Willughby an account of the plants he had observed,‡
but says nothing of birds.

Ray's Third Itinerary. May, June, July, 1662.—On May
8th, 1662, Ray and Willughby, starting from Cambridge,
evidently on horseback, saw the sheep fair at St. Neots, and
passed on thence to Northampton and Rugby. On the 12th
and 13th they noted sundry plants, and on the 14th, continues
the diary, " We diverted out of our Way to see the *Puits*, which
we judged to be a sort of *Lari*, in a Meere at Norbury belonging
to Col. Skrimshaw. They build altogether in an islet in the
middle of a pool. Each hen layeth three or four eggs of a
dirty blue or sea-green, spotted with black ; at the driving
every year, they take commonly above an hundred dozen
young, which they sell at five shillings the dozen."§

This settlement is also described in " The Ornithology "
(p. 347), and afterwards at greater length, in Robert Plot's
" Natural History of Staffordshire " (1686), with a curious

* Printed with " A collection of English Words," 1674 (pp. 81–96).
† Sixteen variants of Solan are cited in " The Gannet," p. 26.
‡ " The Correspondence of John Ray," p. 3.
§ " Select Remains," p. 216.

picture of the driving of the young ones, reproduced in " British Birds," and which by Mr. Mullens's permission can be given again. It must have had a good population of Puits, a thousand at least, but after the Gulls had shifted their quarters once or twice it apparently became extinct.*

After stopping at Chester, they proceeded towards Anglesey —where Ray had been in 1658—intending to visit Priestholm, or Puffin Island, from Bangor. Of Priestholm, a good nursery, afterwards described by Thomas Pennant,† Ray observes : " In the island (Prestholm) are bred several sorts of birds, two sorts of sea-gulls, cormorants, puffins, so called there, which I take to be *Anas arctica clusij*, razor-bills, and guillems, serays [Terns] two sorts, which are a kind of gull."‡ The Great Orme's Head not being in their programme, although Rock-birds might have been seen there in plenty, they next passed on to Bardsey Island, lying at the south-west point of Caernarvon, where there " build the Prestholm puffin, sea-pies, and some other birds . . ." It was here, I make no doubt, that Ray learnt the legend of the Puffin's inability to fly over the land—a fable long believed of the Solan Goose also—as well as another story about a torpid Puffin, which fisherman's myth he relates in " The Ornithology."§

From Bardsey their route was to Pwllheli [Pulhely], and by the way they saw the Lesser Black-backed Gull, and more Terns. On June 2nd, says the journal, they " rode to Aberdovy, seventeen miles, over marsh-land and sand " ; it was here, according to " The Ornithology,"‖ that the Turnstone was identified—a late date for this species. On the sandy meadows near Aberavon, ever on the look out for fresh plants, they

---

* In 1794 they were breeding on some pools at Batchacre, one mile from Shebden pool, and about the same distance from Norbury (" The History and Antiquities of Staffordshire," by Stebbing Shaw, Vol. I, p. 96).
Plot's sketch shows the process of driving the young Gulls, able to swim but not to fly, towards a net, a manœuvre which was done by men with long poles wading in the water. At the present day where gulleries exist, it is the eggs which are eaten.

† Who was there in 1773 ("A Tour in Wales," Vol. II, p. 260).

‡ " Select Remains," p. 226.

§ P. 326. At the present time it is affirmed that Puffins no longer breed at Bardsey, see an excellent account of the birds of that island in the " Zoologist " for 1902, p. 11.

‖ " Select Remains," p. 236.

gathered *Cineraria palustris*, but were in some doubt as to the identity of a mysterious bird, which was only the Common Redshank. Thus following the line of the Welsh coast, the

JOHN RAY.

two naturalists wended their way to St. David's Head, where one can suppose they viewed with longing eyes the wild aspect of Ramsey Island, but it is not stated that they crossed over. They, however, were not prevented from landing upon Caldey island, where they found eggs in abundance of Terns and " puits."* By June 26th the travellers, still stopping to collect flowers as they rode along, had left Wales and were in Cornwall, where the following day an entry in the journal runs : " Friday, June 27th, [1662], we passed on towards Padstow . . . Near Padstow we saw great flocks of Cornish choughs. The gannets, they told us, were almost of the bigness of a goose, white, the tips only of their wings black ; they have a strange way of catching them, by tying a pilchard to a board, and fastening it so that the bird may see it, who comes down with so great swiftness for his prey that he breaks his neck against the board. . . . Monday, June 30th, we rode over the sands to St. Ives . . . We passed over to Godreve Island, which is nothing but a rock, about one league distant from St. Ives, to the north-east near the land, upon which in time of year build great store of birds, viz. gulls, cormorants, razorbills, guillems and puffins. The razorbills are not so numerous on this island as the guillems, or kiddaws, of which many scores of young ones lie dead here. Here they call the puffins, popes ; and the guillems kiddaws. We saw many of those birds which they call gannets, flying about on the water. This bird hath long wings, and a long neck, and flyeth strongly. Possibly it may be the *Catarractes*. He preys upon pilchards, the shoals whereof great multitudes of these fowls constantly pursue. Another bird they told us of here called wagell, which pursues and strikes at the small gull so long, till out of fear it mutes, and what it voids the wagell follows and greedily devours, catching it sometimes before it has fallen down to the water. This several seamen affirmed themselves to have oftentimes seen."†

It is curious that Ray never seems to have realised that the Solan Goose and the Cornish Gannet were one and the same. In " The Ornithology " (p. 349) he says : " We saw many of these Gannets flying, but could not kill one." Had they done so their identity would have been discovered. This being,

---

* This is not without interest, because the Black-headed Gull, or puit, in modern times was not known to Murray Mathew as breeding at Caldey, or on any of the Pembrokeshire islands ("Birds of Pembrokeshire," 1894, p. 95).

† " Select Remains," pp. 268, 273, 275. What Ray was told of the Wagell better fits the habits of the Arctic Skua than any species of Gull. *See* Newton's " Dictionary of Birds," p. 1017.

[Face p. 221.

perhaps, the fullest of the Itineraries, it may not be amiss to indicate, on a map, the actual course taken.

Ray and Willughby's Journey through Europe in 1663–4. —Instead of following Ray in his fourth and fifth Itineraries (when, searching for new plants and birds, he visited Cornwall with Willughby in 1667, and after that again turned his face northwards in 1671 to Northumberland in the company of Willisel, a botanist) it will be pleasant and more profitable to accompany him abroad. Having, after due deliberation, conceived the bold idea of attempting a systematic description of the whole animal kingdom, the two naturalists, Ray and Willughby (of whom one at least was already a master in science), crossed to Calais on April 18th, 1663, bent on exploring western Europe. They had with them Nathaniel Bacon, afterwards a lawyer of distinction, and Philip Skippon, heir to a Suffolk knighthood, but at present Ray's pupil. The intention of the party was to visit Holland, Germany, Switzerland, Italy and France, which they did; but war breaking out they had to hurry back from France on the return journey, escaping at short notice with the loss of valuable journals. Ray's account of the expedition is to be found in his "Travels Through the Low-Countries, Germany, Italy and France," a book somewhat disappointing to the zoologist.*

Striking northwards from Calais, by way of Dunkirk and Ostend, they proceeded to Holland, and visited Delft, of more importance then than it is now. Here one Jean vander Mere kept a museum, where, among other "natural rarities," was a Soland Goose, said—most likely in error— to have come from Greenland.

From Delft† their route took them to Leyden in a canal boat drawn by horses, where they noted the grave of Carolus Clusius (L'Escluse) the famous botanist. From Leyden about the 1st of June, a by-journey in the direction of Rotterdam finds them at a village called Sevenhuys,‡ for the purpose of seeing a grand congregation of Spoonbills, Night Herons,

---

* First edition, 1673; second edn., 1738.

† "Travels," p. 24.

‡ Zevenhuizen, *see* a map illustrating the past distribution of the Spoonbill ("Norwich Naturalists' Trans.," Vol. V., p. 166).

Grey Herons and Cormorants, all of which were breeding in a large wood. Ray's delight must have been great, and his astonishment also at seeing Cormorants, " a whole-footed bird " as he remarks, building upon trees. Perhaps he did not then remember the experience of a certain Englishman, to wit Dean Turner, of their nests in Norfolk. " When the young are ripe," he says, " they who farm the grove, with an iron hook fastened to the end of a long pole, lay hold on the bough on which the nest is built and shake the young ones out, and sometimes nest and all down to the ground." From this composite settlement of birds, the young of the Spoonbill and Night Heron afforded materials for the descriptions to be used afterwards in " The Ornithology." * Besides the four kinds of water-birds in this prolific grove, which was rented as high as three thousand guilders—over £200— merely for the birds and the grass, there were Ravens, Wood-Pigeons and Turtle Doves. From Leyden, Ray and his companions moved to Haarlem, and from Haarlem to Amsterdam, but as there is little in his book of Travels, here or elsewhere about birds, it will be better and simpler in following their route to rely on the pages of " The Orni-thology."

About Collen (Cologne), where the travellers arrived on June 30th, 1663, they discovered the Hoopoe to be very frequent. " It sits for the most part on the ground, sometimes on Willows "; from the stomach of one dissected they took beetles. Here, as usual, Ray enumerates the principal plants which he found growing by the way, a knowledge of which such good use was to be made afterwards.

At Frankfort, July 14th, they ascertained the Hawfinch to be common, and one of the party shot a Golden Oriole, many of which they afterwards saw at Naples, and noted that it was a bird of passage. Here also they first saw the Black Stork.† One of the most important cities which comes

* See pages 279, 288, 329 of Willughby's " Ornithology." Mr. J. P. Thysse states that the last eggs of the Night Heron, which has now vanished as a breeder from Holland, were taken at Lekkerbeck in 1876. Dutch breeding settlements of the Spoonbill are also reduced to two ; the wood in which they nested at Sevenhuys, according to Pennant (" Brit. Zool.," app.) was destroyed some time prior to 1768.

† " The Ornithology," pp. 199, 245, 286.

into Ray's Itinerary is Strasburg, visited by the four friends on July 23rd, 1663, on which occasion our author mentions the Whimbrel, and the Black Stork again, adding : " We suppose those we saw were young ones, for that their bills and legs were green." *   But what was much more to the purpose, Willughby was able to buy a volume at Strasburg containing excellently coloured " Pictures of all the Water-foul frequenting the *Rhine* near that City, as also all the Fish and Water-Insects found there." This welcome prize was " purchased of one Leonard Baltner, a Fisherman."†

It was in Germany that Ray and Willughby first met with the Roller, and one can imagine their pleasure at such a beautiful bird, while in the market at Ratisbone, in Bavaria, they were fortunate in picking up a Great Black Woodpecker. This was in September, on the 15th of which month our travellers arrived at Vienna, where nothing is said about the market, but at the live-bird shops they came across a few novelties.‡

The Nutcracker, illustrated in a plate in " The Ornithology "§ from a dried skin, which they very likely had sent home or brought with them, was met with near this city. We can fancy Willughby's excitement when its harsh callnote was encountered, apparently on September 26th, " in the mountainous part of Austria, near the way leading from Vienna to Venice, not far from a great village called Schadwyen, where there is a very steep, difficult and craggy ascent. . . . ." This is precise enough, and it would be interesting to know if Nutcrackers are still there. In Switzerland, the travellers had leisure to search for many plants, and among birds they were successful, too—the Dipper, Ptarmigan, and Common Sandpiper being added to their growing list. The last-named was noticed in the month of April on the margin of the Lake of Geneva,‖ where its piping note and flirting tail are still to be heard and seen.

* " The Ornithology," pp. 286, 295.
  † Ray's Preface to " The Ornithology." A description of it has been already given, p. 197.
  ‡ Such as the Citril, Serin and Crested Lark, *see* " The Ornithology," p. 265.
  § " The Ornithology," p. 133, pl. XX ; and " Travels," p. 120.
  ‖ " The Ornithology," pp. 149, 176, 302.

Following their road, as it is laid down with much exactness in the " Travels," we see that by the 1st of October, 1663, the four friends had reached the city of Venice. Now we have to depend on the pages of " The Ornithology," from which it appears that they saw several good birds at Venice, viz., Ruffs, Avocets and Water-Rails, besides a Little Egret and a Sea Eagle, and Brambling Finches in profusion.* The Goldeneye Duck was very abundant, although so early in the year, most likely in the market, a resort Willughby would have been sure not to miss. Ray notices its applicable provincial name of *Quattro-occhi*,† the Tufted Duck being called by the natives a *Capo negro*. At one of the palaces they were shown a living Vulture, possibly the palace of Foscari all' Arena, where Evelyn, the diarist, had seen sundry live birds in 1645.‡

Both at Venice and at Padua they saw many Capercaillie, which had been brought from the Alps, where they are still to be found; while at Modena a Great Bustard was hanging for sale in the market, perhaps a migrant, as the date was February 22nd, 1664,§ when snow might have driven it from more eastern quarters.

When they got to Rome they very quickly took notice of Little Owls, standing on their perches, offered for use as decoys, a practice of very old standing. Ray alludes to this form of sport in " The Ornithology," referring to Olina's " Vccelliera," a work of much repute, printed in 1622, where there is a quaint illustration of the mode in which it is carried on.‖ At Rome there were also many great Cranes exposed for sale " in the Winter time, which I suppose had been shot on the Sea-coast."

---

* " The Ornithology," pp. 62, 254, 280, 315, 322.

† " The Ornithology," p. 368: it is still in use, *cf.* "Fauna d'Italia," II, p. 267.

‡ " Diary and Correspondence of John Evelyn," Vol. I, p. 212.

§ " The Ornithology," pp. 173, 179.

‖ *See* Olina (p. 64) for a clever plate, and a pretty full description " del modo d'vccellare con la Ciuetta." The birdcatchers of Italy still repeat the process, just as their forefathers used to do it hundreds of years ago. It is extraordinary what a fascination these Little Owls exercise on birds, especially the smallest sorts, which soon fall victims to the well limed rods artfully set to catch them.

At Rome our travellers found a kindred spirit in the son of Sir Thomas Browne, of Norwich,* who refers in two of his letters to their meeting, remarking that: " Mr. Wray is here at Rome : hee hath been in Sicilia and Malta "; and again, writing to his father: " Mr. Wray hath made a collection of plants, fisshes, foules, stones, and other rarities, which hee hath with him ; and Mr. Skippon, besides a great number which hee hath sent home, though they had the ill fortune to loos one venture with a servant of thers, who is now slane in Tunes."

About French birds there is not very much anywhere in " The Ornithology " : no opportunity was given them for observations of this nature, yet at Montpellier several dried " cases " of the Flamingo, " which is often taken about Martiguez," came under notice. At Montpellier, Willughby (now aged twenty-seven) parted from his three companions, and proceeded to Spain, where he kept a rather brief journal of notes, which contains one reference to Red-legged Part-ridges. A letter which he wrote to Ray from Paris on his way home, is still to be seen at the Natural History Museum. Ray and Skippon remained at Montpellier until December, and then returned by way of Lyons and Paris to England, but unfortunately lost a portion, if not all, the notes taken in Germany.

* " Browne's Works " edited by Wilkin, Vol. I., pp. 77, 87.

Q

CHAPTER XIV

EIGHTEENTH CENTURY.

1753. ERICH PONTOPPIDAN (BISHOP OF BERGEN).

Bishop Pontoppidan, a Danish prelate, born in 1698, claims a distinguished position as the author of a Natural History of Norway, best known in England by the translation

"THE GANNET."

published in 1755. In this fine old work, twenty-two folio pages are devoted to a really very good description of the birds of Norway, with figures which are easily recognisable of twelve of them.*

There is a rather full account of the Gannet, "The Hav-Sule [*i.e.*, Sea-Sule, or Solan] a large sea-bird, which somewhat resembles a Goose," accompanied by a somewhat imaginative figure, with a comb on its head, which cannot be due to a defect in the block, as it is stated in the text to be red.

* "The Natural History of Norway, in Two Parts, translated from the Danish Original," Vol. II., chap. iii. and iv.

1758–59. CAROLUS LINNÆUS.

Karl Linné, better known to science by his Latin designation of Carolus Linnæus, the reformer of Latin names in Natural History, has ever been justly renowned for his attainments. His " Systema Naturæ " was commenced and finished while its author was still quite a young man, the first edition being offered to the Swedish public in 1735. Born two years after the death of John Ray, whose studies and Itineraries were the subject of the last chapter (*supra*, p. 215), the early work of Linnæus is held to have been largely shaped by the influence of his English predecessor. Professor Newton, with somewhat qualified praise, observes that " In his classification of Birds " Linnæus " for the most part followed Ray, and where he departed from his model, he seldom improved upon it."* The Solan Goose is concisely described by Linnæus in the 10th, 12th and 13th editions of the " Systema Naturæ," which were published respectively in 1758, 1766 and 1788, and it is there accorded a position in the genus *Pelecanus*, under the designation of *P. bassanus*. In the 12th edition we are told that it is found " Insula Scotiæ Basse," as if Linnæus was not sure of any other breeding place, and the appellations of " Gentleman" and "Jaen von Gent" are given as provincial synonyms.

The epithet of *gentleman*, a colloquial expansion of the name *gent* or *gant*, as applied to the Solan Goose, is of respectable antiquity, for it is said by Lucas Debes,† from whom no doubt Linnæus, and also Pontoppidan, copied it, to have been used by fishermen as far back as the seventeenth century. In this connection it is instructive to go further and search for the origin of the Dutch and Flemish name of *Jan-van-Gent*, another appellation of long standing, and which is not obsolete yet. *De Jan van Gent* (" Vogels van Nederland," 1854–8, p. 571) is first met with in two works almost forgotten now, a " Voyage into Spitzbergen and Greenland " by Frederick Martin (1675),‡ and Mohr's " Forsog

* "Dictionary of Birds," Introd., p. 8.
† In his "Færoæ and Færoa Referata" (1673).
‡ English edition, 1694.

til en Islandsk Naturhistorie " (1786), in both of which it is cited. It is easy to understand how *Gan, Jan* or *John* would be selected as a common Christian name by seafaring men, who are never slow in applying a nick-name ; indeed there are several such instances in Ornithology.*

1726–98. THOMAS PENNANT.

By far the best authority to consult about birds in the eighteenth century, so far as Great Britain is concerned, although it has been the fashion to underrate him, is Thomas Pennant. A man of great natural ability, he did more to advance zoology in this country from a scientific point of view than anyone else, while to Gilbert White of Selborne is due the great merit of popularising it. Gilbert White's correspondence we fortunately have, and very pleasant and instructive reading the public have always found it to be, but the numerous letters which Pennant must have written in reply to the parson of Hampshire are lost, a circumstance greatly to be regretted.†

No student of this period can go wrong in turning to Pennant's " British Zoology," his chief, as it was his earliest, literary effort. It was begun, the author tells us, in 1761, possibly at the solicitation of the great Linnæus, with whom he had been in correspondence, and by whom he had been elected to the Royal Society of Upsal in 1757, an event which he regarded as the greatest honour of his life.‡

Pennant's careful pages will always repay perusal, if read in the light of what is now known about British birds. A useful comparison may also be drawn between the list of British birds which he has given in an appendix,§ and a similar list drawn up by John Ray at the end of the seventeenth century.‖

---

* Guillemot is said to be derived from the French *Guillaume*, and "Willock," an appellation for the same bird, from *William*.

† At a meeting of the Royal Physical Society of Edinburgh, held in February, 1914, Mr. O. H. Wild exhibited a copy of Pennant's " British Zoology," bearing the following inscription in the first volume : " Gil. White, May 4, 1768. The gift of the author." An interesting relic of their former friendship.

‡ " Literary Life of the late Thomas Pennant," p. 2.

§ " British Zoology," vol. II., pp. 731-749.

‖ " Ornithologiæ Libri Tres." (1676), p. 17.

Altogether Ray reckoned 164 British birds, and Pennant 242, while another well-known naturalist, John Latham, a few years later (1787), puts the total at 268,* which gives an advance of 104 species in about 113 years. In the first half of the eighteenth century progress was slow, only the Golden Oriole, and the Rose-coloured Starling, seem to have been added, but between 1751 and 1796 there was a great stride forwards, sixteen more species being registered as British, thanks to the exertions of Pennant and his personal friends. These species were :—

The Little Bustard in 1751
The Nutcracker in 1753 *fide* Pennant
The Grey Phalarope in 1757 *fide* Edwards†
The Red-necked Phalarope in 1769
The Little Bittern in 1773
The Dartford Warbler in 1773 *fide* Latham
The Spoonbill in 1774 *fide* Sparshall
The Squacco Heron in 1775 *fide* Latham
The Ruddy Sheld-Duck in 1776 *fide* Tunstall
The Red-breasted Goose in 1776 *fide* Tunstall
The Ortolan Bunting in 1776
The Night Heron in 1782
The Cream-coloured Courser in 1785 *fide* Latham
The Little Crake in 1791 *fide* Markwick
The Bee-eater in 1793 *fide* Sir J. E. Smith
The Sclavonian Grebe in 1796 *fide* Montagu

Of the above-named birds four at least are now looked upon as annual visitants, while one, the Dartford Warbler, is a regular breeder in the south of England, in small numbers.

Pennant was a Welshman, born and bred in Flintshire, and it was by a Welsh Literary Society that the " British Zoology " was published.‡ His attention therefore was

---

* " General Synopsis of Birds," by John Latham. First supplement, p. 281.

† Well figured by George Edwards in " The Philosophical Transactions " for 1757 (vol. I., Tab. VI.) as well as in that author's "Gleanings of Natural History " (1760) vol. VI., pl. 308).

‡ In folio in 1766. Reprinted in octavo in 1768 and 1770, *see* " Bibliography of British Ornithology," p. 464, and " British Birds " Mag., vol. II., p. 259. Fifteen years after Pennant's death, a fifth edition was called for, which contains sundry additions by the Rev. John Lightfoot, author of a " Flora Scotica," but they are of little value.

naturally directed to the western side of England, but he
early became aware that on the east coast there lay a greater
scope for the naturalist. Of Pennant's numerous works
none appeals to the naturalist more than his Scotch " Tour,"
published in 1771,* which is principally about North Britain,
but he stopped a while to explore the still imperfectly drained
fens of Lincolnshire on his way.† Thus seeking as he went
for birds and antiquities, he visited Crowland, Swinehead and
Spalding, and thence made his way to Lincoln. This was
in June 1769, but the country was not new to him, for Pennant had already seen something of Lincolnshire in 1768.
Lincolnshire was a land unique in its way, a land which had
been styled by Thomas Fuller the Aviary of England, nor
was that title misapplied, for we can well believe that the
southern portion was still teeming with water-birds, in spite
of the prodigious efforts of Vermuyden to drain it.

In this oasis of plenty, the Ruff was common enough
for one fowler to have netted seventy-two in a morning.
That was exceptional, but in an ordinary season, that is to
say between April and Michaelmas, a single man would take
forty or fifty dozen, which after being fattened on bread and
milk and hempseed, were worth two shillings or half a crown
apiece.‡ §

The wealth of the fenmen were the huge numbers of tame
Geese, which were bred for the sake of their feathers. The
unfortunate birds were made to undergo the cruel operation
of plucking five times a year, the first time at Lady-day, for
their feathers and quills, and after that for the feathers only.
A single person would keep a thousand Geese, each of which
would rear about seven young ones, so that towards the end
of the breeding season he would become master of eight
thousand.‖ A gozzard (i.e., goose-herd) attended the flock,
and twice a day drove the whole of them to water, which

---

* " A Tour in Scotland, and a Voyage to The Hebrides," 1771. The fifth
edition published in 1790 contains several additions.

† *Idem*, pp. 9-12.

‡ " British Zoology," II., p. 460.

§ Pennant's *Gambet* "shot on the coast of Lincolnshire " appears from the
plate in the " British Zoology " (vol. II., pl. LXX.) to have been a Reeve.

‖ " British Zoology," II., p. 571.

kept them in health and exercise. When ready for the market, these Geese, except such as might be retained for further plucking, were driven to London, to supply the poulterers, especially from some of the fens near Revesby. Revesby was where Sir Joseph Banks had a country seat, at which Pennant, who had known Banks for some three years, was a welcome guest, and here he tells us he made " many observations on the zoology of the country."*

Although Pennant has so much to say about tame Geese, very little is told about wild ones in the " Tour," but in the " British Zoology " under the head of Grey-lag Goose, he is rather more explicit. " This species," we are informed, " resides in the fens the whole year, breeds there, and hatches about eight or nine young, which are often taken, easily made tame, and esteemed most excellent meat."†

It was from this stock that the greater part of England's domestic geese had sprung. But that the Grey-lag was the only wild Goose which formerly bred in Lincolnshire, Cambridgeshire and Norfolk, as has been asserted, is more difficult of proof. Of the Bean Goose, and under that name he, no doubt, included the Pink-footed Goose, Pennant remarks that they arrive in Lincolnshire in autumn, " they always light on cornfields, and feed much on the green wheat. They never breed in the fens, but all disappear in May."‡ This seems a plain statement about their habits, which he regarded as opposed to those of the Grey-lag. The west side of the fens was evidently the most accessible, and that is first described by the naturalist in the narrative now to be quoted.

Pennant, who it must be remembered was writing for the general public and not for that little band of naturalists who were his personal friends, does not give us by any means all the ornithological details one now longs for ; nevertheless, we must be grateful. He says :—

" The fen called the *West Fen* is the place where the Ruffs and Reeves resort to in the greatest numbers ; and many other sorts of water fowl, which do not require the

* *See* " Literary Life," p. 8. A good picture of the house is given in Howlett's " Views in Lincoln " (1805).
† " British Zoology," II., p. 570.
‡ " British Zoology," II., p. 575.

shelter of reeds or rushes, migrate here to breed ; for this
fen is very bare, having been imperfectly drained by narrow
canals. . . . . It is observable, that once in seven or
eight years, immense shoals of Sticklebacks appear in the
Welland below *Spalding*, and attempt coming up the river in
form of a vast column.   They are supposed to be the collected
multitudes washed out of the fens by the floods of several
years. . . . . Stares [Starlings] which during winter
resort in myriads to roost in the reeds, are very destructive,
by breaking them down, by the vast numbers that perch on
them.   The people are therefore very diligent in their attempts
to drive them away, and are at great expense in powder to
free themselves of these troublesome guests.   I have seen a
stock of reeds harvested and stacked worth two or three
hundred pounds, which was the property of a single farmer."

With regard to these Starlings it is easy to believe that the
reed owners found them an intolerable nuisance.   According
to Daniel a reed-bed has been known to be damaged to the
tune of a hundred pounds in one night,* this apparently in
Lincolnshire.   It was not only that the Starlings bent the
stems, and even snapped some of them, in either case prevent-
ing their attaining full development, but by their abundant
excrement the reeds became soiled, and consequently less
saleable.   As we have seen the value of a crop, when thatching
was universal, and tiles not much used might be very great,
and the damage a matter of no small consequence.

William Richards, who in his " History of [King's] Lynn,"
has a good deal to say about the fens, with which he was
doubtless personally acquainted, refers particularly to the
Starlings,† and the havoc sometimes made in their ranks
by the long guns of the fen fowlers,‡ who greatly resented
their depredations.

Pennant continues : " The birds which inhabit the
different fens are very numerous ; I never met with a finer

---

* " Rural Sports," by the Rev. W. B. Daniel, vol. III., p. 199.

† Sec. X. and pp. 78, 195, 199 (published 1812).

‡ These men loaded with ample supply of shot, and he relates how a
certain Thomas Hall knocked over 432 Starlings at a single discharge.   But
this tale of slaughter was beaten by Colonel Hawker (" Instructions to Young
Sportsmen," p. 271). and also by a heavy shot at Whittlesea Mere, which
accounted for 504 (" Orn. Miscellany," III., p. 219).

field for the zoologist to range in.   Besides the common Wild-duck, of which an account is given in another place,* wild Geese, Garganies, Pochards, Shovelers, and Teals breed here. I have seen in the *East Fen* a small flock of the tufted Ducks ; but they seemed to make it only a baiting place.   The Pewit Gulls and black Terns abound ; the last in vast flocks almost deafen one with their clamours.   A few of the great Terns or Tickets [? Pickets] are seen among them.   I saw several of the great crested Grebes on the *East Fen*, called there *Gaunts*,† and met with one of their floating nests with eggs in it.   The lesser crested Grebe [same as the preceding], the black and dusky Grebe [Black-necked Grebe in summer and winter plumage] and the little Grebe, are also inhabitants of the fens, together with Coots,‡ Water-hens, spotted Water-hens, Water-rails, Ruffs, Redshanks, Lapwings or Wipes, Red-breasted Godwits and Whimbrels.§   The Godwits breed near Washen-brough|| [and when fattened sell for half a crown or five shillings apiece, B.Z., II., p. 439]; the Whimbrels only appear for about a fortnight in May near Spalding, and then quit the country. Opposite to *Fossdyke Wash* during summer are vast numbers of *Avosettas*, called there *Yelpers* from their cry.   They hover over the sportsman's head like the Lapwing and fly with their necks and legs extended.   Knots are taken in nets along the shores near *Fossdyke* in great numbers during winter ; but they disappear in the spring."

Pennant had not at that time discovered that his Red Knot was only the summer plumage of the Grey Knot as well as of his Flintshire Ash-coloured Sandpipers.   It is, however. correct enough to say that these birds go away in May : their variable plumage continued to puzzle ornithologists.   The following particulars about the Knot are given in " British Zoology " : " These birds, when fattened, are preferred by some to the Ruffs themselves.   They are taken in great numbers on the coasts of *Lincolnshire* in nets such as employed in taking Ruffs ; with two or three dozens of stales of wood

* This reference is to the " British Zoology," II., p. 594.

† Seen on June 27th, 1769, B.Z.

‡ A white coot seen at Spalding, B.Z., II., p. 495.

§ Called Curlew-Knot at Spalding, B.Z., II., p. 430.

|| On the Witham, near Lincoln.

painted like the birds placed within : fourteen dozens have been taken at once. Their season is from the beginning of *August* to that of *November*. They disappear with the first frosts."

To go on with the narrative. " The short-eared Owl," continues Pennant, " visits the neighbourhood of *Washen-brough* along with the Woodcocks, and probably performs its migration with those birds, for it is observed to quit the country at the same time : I have also received specimens of them from the *Danish* dominions, one of the retreats of the Woodcock. This Owl is not observed in this country to perch on trees, but conceals itself in long old grass ; if disturbed, takes a short flight, lights again, and keeps staring about, during which time its horns are very visible. The farmers are found of the arrival of these birds, as they clear the fields of mice, and will even fly in search of prey during day, provided the weather is cloudy and misty. But the greatest curiosity in these parts is the vast Heronry at Cressi Hall, six miles from Spalding. The Herons resort there in February to repair their nests, settle there in the spring to breed, and quit the place during winter. They are numerous as Rooks, and their nests so crowded together, that myself, and the company that was with me, counted not less than eighty in one spreading oak. I here had opportunity of detecting my own mistake, and that of other ornithologists, in making two species of Herons ; for I found that the Crested Heron was only the male of the other : it made a most beautiful appearance with its snowy neck and long crest streaming with the wind. The family who owned this place was of the same name with these birds, which seems to be the principal induce-ment for preserving them. In the time of Michael Drayton,

> *Here stalked the stately crane,*
> *As though he march'd in war.*

But at present this bird is quite unknown in our island . . ."

This testimony about the Crane is repeated in the " British Zoology," and has been already quoted (*supra*, p. 168). Nevertheless, some Cranes must have still existed in Lincoln-shire, if we are to credit John Hill, who, writing in 1752, affirms that he had seen large flocks of them in that county, yet it must be admitted that Dr. Hill was not a very trustworthy observer.*

The Cressi heronry, which Pennant saw, and which is also alluded to in the " British Zoology,"† must have been an exceptionally fine one. Pennant did not fail to transmit some account of it to Gilbert White, but that is lost, although we have White's characteristic reply.‡ It was situated near the town of Gosberton, not far from Sir Joseph Banks's Abbey at Revesby, where Pennant, on his first visit to Lincolnshire in May, 1768, had been fortunate enough to shoot the Sedge Warbler.§

On less competent authority so many as eighty nests on one oak tree would hardly have been accepted as credible, nor has Pennant's counting met with a modern parallel in England. Lincolnshire heronries appear to have been larger than at the present day, but it is hardly likely that the birds themselves were more numerous. Pishey Thompson, a local historian, writes of a very large tree at Leake, in the same neighbourhood, which was literally covered with Herons' nests,‖ but he does not tell us how many, or whether anybody counted them.

---

* " History of Animals," by John Hill, forming Vol. III. of a general Natural History.

† II., p. 422.

‡ Letters to Pennant, XXII., XXIII.

§ Thereby adding a bird to the British list, *see* White's letter XXIV.

‖ " Boston and The Hundred of Skirbeck," 1820, p. 368. Dawson Rowley says that the tree at Leake was an ash, and that it was still standing in 1822 (" Orn. Misc., III., p. 71).

INDEX.

ImTheStory.com

CPSIA information can be obtained
at www.ICGtesting.com
Printed in the USA
BVHW041639150519
548351BV00027B/1939/P